D1526207

From Physics
to Politics

Robert C. Trundle, Jr.

From Physics to Politics

The Metaphysical Foundations of Modern Philosophy

Second Edition

with a foreword by
Peter A. Redpath

Transaction Publishers
New Brunswick (U.S.A.) and London (U.K.)

Paperback second edition 2002
Copyright © 1999 by Transaction Publishers, New Brunswick, New Jersey.

This book is printed on acid-free paper that meets the American National Standard for Permanence of Paper for Printed Library Materials.

Library of Congress Catalog Number: 2001048080
ISBN: 0-7658-0901-X
Printed in the United States of America

Library of Congress Cataloging-in-Publication Data

Trundle, Robert C., 1943-
    From physics to politics : the metaphysical foundations of modern philosophy / Robert C. Trundle, Jr.; with a foreword by Peter A. Redpath.—2nd ed.
        p. cm.
    Includes bibliographical references (p.) and index.
    ISBN 0-7658-0901-X (alk. paper)
    1. Truth. 2. Ideology. 3. Philosophy, Modern. 4. Metaphysics—History. I. Title.

BD171.T69 2001
121—dc21   2001048080

For
Janeanne

Contents

Contents

Contents

Foreword

———————※※※———————
Fascism, Nazism, Marxism, political correctness
and moral relativism reflect a "self-reinforcing
circular reasoning" of the dominating class
that currently acts as a substitute
for metaphysics.
———※※※———

Berkeley, Hume, Rousseau, Kant, Hegel, Nietzsche and others reconstituted Descartes' impossible dream of replacing the philosophy of antiquity with a wondrous new science of clear and distinct ideas: a practical scientific system of indubitable ideas produced by pure reason. Few contemporary intellectuals realize the repairs these thinkers made to the Cartesian dream of systematic science to salvage Descartes' musings from the scrapheap of philosophy. And few contemporary thinkers recognize the damaging repercussions that this tinkering has caused us intellectually, culturally, and politically. Robert Trundle is an exception.

Trundle knows that our concepts of scientific truth, logic, and necessity are essentially connected. The locus of necessity dramatically influences our understanding of logic and scientific truth. Modern philosophy restricts our understanding of necessity to political dreams and aspirations of Enlightenment intellectuals. As a result, it refuses to acknowledge as factual or meaningful whatever is not intelligible within the practical goals of the Enlightenment project of establishing science as a system of enlightened ideas.

The net effect of this subordination of truth to the Enlightenment project is that, in our time, metaphysical principles, speculative truths, our understanding of science, and the nature of logic are subordinated to, and shaped by, ideological dreams. Fascism, Nazism, Marxism, political correctnes, and moral relativism are actually essential acts, not historical aberrations. They reflect, what Professor Trundle calls, a "self-reinforcing circular reasoning" demanded by an apologetics of the dominating class that currently acts as a substitute for metaphysics.

One does not have to be a professional logician to concur with Trundle's underlying thesis, which is clear and tenable, that scientific truth demands a modal defense. Metaphysical principles ultimately justify the nature and scope of intelligible discourse. Hence, the specialized logics of practical thought ultimately presuppose a logic of theoretical discourse grounding the intelligibility of ordinary language. By subordinating theoretical and metaphysical truth to practical goals of the Enlightenment project, modern intellectuals subordinate modal logic to the hypothetical goals of a contingent necessity. In the end, as Trundle notes, this means that science becomes a complicated form of circular reasoning.

Trundle's work is groundbreaking and daring, with widespread ramifications. His argument transcends the domains of logic and scientific method. It extends to metaphysics and the history of philosophy. As a result, it is a significant achievement demanding exceptional skill to compose. I think his work complements my recent research in the history of philosophy. I encourage people to read this book because I have learned many things from it. I think others will too.

Peter A. Redpath
Professor of Philosophy
Saint John's University
Division of Theology and Philosophy
Staten Island, New York 10301 USA

Author's Preface

"Never before in human history has so much cleverness
been used to such stupid ends. The cleverness is
in the creation of... power; the stupid ends are in
the destruction of community, responsibility,
morality, art, religion and the natural world."

***

In this revised edition, some formulations of logic were deleted
and others added for clarity, such as those on page three. Also,
since the momentum of politicized truth has continued by a
thoughtless inertia, new material is added which may fortify
misgivings about an entanglement of academia and political
ideology. Negatively, apart from its origins, the ideology is
detailed courageously in *Tenured Radicals: How Politics Has
Corrupted Our Higher Education* (1998) by R. Kimball, *The
Shadow University: The Betrayal of Liberty on America's
Campuses* (1999) by A. Kors and H. Silvergate, *Literature Lost:
Social Agendas and the Corruption of the Humanities* (1999)
by J. Ellis, and *Dumbing Down: Culture, Politics and the Mass
Media* (2000) by I. Mosley.

Mosley notes in his introduction: "Never before in human
history has so much cleverness been used to such stupid ends.
The cleverness is in the creation of... power; the stupid ends
are in the destruction of community, responsibility, morality,
art, religion and the natural world." These developments beg
for attention to the nefarious origins of viewing 'truth' in
terms of power. Positively, there is needed a revitalized articulation of sane and coherent truth-conditions.

Were the conditions abandoned when modern philosophy
departed from a philosophical theology which would have
rendered coherent moral and scientific truth? In warning
of 'winds of doctrine,' theology might be prophetic if modern
ideologies are rooted in certain philosophical doctrines. One is

that the visible world cannot be a basis for reasoning to God. Hopefully, without a straw man criticism in the spirit of Hume, who related 'God' to superstition, this work will not merely show that the departure led to the incoherence. In addition, it will reveal that the departure resulted in ideologies in response to *who* determines 'truth'? The question of 'truth' converges on three developments.

First, Kant's Copernican Revolution undercut ascriptions of 'truth' to even well established theories of physics, understood paradoxically as ideal knowledge, and rendered chimerical moral truth. For 'truth' afforded by moral and scientific inquiries presupposed a metaphysics of freedom and causal determinism. Kant held that the latter were not known to be true. How this dilemma evolved is illustrated most concisely by his mediation between a Cartesian metaphysics and empiricism of Hume. A Humean-Kantian tradition of philosophy need not be perused deeply to see that the question 'Whence comes truth if not from metaphysics?' has resulted in antimetaphysical responses.

Second, in being ineffective stratagems, the responses of anti-metaphysical philosophies inspired ideological answers in the nineteenth century. This century witnessed the ideas that 'truth' comes from either dominating classes in a progressively *determined* history or, despite Nietzsche's disassociation from fascism after World War Two, an unfettered *freedom* of superior men to create it. Thus although moral and scientific truth were excluded covertly by Kant, ideological appeals to a metaphysics of freedom and determinism turned his Revolution on its head: In accord with a perennial dictum *ta meta ta phusika* (things after physics), his Revolution had at least accepted as a 'practical matter' an objectivity of the inquiries from which were inferred the metaphysics.

Third, metaphysics had previously included modalities that, despite Kant's category of modality, did not penetrate modern logic. Certainly, the logic of Greek and medieval philosophy was entangled with metaphysics. But a metaphysical modal reasoning might have afforded ascriptions of 'truth' to both modern theories of physics and their presupposition. And dare it be said? The presupposition may entail a First Cause, or God of Nature, which had been inferred modally in philosophical theology.

In sum, theology bears on Nature and, with no Naturalistic Fallacy, on the natural and human sciences as well. In describing our nature, these sciences implicitly prescribe how it ought to be fulfilled. The fulfillment contrasts to anti-metaphysical philosophies which cannot even articulate scientific truth, let alone relate it to ethics or politics. Thus the fulfillment averts political ideologies unique to modern society. The ideologies have evolved virulently from seeking to mold our nature to concocting ethnic *Weltanschauungen* (worldviews). The worldviews foster not only incoherent views of knowledge in which 'truth' is relative to whoever has power but views which inflame tribal strife. And hence by pathological *ad hominem* attacks on race, gender and class, which beg for a curative reasoning at hand, there has come to be an unprecedented apologetics for global ethnic conflict.

Acknowledgments

Much gratitude is owed to Dr. Irving Louis Horowitz, Chairman of the Board and Editorial Director of Transaction Publishers. A world renowned social scientist and intellectual historian, he quickly espied needed improvments in this work which not either I or seasoned reviewers had noticed. And without the following scholars who afforded a cultivation of my ideas in research journals, this book would not have been possible: Professor Jean Paul van Bendegem, Chair, Department of Philosophy, Vrije Universiteit Brussel, Editor of *Logique et Analyse: Belgium Center for Research in Logic*; Professors Kris Deschower and E. Van Evenstraat, Politologisch Instituut, Katholieke Universiteit Leuven, of the *Res Publica: Belgium Journal of Political Science*; Dr. Lionel Ponton and Dr. Thomas De Koninck, Department of Philosophy, Laval University, Quebec, Director and Editor of *Laval Theologique et Philosophique*; and Professors Michael Heller, William Stoeger, S.J., and Josef Zycinski, Editors of *Philosophy in Science*, affiliated with the The Pachart Foundation in Tucson, Arizona.

I am especially indebted to Dr. David Lamb, Honorary Reader in Philosophy, Department of Biomedical Science, School of Medicine, The University of Birmingham, England, Editor of the Avebury Series in Philosophy and Philosophy of Science for Gower Publishers, who oversaw my project *Ancient Greek Philosophy* (1994) and work in *New Horizons in the Philosophy of Science* (1992).

Acknowledgments

Finally, I am beholden to the following publishers for the use of quotations: The Modern Library, New York, for Rene Descartes' *Meditations on First Philosophy*, translated by N. K. Smith in *Descartes: Philosophical Writings*; Oxford Clarendon Press, New York, for David Hume's *Enquiries Concerning Human Understanding and Concerning the Principles of Morals*, Introduction by L. A. Selby-Bigge; Macmillan & Co., New York, for Immanuel Kant's *Critique of Pure Reason*, Unabridged First and Second Editions, translated by N. K. Smith; Macmillan Publishing Co., New York, for Karl Marx's *Capital: A Critique of Political Economy*, from *Marx*, edited by A. Wood; Random House, New York, for Friedrich Nietzsche's *The Will to Power*, translated by W. Kaufmann and R. J. Holindale; Oxford University Press, Oxford, for *The Oxford History of Western Philosophy*, edited by A. Kenny; and The University of Illinois Press, Chicago, for *The Structure of Scientific Theories*, edited by F. Suppe.

Chapter 1

Introduction: The Enlightenment's Paradigm Physics

After the Greek Enlightenment and despite it,[1] the idea of a Cause, as a God of Nature, became explicit. In including both natural and voluntary causes, metaphysics tied physics to theology in currently ignored ways. These involved a modal reasoning infused into metaphysics which might have rendered rational modern physics as well as its relation to ethics and politics. Instead, a sixteenth-century Reformation severed itself from the theological tradition and the Enlightenment revolted against the entire spectrum of medieval reasoning that underlaid science.

Among the sciences, physics became an epistemological paradigm for an oxymoronic metaphysical anti-metaphysics. Momentous achievements in physical science, such as those of Galileo and Newton, found expression in Copernicus' revolution to which Kant compared his philosophy. And this philosophy further fractured a tradition that the Reformation had already displaced. Though most scholars have long exalted the displacement, the ironic question ensues of whether the physics paradigm has led to an inability to even ascribe 'truth' to well established scientific theories. The inability would have grave consequences for society.

---

[1] Whereas the sixth-century B.C. Greek Enlightenment sprang from a Sophistic-Atomistic revolution in metaphysics that excluded a coherent 'truth' in physics, the modern Enlightenment arose from a revolution in physics. Physics was viewed as a paradigm of knowledge that, paradoxically, presupposed a metaphysics whose truth was not known because it was *synthetic a priori*.

Herein, there is concern for a link between the societal consequences and a covert modern metaphysics that underlies physics. Paradoxically, an advent of formalized physics has influenced a development of anti-metaphysical philosophies. Having themselves impacted the philosophy of science, the philosophies have come to exacerbate a questionable scientific rationality. There is not only the view that science functions independently of metaphysics and that physics is an epistemological ideal. In addition, this ideal is viewed through a lens of the Enlightenment. The latter has induced an optimism of inevitable technological and political progress with increasing historical happiness.[2]

§

A worldview bereft of Nature's God and its implication for human free will, led to a deterministic-materialistic idea of human nature and Nature.

§

Cultural critics outside the academic world may better see the forest for the trees. In *On the Eve of the Millennium*, a sober case is made by Conor Cruise O'Brien that the lens has filtered out millennial insights into human nature and obscured how enlightened ideals were transformed into pseudo-scientific ideologies. The ideologies have led to thought control, cultural revolutions, political correctness, and ethnic cleansings.[3] How could these cleansings, and the other pathologies expressed euphemistically, have any relation to such noble goals as the intellectual autonomy to pursue objective truth?

Initially, the ideal of this truth begs for qualification. The quest for objective truth in psychology, biology and physics would no more disconcert most modern theologians than many medieval ones. The latter included St. Augustine of

---

2 Cf. M. C. Jacob, *Living the Enlightenment* (NY: Oxford University press, 1991), p. 143. Typically confusing a dogmatic rationality with a rational realism, proponents of the modern Enlightenment may be traced back to thousands of "academicians familiar with 'the light'... [who were politically] sponsored."

3 Conor Cruise O'Brien, *On the Eve of the Millennium: The Future of Democracy Through an Age of Unreason* (NY: Free Press, 1996).

Hippo and St. Thomas Aquinas who held that since God created the psychobiophysical world, He created the truth-condition for cognitive truth. There was ample ground, in terms of a *modal reasoning*, to disavow that this truth could be strictly studied apart from theology and a scientific reason rooted in sense experience.

What is this experiential modal reasoning? It contrasts to a material conditional $p \rightarrow q$, where '$\rightarrow$' reads 'If... then' and we ordinarily admit that $\sim q$ is possible when p. The conditional 'If John chews gum, then he'll blow bubbles' permits a reasonable possibility that John did not blow bubbles when he chewed gum. But a modal conditional holds that it is *impossible* that $\sim q$ when p. There are conditionals, for instance, such as 'If John was conceived, there were prior biological processes.' Given our reproductive nature, it is either irrational or *more* than unreasonable to admit of a possibility that there were not the processes when he was conceived.

The modal conditional specifies that 'p entails q' if and only if 'p therefore q' is a valid inference. That is, $p \rightarrow q$ must be necessarily true, without triviality, where the truth can be expressed as $N(p \rightarrow q)$ or $\Box(p \rightarrow q)$. In this manner, experience bore reciprocally on theology and science. Science began with an experience of the impossibility that there is an event when there is no cause. Later formulated as a causal principle, the impossibility can be recast as a necessity. This may be expressed nontechnically as it is necessarily the case that if there is no cause, there is no event.

The events and causes cannot proceed *ad infinitum* since the series would be scientifically unlike all the things which compose it. Thus with no fallacy of composition anymore than concluding that something has mass when mass is a property of things composing it, the series is a totality which begs for a Cause. And if this Cause was itself caused — though its being caused is not required modally in the semantics of a purely voluntary cause, we return to the impossible infinity. Thus 'Necessarily if there is no first Cause, there is no series a part of which we experience.' This conditional does not express a logical necessity but bears on a rudimentary nature of things. It is stronger epistemologically than the ordinary empirical

3

truth of a material conditional because this conditional admits merely of a logical possibility that there is the series when there is no first Cause.

§

Every structure, mechanism and vehicle in the modern world owes its design to physical laws set forth in 1687 by the *Principia*.

§

Based on experience, reason led to this Cause as Nature's God. God was a voluntary Agency who created the world. A worldview bereft of it and its analogical human agency, of free will and reason, led to a deterministic and materialistic view of our nature and Nature. With an onslaught of the Enlightenment, a morally relevant metaphysics of Nature was abandoned by science. Ironically, however, the science did not conflict with the metaphysics! Relevant is Thomas' *Summa Theologica* (I, I, 2), in which the "astronomer and... physicist may both prove" that the earth "is round."

A rejoinder that Duns Scotus presaged Hume's skeptical critical thought about Nature's uniformity, in contrast to Thomas, disregards Thomas' scientific insights and his modal reasoning for a 'necessity' of the uniformity which is based on efficient causes. The latter included voluntary causes beyond the natural ones of a modern causal principle. Then, there is an objection that it was Occam's razor which later shaved off a superfluous medieval metaphysics. But this ignores that a modern mechanistic materialism, in addition to being metaphysical, rendered incoherent a truth of physics.[4]

Besides evoking questions about a coherence of 'truth,' the sciences were unable to provide any foundation for either morality or a humane politics. This was a short step to claims about political rights and responsibilities being meaningless pseudostatements. In entering into physico-scientific language, often under a rubric of physics, the deterministic metaphysics

---

4 W. T. Jones, *The Medieval Mind* (NY: HBJ 1969), pp. 308, 323. See R. Trundle, "Thomas' 2nd Way: A Defense by Modal Scientific Reasoning," *Logique et Analyse* 146 (1994) 145-68.

resulted surreptitiously in a reductive belief. That is, human behavior cannot be morally praised or blamed because 'root causes' rule out free choice of will.

From Metaphysics to Physics

Until the Enlightenment's influence on an anti-metaphysics of modern philosophies, there was the assumption that biophysical *descriptions* of our nature provided the morally relevant basis for *prescriptions* of how our nature ought to be fulfilled. Having a long history in an Aristotelian-Thomistic metaphysics, this assumption came to be called a moral and theological 'naturalism.' As part of a metaphysics of physics, the naturalism was largely undermined by the modern transposition of efficient causality into a deterministic sequence of physical events. The transposition reflected a virtual world view which, though metaphysical, was often confused with either physics or a 'physical' cosmology.

Accordingly, the world was viewed as a mechanical clockwork system composed exhaustively of material particles whose interactions deterministically obey mathematical laws.[5] Though the laws made no immediate reference to deterministic events, lawfully related properties and processes were tied conceptually to future state descriptions of physical systems coordinated causally to present descriptions. Formulated in terms of a causal principle that all events are caused, causal determinism became a foundation for the new physics. But traditional moral praise and blame became incoherent because they presupposed indeterministic realities of freedom, the 'good' and God which were also immaterial.

In addition to immaterial realities not being empirically measurable or verifiable, their presupposition collided head-on

---

[5] Cf. physicist Edward A. MacKinnon, *The Problem of Scientific Realism* (NY: Appleton-Century Crofts, 1972), p. 16. MacKinnon quotes the eighteenth-century mathematician and astronomer Marquis de Laplace, in *The System of the World*: In being "assured that nothing will derange the connection between causes and their effects we can extend our thoughts forward to... the series of events which shall be developed in the course of time... It is surely in the theory of the system of the world that the human mind has, by a long train of successful efforts, attained to this eminence."

with the new materialistic-deterministic picture. God and free will had no place in Newton's stunning inverse-square formula for gravitational force, nor in other laws or symbolic interpretations. In being formalized as mathematized theoretical concepts that made precise the inexact empirical predicates, his revolutionary physics was an ideal knowledge-yielding enterprise. Encoded paradigmatically in Newton's *Principia*, its prestige was so pronounced that scientists in other fields looked to the day when their sciences would have a formalized maturity with similar predictive and manipulative powers:

> It is, perhaps, the greatest single work of the scientific canon — and undoubtedly the most influential. Every... structure, mechanism and vehicle in the modern world, for that matter, owes its design to mathematical techniques and physical laws first set forth in 1687 by Isaac Newton in his *Philosophiae Naturalis Principia Mathematica*.[6]

§

But a scientific prediction of what *is* the case is not the same as saying what *should be* the case: To say that physical systems change is not to say they progress.

§

Physics: Paradigm for Philosophy

Increasingly, ordinary persons abandoned a reliance on God by one on scientists. Their prestige took a quantum leap. There arose a utopian notion that a progressive human condition does not depend on faith. The notion found quintessential expression in Baron d'Holbach's *System de la nature* (1770), in which unhappiness stems from ignorance of Nature, as well as in Auguste Comte's *Cours de Philosophie Positive* (1830). Credited with pioneering sociology, he held that a sociologico-

---

[6] See L. A. Marschall on "Newton's Principia...," *The Sciences: NY Academy of Sciences* 35 (1995) 45-46. Interestingly, Newton is quoted as stating: "To avoid being baited by little smatterers in mathematics... I designedly made the *Principia* abstruse; but yet so as to be understood by able mathematicians who, I imagine, by comprehending my demonstrations would concur with my theory."

scientific phase of history would evolve out of a philosophical phase as the latter had from a theological one.

This anti-theology anticipated Marx. Comte predicted the evolutionary progress of a new physics into an increasingly comprehensive chemistry, biology and sociology of man with utopian political effects.[7] And Marx compared himself to a physicist by holding *sub specie aeternitatis* (without reference to his own changing conditions) that even the idea of a 'mechanistic determinism' was caused by a deterministic dialectic. A dialectic of matter would lead historically to the politico-scientific consciousness of communism. On this enlightened view, the oppressed would be liberated socially and politically by an egalitarian *quantification* inspired by the scientific model.

The new model rejected *qualitative* distinctions of 'elitist' medieval hierarchies. These included the traditional Church, state, and family. And their progressive decline would be aided by the industrial revolution. Though part of a reactionary history to be itself overcome, the revolution augmented the political egalitarianism. A brute 'sameness' was created by assembly lines which stamped out identical products in mass quantities. The capitalist words '*caveat acheteur*' (let the buyer beware) as well as 'the price of everything and value of nothing' signified a phase which was to be superseded by a more scientific economics.

Great wealth would not be governed in virtue of either wisdom or the old aristocratic status. The wealth would be bestowed with equal opportunity on those with cunning and persistence whose economic power would further topple the medieval remnants. In short, a reformed theology was accompanied and influenced by a scientific revolution which evolved into a peculiar ideal for philosophy. Paradoxically, a philosophical paradigm of physics resulted in a metaphysical anti-metaphysics. And the anti-metaphysical agenda has

---

[7] Cf. Stanley L. Jaki's "The Last Word in Physics," *Philosophy in Science* V (Oct 1993) 9-32. Jaki suggests a pessimistic induction in which the history of science inductively warrants pessimism about an unqualified truth of any theory and *a fortiori* about its political implications.

shaped virtually all philosophical movements since the time of the eighteenth-century Enlightenment.

Philosophy and Anti-Metaphysics

Surely, there continued to be a philosophical recognition of such things as a Physical Possibility Principle. In specifying that it is wrong to demand that we ought to do what is either physically impossible or contrary to our nature, the specter was raised of a naturalistic ethics. But ethicists still had to contend with the physics ideal. The ideal found expression in 'neutral territories' of reason and empirical experience as a basis for all modes of inquiry.[8] A dilemma was that inquiries would involve distinguishing scientific predictions of what *will be* from what *should be* the case: To say physical systems change is not to say they progress. Accordingly, the inquiries would beg for distinguishing the morally desirable from that which is in fact desired. That is, there must not be the dreaded Naturalistic Fallacy.

§

Central to Kant's revolution was that 'determinism' and 'freedom,' in being expressed meta-physically, had no known truth.

§

Following the Naturalistic Fallacy, in Hume's empiricism, there ensued a mischievous stance: In asserting how we *ought* to fulfill our nature on the basis of how it *is*, we fallaciously

---

[8] Consider the impact on Professor Richard T. De George, former head of the American Philosophical Association (Central Division). De George argues that philosophers rely on empirical experience and reason alone. Reason is called a 'neutral territory' in his "Theological Ethics and Business Ethics," *Journal of Business Ethics* 5 (1986) 421-432. And beyond him, a broad spectrum of the impact is poignantly evident from Professor F. Suppe's assertion that the "history of epistemology (and metaphysics) *is* the history of the philosophy of science" to Professor Abraham Edel's criticism that moral philosophy is "not much further advanced than the Pre-Socratics were in physics." See Suppe's *The Structure of Scientific Theories* (Chicago: University of Illinois Press, 1979), pp. 716-717 (emphasis added), and Edel's "Romanell Lecture" in *Proceedings of the American Philosophical Association* (1987) 823-840.

deduce an *ought* from an *is*. Moreover, moral and theological truth-claims were not rational certainties because their denials were not self-contradictory. This thinking is a central reason why the paradigm of physics led to an anti-metaphysics. In Hume's critique of Rationalism, metaphysical claims were not, as the claims of physics, empirically verifiable. Ostensibly, unverifiable metaphysical claims confused psychological with logical certainties.

Certainly, an Enlightenment counterpart of empiricism, in Descartes' rationalism, was based on an indubitable pure reason. Reason was 'neutral' in being unbiased by theological assumptions and could deduce moral and scientific truth. Kant acknowledged such truth and a role for reason. But Hume's empiricism was equally influential. Thus in regard to science, Kant held that 'truth' was not either based on pure reason or absolutely objective because the mind interpreted only a raw material of experience.

Finally, sense experience could not produce ideas of freedom, 'good,' and God since they are not material things. Thus, things-in-themselves (*noumena*) had to be distinguished from phenomena. Religious and moral truth did not refer to phenomena but only to possibly real noumena of practical reason. In Kant's *Critique of Practical Reason*, this reason's scope was limited theoretically by his *Critique of Pure Reason*. Tellingly, the latter was viewed by Kant as a Copernican Revolution in philosophy.

Kant endeavored to do for philosophy what Copernicus had done for astronomy. The revolutionary assumption that the earth is active in orbiting the sun had resolved mounting scientific anomalies. Kant held that increasing epistemological problems in the history of philosophy could be surmounted by assuming that our mind is active in the acquisition of knowledge. This analogy of explaining knowledge to explicating celestial bodies, which evoked his awe of the starry heavens above, showed clearly that all substantive knowledge should be patterned on natural science and not on a metaphysics of philosophical theology.

While inquiries into salvation, political responsibility, and moral inquiry presupposed a metaphysics of *inner* freedom, scientific inquiries presupposed a metaphysics of *outer* determinism. A revolutionary part of Kant's articulation of determinism and freedom was that, in being metaphysical ideas, they had no known truth. The judgments were *synthetic a priori*. Synthetic meant that the concepts 'events' and 'caused,' in the judgment 'All events are caused,' had different meanings. The same held for 'persons' and 'free agents' in 'All persons are free agents.' Since the concepts were different, the judgments were not logically true *(analytic)*. And since they did not follow from experience *a posteriori*, but were assumed *a priori* for intelligible inquiries, they were not empirically true.

§

As philosophers realized that scientific and moral truths were undercut by metaphysical presuppositions to which truth was not ascribed, there arose anti-metaphysical views.

§

On the one hand, the judgment 'All events are caused' was presupposed by scientific inquiries and 'All persons are free' was assumed by moral inquiries. Still, political science assumed determinism as well as freedom insofar as it addressed rights and responsibilities. Kant parodied a medieval reliance on metaphysics. Though a metaphysics of freedom and determinism are not known to be true, they were assumed. But he made plain that, despite the Enlightenment, moral inquiry should not be disparaged. 'Truth' afforded by the inquiries of morality and science were equally undercut since they presupposed a truth-valueless metaphysics. In this sense the metaphysics had an *epistemological equality*!

On the other hand, the metaphysical judgments had an *ontological inequality* rooted in the scientific model. This model had phenomena as its object of inquiry. Admittedly, the inquiry involved mental categories that transposed a raw material of experience into ideas such as that some things are impossible and phenomena are causally related. But phenomena referred to a real material world and this world contrasted to a mere possible reality of noumena.

10

In this sense, a noumenal freedom was acknowledged only as a concept in the mind presupposed by religious, moral, and political inquiries. However, phenomena had a stronger onto-logical, if not epistemological, status of involving concepts in the mind *and* really existing things.

The Metaphysical Dilemmas

There were momentus consequences of the Kantian idea that a metaphysics of freedom and determinism were *equally* without known truth but, at the same time, that a noumenal freedom and deterministic phenomenon were *not equally* real. Several points beg for consideration. First, scientific inquiries which supposedly yield truth presuppose a truth-valueless metaphysics. In having no known truth, this metaphysics precludes the truths of science. Moreover, scientific success in predicting phenomena did not imply true theories in any standard inferences of modern logic.

Though the limits of logic did not become clear in the 1930s with the Vienna Circle's *Die Wissenschaftliche Weltauf-fassung* (*The Scientific View of the World*), but rather with Sir Karl Popper's *Logik der Forschung* (*Logic of Scientific Discovery*), there was no naive stance to the contrary among philosophers of science. This lack of any contrary stance, together with overzealous celebrations of scientific knowledge over mere religious and moral belief, did not bode well for an intellectual integrity of the academic community which so heavily influenced education and public policy.

Second, theories of physics were an epistemological ideal because they yielded systematically *true* predictions which could be exploited for unparalleled technological and industrial progress. The stunning progress led philosophers to abandon any pretension of metaphysics yielding truth about the physical, biological and psychological worlds. Scientific success in these worlds evoked painful searches for what is the proper scope of philosophy. As philosophers realized that scientific and moral truths were undercut by metaphysical presuppositions to which truth was not ascribed, there arose an anti-metaphysics in which *(i)* moral truth-claims were deemed to be a pejorative metaphysics since, besides not

11

yielding predictions, they referred to an unverifiable 'good' and God. *(ii)* There were unsuccessful attempts to show that apparent truths, afforded by scientific inquiry, did not presuppose any metaphysics such as a causal principle. And *(iii)* there were ingenious endeavors to either defend a tenability of science without 'truth' or articulate 'truth' apart from metaphysics.

§

A denial of the reasoning did not merely lead to singular problems of objective 'truth.' Philosophers and scientists began to flirt with the most thinly veiled politicized metaphysics in their midst.

§

Traditionally, 'truth' was understood in terms of a realism in which statements or theories are true when they reflect the way reality really is. This was evident in a medieval dictum *adequato rei et intellectus* (truth as conformity of thought with reality). But realism came to be seen as a mere metaphysics that was not itself true. From pragmatism to positivism to analytic philosophy, philosophers increasingly deferred to physics insofar as they held that metaphysics was not itself true and could not, as physics, predict or manipulate phenomena. Though phenomenal success may not imply true theories, theoretical physics became an epistemological ideal which influenced many academics to assume that physics had positively superseded philosophy.

In hindsight, it was admitted by several contemporary philosophers of science that "one of the most hopeless illusions of nineteenth-century science was" the attempt "to give physical answers to questions posed in classical philosophy."[9] Admittedly, there was not merely a revolt against classical philosophy. Pragmatists and existentialists rebelled against the de-humanizing effects of science. But misgivings about science did not counter a Kantian dilemma: Where does 'truth' come from if not from metaphysics?

---

9 J. Zycinski et al, "Editorial Note," *Philosophy in Science* V (1993).

Introduction: The Enlightenment

In general, some main anti-metaphysical responses can be summarized. Preceded by Kant's term *'pragmatisch'* one hundred years earlier, pragmatism tended to interpret beliefs to be true when they 'truly' made a difference in life and to posit an instrumentalist view of science. Scientific theories were said to be true, without implying an existential truth about theoretical entities, when they effectively manipulated and predicted phenomena. Logical positivism, in turn, led to conservative and liberal verification principles. The former specified that sentences are meaningful if and only if they are synthetic or analytic and the latter that they are meaningful if and only if something counts for and against them.

Finally, having largely evolved from positivism, analytic philosophy considers a richness of ordinary language which is said to have no metaphysical presuppositions. In the context at hand, this language is a source of presuppositionless scientific languages whose truth-claims 'do work' in limited domains. And contrary to popular belief, atheistic existentialism did not reject science. Scientific 'truth' is disavowed when it is taken as an 'essence preceding existence'.

Generally, knotty epistemological dilemmas have gone unanswered. How could pragmatists confirm that theories are effective apart from a rejected metaphysical realism in which predicted observations reflect reality? Could positivists verify a verification principle that is not itself analytic or synthetic, or tenably hold a liberal verification principle against which nothing is permitted to count? Could analytic philosophers avoid a traditional metaphysics of 'things after physics' *(ta meta ta phusika)*, in a language game of formalized science, when coordinating present to future states of a physical system is necessary for a coherence of predictions?

And the everyday existence of existentialists belies no doubt about the truth of such things as an applied engineering physics, apart from what is willed, for a structural integrity of the proverbial cafe where they philosophize. Does not a philosophical spontaneity, which they traditionally stress, suppose a predictable truth at odds with what is distinctive in the genre of either Friedrich Nietzsche's *will-to-power-to-truth* or Jean-Paul Sartre's *etre-pour-soi* (being-for-itself)?

13

The apparent paradoxes suffered by modern philosophy bear on its politicization of 'truth.'

Dilemmas of Politicization

Was medieval metaphysics confused with a *metaphysico-modal* reasoning which integrated causal determinism and freedom? In accord with human nature and the natural sciences which pertain to evolution, a mode of the reasoning might be expressed by an impossibility which — while not logical — bears on a rudimentary experience of phenomena: It is impossible for anything to exist, person or particle of mass, when it has no voluntary and natural cause because our psychobiophysical nature is rooted in Nature. The connection to a coherent notion of evolution seems patent even if it is studiously avoided. One medievalist strongly suggests a metaphysical logic in regard to the reasoning.[10]

§

Heidegger only briefly upheld fascism but had the ideological vision right when he exalted a power of the Fuhrer, as a virtual truth-condition, who "*is* the German reality."

§

A denial of the traditional reasoning did not merely lead to singular problems. Philosophers and scientists flirted with the most thinly veiled politicized metaphysics. In *Biology as Ideology*, R. Lewontin joins a growing chorus in academia. He chimes that science "is shaped... by social and political needs" and that scientists are "molded by... social and economic forces."[11] An abdication to the forces, which foster a pursuit of power for molding 'truth,' has led to regrets that "one of the greatest dangers to academic freedom... is the growing politicization of the university" and that it is a "cheerless fact that trained philosophers are just as captivated by political

---

[10] John F. X. Knasas, *The Preface to Thomistic Metaphysics* (Bern, Switzerland: Peter Lang Publishing, Inc., 1990), p. 159.

[11] R. Lewontin, *Biology as Ideology* (NY: Harper Collins Publishers, 1997), from the author's own abstract.

fashions...as other people are."[12] Whence comes 'truth' if not from metaphysics?

Marx appealed to a metaphysics disguised as physics in which dominating classes *determine* truth. What is true for one class may be false for another. Nietzsche held an equally incoherent metaphysics of Supermen whose unfettered free will afforded a will-to-power to *freely* mold cultures. In effect, cultures became inconsistent truth-conditions for truth. Both views appeal to truth-claims of political classes or *Uebermenschen* for what reality is like. That the relativism found its way into mainstream thought is evidenced by the observation that Weltanschauung analyses, from Toulmin to Feyerabend and Thomas Kuhn, are "heir to the philosophical tradition which includes Nietzsche... Accordingly, it can be viewed as a kind of neo-Kantian pragmatic position."[13]

America's *Chronicle of Higher Education* states that Kuhn's position "rivals Merton's [sociology] in its range of impact."[14] Questions about American education ensue when, in mere virtue of the impact, educators gush that he deserves a Nobel Prize. Misgivings about education, if not the Prize, are raised by Kuhn himself. Over a half decade earlier, he voiced embarrassment that many social scientists "loved" his *Structure of Scientific Revolutions*. The latter either gave hope that social scientists may "attain the same level of legitimacy... as physicists" or "was seized on by radicals..." since evolution is not "toward anything... truth in the case of science." [15]

A scientific realism which permits testable truth, by a truth-condition of experienced reality, found strange rivals in both Kuhn's paradigms and university radicals of the 1960s who sought power. Without denying his many insights, Heidegger may be noted. He only briefly upheld fascism but had the ideological vision right, epistemologically, when he

---

[12] S. Hook, "Reminiscence" *APA* 60 (1987) 511-13 and N. Rescher, "Where Wise Men Fear to Tread," *APQ* 27 (1990) 259.

[13] Suppe, *The Structure of Scientific Theories*, pp. 126-27, fn. 258.

[14] M. McPherson, "Needed: A Nobel Prize for the Giants of Social Science," *The Chronical of Higher Education*, 30 January 1998, p. B7.

[15] See J. Horgan's interview of Kuhn, in "PROFILE: RELUCTANT REVO-LUTIONARY," *Scientific American*, 9 May 1991, p. 49.

exalted a power of the Fuhrer, as a virtual truth-condition, who "*is* the German reality."[16]

§

Predictably, ideology is rationalized by imputing concerns about political correctness to right-wing students or to an uneducated public.

§

Reality as God was rejected by the Fuhrer whose view of theology was "derived from the... Enlightenment."[17] Professor Hazel Barnes may contrast the Enlightenment to an *Offenbarkeit* (manifestness) of Being in Heidegger's philosophy. But she ties his philosophy, with its religio-political import, to his Armistice-Day speech on behalf of Nazism. She is not willing as most of her colleagues to "soft pedal" bonds of what he said to "his philosophical works."[18]

These works bring to mind Nietzsche. In considering how his metaphysics gripped the mind of Nazi intellectuals who used taxpayer money to research his thought, despite an anti-Semiticism of his sister, one may be surprised by a ubiquitous deference to his relativism by sprouting postmodern interpretations of 'fact.' Defenses of the interpretations are largely devoid of any critical analyses of metaphysics which normally evoke caution in mainstream philosophy.

Feminism has not concealed its reliance on Nietzsche's relativism in which 'truth' stems from a political power to *freely* shape reality in moral and scientific realms.[19] And in

---

16 M. Heidegger, "Deutsche Studenten," *Heidegger & Modern Philosophy*, Ed. M. Murray (New Haven: Yale University Press, 1978), p. 318.

17 P. E. Schramm, *Hitler: The Man and the Military Leader* (Malabar, Fla: Krieger Publishing, 1986), p. 47.

18 H. Barnes, *An Existentialist Ethics* (Chicago: University of Chicago Press, 1978), p. 418. The German scholar A. Schwan is noted.

19 Rosanna Vitale says that the "right will be swayed into flexibility by the maternal left" by feminists in virtue of Nietzsche; Kathryn Parsons connects Nietzsche's relativism to Kuhn; and Susan Hekman agrees that "to interpret feminist... theory, we should look to Kuhn." See Vitale's "Modern Europe," *History of European Ideas* 20 (1995) 665, Parsons' "Nietzsche and Moral Change," *Nietzsche*, Ed. R. Solomon (NJ: Anchor Books, 1973), pp. 169-193, and Hekman's "Truth and Method," *Signs* 22 (1997) 356.

recalling how much of the cold-war world was suppressed in the name of Marxian science, one may be surprised by the fervent belief in its *deterministic* metaphysics in Western universities. In the 1970s "Marxism in the East was universally taught and... disbelieved," notes one eminent philosopher, "while Marxism in the West was taught to... passionate believers."[20]

Having inevitable consequences for Western societies that were ironically to be models for reformed communist ones, the intellectual anomalies return us to basic questions: Was a modal reasoning about human nature and Nature, from Aristotle to Thomas, confused with metaphysics by modern philosophers, despite Kant's category of modality? Was the confusion coupled to both an increasing lack of acquaintance with the nature of metaphysics and its relegation to amateurs in other academic areas? Whereas Yale's John Smith traces a distressing exit of metaphysics to other disciplines, Peter Strawson notes that Wittgenstein's dictum "Philosophy leaves everything as it is" distinguishes his descriptive metaphysics from a traditional one "in the bad sense." Oxford's Bryan Magee adds that "When I was an undergraduate..., metaphysics was a dirty word — to refer to a man as a metaphysician was to dismiss him with contempt."[21]

Finally, substitutes for a realism of human science, in which scientific 'truth' has a truth-condition of our nature, arose with mass movements which tend to deny natural behavior and stress only political nurture. P. Gross notes "antiscience attitudes... and 'science bashing' from an array of... fashionable view points — postmodernism, feminism, radical environmentalism, multiculturalism, and AIDS activism."[22] These movements find an apologetics in modern

---

[20] A. Kenny, ed., *The Oxford History of Western Philosophy* (Oxford: Oxford University Press, 1994), p. 368.

[21] See Smith's *The Spirit of American Philosophy* (NY: SUNY Press, 1983), pp. 218-220, and Magee's *Modern British Philosophy* (NY: St. Martin's Press, 1971), pp. 125-127, for quotes of Magee and Strawson.

[22] P. Gross and N. Levitt, *Higher Superstition: The Academic Left and its Quarrels with Science* (MD: The Johns Hopkins University Press, 1994) and this quote from *New York Academy of Science* (1996) 8.

epistemology as well as strong institutional support in most American universities.

§

A new mode of reasoning, without an incoherent modern metaphysics, may integrate science as well as perennial insights of religion.

§

For instance, women's studies invariably take a feminist perspective. A radical relativistic version, now called 'gender feminism,' is inordinately influential. This version has been the engine behind other movements which seek to subvert traditional truth. Anchored in a metaphysics based on an experience of ages, traditional 'truth' was ultimately undercut by the studies which, unbeknownst to many of their minions, is rooted in the so-called critical thought of Hume and Kant. They displaced thinking from the natures of men and women as well as ushered in ideology for changing it, as echoed by H. Aiken's classic *Age of Ideology*.[23] Predictably, ideology is rationalized by imputing concerns about political correctness to either right-wing students or an uneducated public.[24] These points lead to my present endeavor.

In highlighting only some of the most influential modern philosophers for the purpose at hand, this work focuses on how the philosophers have contributed to ideologies. Ideologies are traced to a confusion, of metaphysics with modalities, which resulted in peculiar dilemmas.

Some Conclusions

Dilemmas are clear in a K-K thesis: "exploitation of... 'causal' regularities in obtaining a posteriori knowledge must not require prior knowledge of those regularities."[25] Given that the regularities are not known either *a posteriori* (empirically) or

---

[23] H. Aiken, *Age of Ideology* (NY: New American Library, 1957).

[24] Having myself heard this, S. Balch notes that academic ideologists have sought to corrupt the university's "essential mission." See G. Punishes, "The Incubus of Deconstruction," *Modern Age* 32 (1989) 290-293.

[25] F. Suppe, *The Structure of Scientific Theories*, p. 722.

logically, scientific truth not only presupposes what is not known to be true but 'truth' is incoherent. Ignored is that an efficient causality, positing voluntary and natural causes, may afford coherence and permit the truth of a more liberal causal principle. Its epistemic status would evidently border the falsely dichotomized truth.

Skepticism over the causal principle, by excluding alternatives to empirical or logical truth, is exacerbated at the level of theories. They would be either trivially or empirically true. That empirically true theories are not implied by predictive success is not assuaged by a lack of success which affords a rational choice between theories. Thus there ensues a problem beyond the causal principle having an ignored modal truth that skirts what is logically necessary and empirically reasonable. Is there a reasonable necessity wherein the problems have a complementary solution?

Arguably, it is *more* than reasonable to ascribe empirical truth to theories in virtue of their systematic success in given domains. The success is inexplicable unless the theories truly describe what those domains of physical reality are approximately like. *Pari passu* it would be equally reasonable to ascribe truth to a causal principle since its truth is necessary for the accepted theoretical truth. This is one understanding. But it is not captured by a material conditional 'If T then C': If as a *matter of fact* theoretical truth is yielded by scientific inquiry *(T)*, a causal principle is true *(C)*. The thought is captured by an epistemic impossibility that C does not obtain when does T: *Necessarily (T → C)*. This is to say that it is logically, but not modally, possible that $\sim C$ when T.

To accept T, and therefore C, is to accept not only the causal principle's limited truth but our limited free choice of will. Held by Kant to be as truthless as the causal principle, the principle that persons are self-conscious free agents is necessary for the very intelligibility of the causal principle's truth as well as for a truth of scientific theories themselves. Otherwise, our behavior would be determined along with scientific truth-claims. Incoherently, contradictory claims would both be true. For the truth-condition for truth is the way in which *is* reality. Given that it is entirely determined, a determined reality would be the condition for truth and inconsistent claims would be equally true because equally caused. There would be no way to rationally assess any truth-claim including, paradoxically, that everything is causally determined. Assessments of claims and counterclaims would not be *free from* a deterministic spatio-temporal realm of which we would be exhaustively a part.

§

In modern thought, 'truth' was not even ascribable to theories of physics; physics was confused with a metaphysics of ideologies; and they worsen the human condition by replacing idle metaphysical interpretations of the world with murderous efforts to change it.

§

We conclude with two intriguing questions. Does a metaphysics of determinism and freedom, wherein our voluntary and deterministic natures are complementary, have a strong epistemic status that borders empirical and logically necessary truth? If the answer is possibly 'yes,' may prevailing anti-metaphysical philosophies be based on a falsely dichotomized truth? If there is another possible 'yes,' there are astonishing considerations. A new mode of reasoning which undergirds physics, without a naive incoherence of modern metaphysics, may again integrate science as well as perennial insights of both morality and theology.

Certainly, a *philosophical* determinism or materialism is not the same as a *methodological* one. The philosophical one is dogmatic and the latter is not because it accepts only the unqualified determinism or materialism for limited purposes of scientific inquiry. But the methodology does not erase the problem if there is not a more liberal metaphysics and modal reasoning which render coherent truth-claims. Since scientists cannot ascribe 'truth' to a metaphysics of determinism or materialism in either case, and since they deny a consistency of the metaphysics with free will, many of them studiously ignore the dilemma or side with 'science.'

20

For example, Dr. Elaine C. Scott, Director of the National Center for Science Education, admits of her *philosophical* acceptance of materialism. In knowing the difference but evidently not the problem of coherence, she contrasts herself to Gregor Mendel who "decoupled methodological from philosophical materialism."[26] In addition to an evident unawareness of the incoherence, her remarks exhibit an apparent willful dogmatism. This raises troubling questions about the NCSE. For it seeks to impress on American education a rationality of the scientific enterprise, especially as it contrasts to theology. To what can such a false dichotomy between theology and science be traced?

In order to trace the false dichotomy and resulting schism of philosophy from areas to which it is related, Descartes is initially examined. While he is the 'Father' of modern philosophy, he did not divorce metaphysics from physics in a mode of later philosophers. Still, he may have contributed to an epistemic ideal of physics and to an ensuing anti-metaphysics. The latter bears on confused ideas of scientific rationality that resulted in irrational anti-scientific ideologies. The ideologies led to tragic societal pathologies.

Thus although the following pages focus on a central trend of modern philosophy — peppered with references to philosophers from Merleau-Ponty to Wittgenstein, the discussion is hopefully sufficient for evoking sober consideration of something akin to a process of cultural suicide in the West. At the very time that the West exalts physics as an archetypal knowledge-yielding enterprise, there are peculiar anomalies: 'Truth' cannot even be ascribed to well-established theories of physics; physics is often confused with a metaphysics adopted by anti-scientific ideologies; and ideologies worsen the human condition by replacing idle metaphysical interpretations of the world with murderous efforts to radically change it.

---

[26] See Elaine C. Scott, "Monkey Business," *The Sciences* 36, No. 1 (Jan/Feb 1996) 20-25.

Chapter 2

Physics and a Metaphysical Rationalism

Oddly, radical efforts to change the world have tacit roots in Descartes. He declared that he must rid himself of all learned opinions "hitherto given credence."[1] This approach is unique to the modern mind which abandons millennial intellectual traditions. Nothing more poignantly indicates a revolt against them than his quest for a universal knowledge which exceeded medieval physics. The latter posited *many* less than rigorous formula such as that velocity is proportional to compulsory force and weight, and inversely proportional to resistance *(v α F/R* and *v α W/R)*.

In seeking logico-mathematical ultimates in a framework of a hypothetico-deductive method, he foresaw one given universal law (L_o) in the mode of Galileo:[2]

$$a_{av} = v - v_o / t \ (L_o)$$

Here, average acceleration (a_{av}) is change in velocity ($v - v_o$) divided by change in time (t). In applying L_o by assigning values to time and change in velocity (L_1), a hypothetical *modus ponens* obtains for deducing a prediction of $a_{av}(P)$:

$$L_1 \wedge (L_1 \rightarrow P) / \therefore P$$

---

[1] R. Descartes, *Meditations on First Philosophy*, from M. Beardsley, Ed., *The European Philosophers* (NY: Random House, Inc., 1960), p. 28.

[2] Descartes' contemporary Galileo (1564-1642) was a pivotal basis for Newton. Also, he was credited by professors A. W. Smith and J. N. Cooper, in *Elements of Physics* (NY: McGraw-Hill, 1979) pp. 31-33, for the kinematics $v_{av} = v + v_o/2$.

Though Descartes believed that L_1 and an unapplied law L_o gave rational expression to reality, he did not hold either that L_o could be formulated without observation or that observation was indubitable. His notion of 'indubitable ideas,' in terms of which he was criticized for being dogmatic, will become clear after noting his philosophical background and astonishing scientific achievements.

§

Anti-science attitudes are more a result, than violation, of the Enlightenment which underlies modern ideals.

§

Rene Descartes (1596-1650) was a Continental Rationalist. In most prominently including Spinoza and Leibniz — who discovered the calculus at about the same time as Newton, the rationalists turned to reason *par excellence* as a basis for 'truth' in virtue of our rational nature as human beings. Called the 'Father of modern philosophy,' Descartes assumed that whatever could be clearly thought existed outside the mind and, with Leibniz, that innate ideas not only become self-evident with certain experiences but enable deductions to moral, theological, and scientific truths.

Though he held a mechanistic worldview with its idealization of physics, he avoided a metaphysics of deterministic materialism by a duality of material and immaterial substance. And while he is associated with an overly optimistic Enlightenment, second thoughts about its naivete may arise by noting his scientific achievements. Some are credited to his *Discourse on Method*.[3] Criticism that he is a dogmatic rationalist in this work and others, such as the *Meditations,* might seem to be offset by a success of his scientific ideas as by analogy a success of theories might offset criticism of them.

---

[3] See, for example, Descartes' *Discours de la Methode pour bien conduire sa raison, & chercher la verite dans les sciences* which, first published in 1637, introduced the Dioptrics, Meteors, and Geometry which illustrate the method of his reasoning.

A Metaphysical Rationalism

Second Thoughts on the Enlightenment?

In virtue of inspiring a host of scientific discoveries as well as a hypothetico-deductive method of science, the achievements attributed to such works as the *Discourse* were so impressive that L. Lafleur notes:

> these achievements are... astonishing, for, in the four essays which appeared together in 1637, he exhibits the most remarkable... accomplishments which have ever been given to the world by one man at one time.[4]

Relating to why an Enlightenment stress on science seemed so tenable and to how theory bears on technology, Descartes' technologico-theoretical discoveries are rarely enumerated. In the Dioptrics they include: *1)* a wave theory of light, *2)* vector analysis of motion, *3)* law of sines in refractions, *4)* first theoretical account of far and near-sightedness, *5)* first viable theory of space perception, *6)* first theoretical explication of lenses, *7)* first recognition of spherical aberration and method of correcting it, *8)* determination of light gathering power in telescopes, *9)* principle of the iris diaphragm, *10)* draw tube, *11)* telescope finder, *12)* use of illuminating equipment for microscopes, and *13)* parabolic mirror.

In view of these achievements alone, one can easily see why a rationalism of the Enlightenment is still esteemed in scholarly literature. This includes *The Flight from Science & Reason* by P. Gross, N. Levitt, and M. Lewis. They document how the twentieth century has violated rational ideals of the Enlightenment by, most distressingly, the American academic community itself.[5] One may concede that this community is threatened by irrational ideologies parading as science and by anti-science attitudes. Herein, nonetheless, it is argued that

---

[4] See L. J. Lafleur, *Philosophical Essays* (NY: Liberal Arts Press, Inc. 1964), pp. x, xi. There is no reference to a hypothetico-deduction, though there is in the Bobbs-Merrill edition by Paul Olscamp. A verificationist *modus-ponens* contrasts to a later *modus tollens* $L_o \rightarrow P_o$ /$\sim P_o$ // $\sim L_o$, where a law is falsified ($\sim L_o$) by a false prediction ($\sim P_o$).

[5] P. Gross, et al, ed., *The Flight from Science & Reason* (NY: Annals of NY Academy of Sciences, 1996), V. 775.

the attitudes are more a result, than violation, of the general philosophy which underlies the ideals.

By focusing on the ideals, however, an improbability of Descartes' scientific success might be taken prima facie to warrant belief in a probable cogency of the philosophy to which he credits his discoveries. The above discoveries were buttressed by others such as his discourse on physiology. Though his theory of anatomy turned out to be incorrect, it presaged the principle of the steam and internal combustion engines. Also, he distanced himself from theology in achieving discoveries in his Meteorology: *1)* a rejection of Divine intervention to explain events, *2)* a kinetic theory of heat, anticipation of Charles Law, and concept of specific heat, *3)* first outline of a meteorology in his treatment of winds, clouds, and precipitation, *4)* description and explanation of primary, secondary and reflection rainbows, and *5)* description of the division of white light into colors by a prism and set-up of the slit spectroscope.

§

In ostensibly arising from rational rules, as relevant to theology as physics, his achievements evoke an 'inner light' of the Enlightenment.

§

Finally, Descartes' analysis of geometric structures and properties by algebraic operations on variables, defined in terms of position coordinates, led to analytic geometry. From it came a foundation for advanced mathematics and its applications to science. National Science Fellow at Stanford and former editor of the *American Mathematical Monthly*, E. P. Vance, credits Descartes' rectangular system of coordinates, named 'Cartesian', for extraordinary "progress in mathematics and... [its] application in science"[6]

Indeed, international scientists augment the praise. For example, physicists B. M. Yavorsky and Yu. A. Seleznev note Descartes' important contributions to projections of either the acceleration of a point particle or a translationally

---

6 E. Vance, *Modern Algebra* (London: Addison-Wesley, 1962), p. 75.

moving body. In terms of specifying finite dimensions onto axes of a Cartesian coordinate system, the projections bear on Newton's second law in the form a = F/m:[7]

$$a_x = F_x/m,\ a_y = F_y/m,\ \text{and}\ a_z = F_z/m$$

Descartes' contribution to point-particle accelerations and to technology suggests how technology can advance theory and theory the technology, say one for more accurately calibrating acceleration. A needed technology may otherwise be unimaginable and itself raise anomalies, say about mass *(m)* for bodies that approach the speed of light, which begs for a new theory such as Einstein's and it to new technology. In ostensibly arising from rational rules, as relevant to theology as physics, his achievements evoke an 'inner light' of the Enlightenment.

The *Meditations on First Philosophy* warrants special study since it best reflects an essential rationalism: It "speaks to the philosophical novice as well as the sophisticate," says one Cartesian scholar, because it "introduces basic issues... in a way that is brief, compelling, and penetrating."[8] This work was often taken to reveal an inner light. But we will see how it was criticized by Hume and Kant as a matter of confusing *a priori* with *analytic* ideas.[9]

Doubt and Science

Descartes' *Meditations* seeks indubitable ideas by doubting anything uncertain. After increasingly stronger doubts, an idea that can not be doubted is a basis for deducing other veritable ideas. Some have epistemic qualities that characterize, or are similar to, the initial idea that is most indubitable. That is, though there are differences of an initial indubitable idea from later true ones, the former is not merely the ground for

[7] B. M. Yavorsky and Yu. A. Seleznev, *Physics*, Tr. from the Russian by G. Leib (Moscow: MIR Publishers,1979), p. 55.

[8] G. Dicker, *Descartes: An Analytical and Historical Introduction* (NY: Oxford University Press, 1993), p. vii.

[9] Hume's attention to a triviality of logical necessity led to Kant's distinction of necessary analytic judgments from necessary a priori ones.

contingently true ideas. Some of the latter seem modal in nature and are not captured by recent analyses restricted to ontological notions or proofs.[10]

Having made these points, his assertion that doubt "frees us from all prejudices" is followed by a caveat that to doubt is not necessarily to proclaim falsity.[11] Besides falsity not being implied by doubt, he expresses a doubt which does not have as much philosophic interest *per se* as others. Thus although he rids himself of all opinions that were "hitherto given credence," that include ones rooted in ancient and medieval authority, he delves into three levels of 'philosophically significant doubt.'

§

St. Augustine handled the problem of perceptual truth in a manner that has an intriguing resemblance to both Descartes' statement of the problem and his resolution.

§

There is a first-level doubt about his senses which deepens with possibilities at a second of dreaming and third of an evil god-like genius. While the first two levels have objections that serve to intensify his doubt, the third results in an indubitable idea. His use of '*I*' reveals a judicious use of language in his doubting approach. And significantly, while the approach calls for caution in not glibly accepting a dubiousness of traditional thought, it brings to mind exactly that thought in terms of a 'Cartesian realism.'

The realism, some say is naive, defends a common-sense reality of ordinary objects and a scientific truth wherein true theories, in given domains, correspond to what reality is really like. Challenged by quantum and relativistic physics when they

---

10 Cf. P. Herrick's *The Many Worlds of Logic* (NY: Harcourt Brace, 1994), pp. 309-17: Cosmological proofs are not criticized modally.

11 Descartes, *Meditations on First Philosophy*, from Beardsley, *The European Philosophers*, pp. 25. Future reference is to the *Meditations*, with pages in Beardsley's work, is from N. K. Smith's translation in *Descartes: Philosophical Writings* (NY: Modern Library, 1958).

are taken to show that physical reality is unlike its ordinary appearances, Descartes might respond in a way in which he might have the last word. This holds even if he, as the 'Father of Modern Philosophy,' influenced future philosophers who denied any metaphysics.

The Dubious Senses

The senses may be more commonly understood in terms of sense experience or perception, in everyday language, and sense data in later modern philosophy. When Descartes says "I have sometimes found [the senses] to be deceptive,"[12] the 'I' indicates he is not speaking for others. The idea that others exist would be a question-begging one since it assumes a reliability of the senses in question. Since a question of his senses is not assuaged by further levels of doubt, reference to himself continues until ideas that cannot be doubted provide a basis for inferring other existing things.

Importantly, St. Augustine had responded to the problem of perceptual truth in a way that has an intriguing resemblance to both Descartes' statement of the problem and his later resolution. As soon expanded on, the resolution strengthens the idea that 'truth' may be ascribed rationally to observable predictions, if not to the theories in terms of which the theories are understood.

Perennial questions about a reliability of our senses is evident by cursory considerations. In appealing to common experience, we may believe that we see a given person who turns out to be someone else or, in washing our cold hands, that the water is hot when it is actually tepid. There is a difference between water being hot and feeling that way. The feeling is not what is doubted but rather the water's approximate temperature. A mere possibility that the senses may induce false ideas indicates they are not reliable sources for indubitable ideas.

Now a hallmark of seasoned philosophers is to be their own worst critics by anticipating objections in order to prevent glib rejoinders. In presaging such rejoinders, Descartes

---

12 *Ibid.*, p. 29.

entertains the objection that there are higher qualities of sense experience. There may be more self-evident experiences that do not admit of such things as confusing 'feelings' of heat with what may not be hot. The experiences may include looking at one's hand or sitting by a fire. One might have an indubitable idea that something exists, much more that it is either a hand or fire.

Am I Dreaming?

Though some indubitable ideas may seem to be "known by way of sense...," Descartes cautions that often "I *dreamt* of myself being in this place, dressed and seated by the fire, whilst... I was lying... in bed!"[13] Therefore, even ideas in high-quality experiential contexts do not seem indubitable because he cannot be certain that he is not dreaming.

§

Given that various geometric ideas have a patent truth which is not averted by either ordinary language or phenomenology, a cavalier dismissal of Descartes' object-ion seems problematic.

§

However, he is talking about dreaming when he thinks he is awake. Before considering his own objection, other recent ones might be briefly noted in order to better appreciate its possible depth. When he adds that he may be deceived while "looking at this paper" and extending "this hand,"[14] for example, we recall Wittgenstein's distinction of philosophical and genuine doubt. Apart from extraordinary circumstances, such as one's hand being extended during a muscle spasm, expressing doubt about the ordinary might belie a disingenuous philosophical doubt. This doubt does not seem to be genuine and genuine doubt does not seem to be philosophical.

---

13 *Ibid.*, p. 29. Below, some puzzlement may be captured by noting that Descartes' talk of possibly dreaming may seem self-refuting if he relies on a veracity of being awake in order to question whether or not he is awake or dreaming.

14 *Ibid.*, p. 29. Emphasis added.

Or, for instance, Merleau-Ponty says there are behavior patterns of the body "which uses its own parts as a general system of symbols."[15] Here, relations of analytic philosophy to phenomenology raise other objections.[16] Phenomenology stresses our awareness of perception and analytic philosophy questions talk about perception as mere thinking. Is there any more sense in saying that 'I am thinking but unaware of it?' than 'I perceive something but am unaware of it'? By analogy, while it might make sense to speak of dreaming without awareness, does it make sense to assert 'I am unaware of being awake'? If what holds for dreams does not hold for being awake, when one is awake it may be senseless to calmly utter 'I see my hand but may be dreaming.'

The above objections may seem tenable. But the fact that the objections may be only apparent is precisely the point. The point is to doubt whatever can be doubted. Hence, the question ensues of whether a given mathematical idea *per se* is doubtful, even in dreams, in contrast to perceived geometrical objects and less than rigorous concepts in ordinary language. In this respect, Wittgenstein notes that one "can give the concept 'number' rigid limits" as opposed to Merleau-Ponty who notes that perceived triangles do "not necessarily have... angles the sum of which equals two right angles."[17]

Merleau-Ponty notes relativistic physics. His point about triangles holds "if it is true... space... is no less amenable to non-Euclidean than to Euclidian geometry."[18] In addition to a pessimism about geometrical ideas, his words "if it is true" suggest an inductive pessimism. Given a historical supersession of scientific theories, it is inductively reasonable to be pessimistic about a current theory's truth-claims— say that objects with appreciable mass cannot accelerate instantaneously. For this might be possible in terms of a future theory. Still, this

---

15 M. Merleau-Ponty, *Phenomenology of Perception*, Tr. C. Smith, (London: Routledge & Kegan Paul, 1978), p. 237.

16 See, for instance, N. Gier's *Wittgenstein and Phenomenology* (NY: State University of New York Press, 1981).

17 L. Wittgenstein, *Philosophical Investigations* (NY: Macmillan, 1971) #68; Merleau-Ponty, *Phenomenology of Perception*, p. 391.

18 *Ibid.*, p. 391.

pessimism may not undercut even ideas in dreams such as 'triangles are three-sided.'

§

Colliding head-on with an Enlightenment he influenced for which the mere specter of a devil was as offensive to 'scientific reason' as God, this evil god led some modern readers to view his rationalism as an antiquated medievalism.

§

Given that some ideas of geometry and mathematics have a patent truth which is not averted by either ordinary language or phenomenology, a cavalier dismissal of Descartes' objection seems problematic. His objection is that it does not seem possible that "2 and 3 are 5" and that a "square has no more than four sides... can ever be suspected of falsity."[19] Thus if the false ideas are inconceivable, how could they be conceived even in dreams? And if they cannot even be dreamed, might they not be indubitable?

Evil and Rationality

"Yet even mathematical and geometric truths," he says, "can be questioned."[20] There may be an all-powerful evil God who not only creates appearances of earthly and celestial realms, that merely appear composed of things with magnitude, but merely apparent indubitable truths that are grasped in virtue of a rational nature also in doubt. He had previously opined the existence of an omnipotent creating God. Why is it not possible that he is also now deceived as others were about what they opined was best known? Descartes does not suppose he has an indubitable idea that other persons exist. Rather, his present idea about their mistaken 'certainties,' if they exist, warrants doubt about what *he* now thinks is best known. "How do I know that I am not myself deceived every time I add 2 and 3... or judge of things yet simpler... ?"[21]

---

19 Descartes, *Meditations*, p. 30.
20 *Ibid.*, p. 30.
21 *Ibid.*, p. 31.

The objection that a supremely good God would not constantly deceive him is discounted since God's allowance for a limited deception permits a constant one as well. Also, the further objection that this God is a 'fable' adds more force to the possibility of constant deception. For in order to explicate how "I have come to be what I am,"[22] there would not be appeal to a God who is supremely good but to fate, chance, or an invariable succession of events. So, his less than good or imperfect origin would accord with a possible deception which is "increased in proportion as the power to which... my origin is lessened."[23]

Now all ideas about his origin, from science to supremely good God, are to be treated as "long-established customary opinions." And the opinions are held as "entirely false" in order to avoid assuming that what is possibly false is true.[24] Possible truths were entertained to show that they did not counter his present doubt. Nevertheless, the doubtful idea of a supremely good God posed the greatest likelihood that he is not constantly deceived even about what is supposedly best known. Accordingly, his attempt to avoid all "old-time prejudices" leads him to pose the opposite possibility of a malignant god, or evil genius, who succeeds in systematic deception in virtue of *his* omnipotence.

Colliding head-on with an Enlightenment he influenced for which the mere specter of a devil was as offensive to 'scientific reason' as a Judeo-Christian God, this opposite evil god has led some modern readers to associate Descartes' rationalism with an antiquated medievalism. Though nothing could be further from the truth as his reasons make abundantly clear, neo-enlightened aversions to a 'mystery' of evil, much more to a supernatural devil, are reflected in many cultural modes. These include banned novels such as the award-winning *Master and Margarita* (1967) by former Soviet dissident Mikhail Bulgakou. His censored novel ridiculed communism by a literary devil who is angry since for Marxian science to discount God is for it to dismiss the devil. There were even

---

22 *Ibid.*, p. 31.

23 *Ibid.*, p. 31.

24 *Ibid.*, pp. 31, 32.

petty attempts in the West to 'demystify' a folklore genre of supernatural creatures, from the devil to vampires, whose evil is either inimical to child development or anomalous to scientific rationality.

The rationality is not itself scientific but has nevertheless intimidated authors in that genre such as Anne Rice. In her *Interview with the Vampire* (1995), she spoke apologetically of 'vampires' as mere symbols of a human conflict, progressively overcome by rational social-science action.[25] Having noted lingering neo-enlightened influences which eschew any mystery of evil, the 'evil genius' may be situated in spiraling doubt-laden possibilities:

(1) **Possibility of Sense Deception**
   Objection: Immediate high-quality perceptions?
(2) **Possibility of Dreaming**
   Objection: Geometrico-mathematical truths?
(3) **Possibility of Evil Genius**
   Objection: I cannot doubt that I am doubting?

Three Levels of Doubt

Science and Certainty

A certainty about the senses, which bears on empirical tests of theories and theoretical interpretations of observation, *e.g.* observed light as a wave (λ), is later related to the idea of a 'perfect God' which conflicts with the existence of evil genius. Doubt about this genius initially deepens doubt about his senses and dreaming. However, even if he undergoes the ultimate doubt of doubting his deception, he infers that if this genius "is deceiving me, I exist."[26] Since deception involves doubt and to doubt is to think, *ego sum, ego existo* "is

---

25 Professor L.T. Sargent ties a rational social-science vision in liberal democracy, which reflects Rice's embarrassment over vampire movies that foster religious superstition, to an illusory rational science of Marxism mocked by Soviet dissident M. Bulgakou. The Enlightenment engendered an approach that was "rationalist, whether Marxist or liberal democratic" wherein all problems "could be solved by... reason and science." From *Contemporary Political Ideologies* (Chicago: Dorsey Press, 1987), p. 116.
26 Descartes, *Meditations*, p. 34.

necessarily true every time I... [think] it." *Cogito ergo sum* (I think, therefore I am) is, accordingly, his first indubitably true idea.[27]

"Thinking?," he asks. "Here I find what... alone cannot be separated from me: *I am, I exist*. This is certain."[28] The certainty raises a question about the "I." His answer resulted in one of the greatest controversies among philosophers and those in the human sciences. Further, it is often overlooked that the answers bear on the intelligibility of truth-claims in the natural sciences, such as physics, to which we turn after Descartes' reply.

Idea of the Self
The existing 'I' or 'self' cannot be the body since there is still doubt about the senses. There would have to be a reliance on the senses for an indubitable idea of a body. For instance, if part of the body becomes numb such as a foot, feeling in it may be lost. But doubt about its existence may not ordinarily arise since it can be seen or felt with the hand. By contrast, Descartes doubts the feelings in his hand and all the other senses. This excludes appeal to them for not doubting the body. Since the body is not 'thought' and he only knows he thinks, it is only "necessarily true" he is "a thinking thing, that is to say, a mind... or reason."[29]

But when he adds that the words 'reason' or 'mind' have a new "significance... unknown to me,"[30] his inquiry yields several insights. First, he sees *clearly* that imagination cannot grasp the significance of the words since it is no more reliable than dreaming. Thus apprehending the 'self' with perfect *distinctness* involves the imagination's restraint. Second, by restraining it, he distinctly and clearly apprehends his 'self' as an unextended immaterial thinking thing. And he submits that "everything I apprehend in a genuinely *clear* and *distinct*

---

27 *Ibid.*, p. 34.

28 *Ibid.*, p. 35.

29 *Ibid.*, p. 35.

30 *Ibid.*, p. 35. Among other things, Descartes speaks of the mind in terms of a soul.

manner is true."[31] Hence, from the first indubitably true idea 'I think, therefore I am,' taken with doubt about his body, he infers a first clear and distinct idea which is substantial. The idea comprises the substantive first knowledge that he is a 'thinking thing.'[32]

Interestingly, a certainty of the first indubitable idea 'I think, therefore I am' may be stronger, epistemologically, than a certainty of the first clear and distinct idea 'I am a thinking thing.' Consider the inference rule of simplification $p \wedge q / \therefore p$. The proposition p may be weaker than a conjunction from which it is inferred. The inferred idea 'I am a thinking thing,' by analogy, may be weaker than the *cogito* even if both ideas are certain per se.

§

Caught in the pincers of his own novel usage, Descartes' inability to articulate how mind and body 'met' in a pituitary gland influenced the everyday speech over which he puzzled.

§

Here, 'thinking thing' or 'mind' as immaterial substances can be contrasted to substance that is material and extended. 'Extended' means occupying space and time as well as having volume. Extended things include the body and, herein, lies a uniquely modern 'mind-body problem.'

On the one hand, Descartes refers to soul as 'mind'. His reference has been viewed as a subtle agenda that has more to do with liberating modern philosophy from an Aristotelian-Thomistic "Scholasticism than... defeating materialism."[33] Despite ties of materialism to a modern mechanico-clockwork

---

31 *Ibid.*, p. 41. Emphasis added. 'Clarity' is said of ideas when they are "presented... to my mind" as opposed to coming "by way of the senses" (41); 'Distinctness' when the senses do not beget images in the mind which obfuscate the things presented (*cf.* the 'imaginative faculty' [39]).

32 *Ibid.*, p. 41.

33 See M. Rozemond's "The Role of the Intellect in Descartes's Case for the Incorporeity of the Mind," in *Essays On The Philosophy And Science Of Rene Descartes*, Ed. S. Voss (NY: Oxford University Press, 1993), p. 102.

cosmology with which he was sympathetic, this view suggests that his doubt, which is related to thinking, was contrived. The contrivance conflicts with a heartfelt diary-like quality in his *Meditations*. And it ignores a tradition from Aristotle's *Metaphysics* (984^b) to Thomas' *Summa* (I, 14, 9) wherein a psyche is conceptually distinct from a body. The distinction renders coherent ascriptions of 'truth' to thought about the body. Scientists do not strive for material bodies to be true but for a truth of thoughts, expressed as empirico-theoretical descriptions, about matter.

A deterministic and materialistic Atomism, as well as a relativistic Sophism, were touted euphemistically as the Greek Enlightenment. But this Enlightenment fostered an opposing tradition with which Descartes was in partial accord and which renders intelligible scientific 'truth.'[34]

On the other hand, he suspended traditional principles as old-time prejudice. Though his idea of a 'thinking thing' was novel, it was infused into meanings with which he was uneasy — per his letter to Mersenne in 1641.[35] In inferring a mind-body duality that was his real break with a medieval tradition, he was also at odds with its general view of an essential unity based on experience. An experienced reality was a truth-condition for 'truth.' Truth as the conformity of thought to reality *(adequato rei et intellectus)* reflects St. Augustine's view. Whereas everyday talk accords with the mind and body being conceptually distinct but still experienced as "one inseparable life," it is noteworthy Descartes expresses concern about being hampered by "ordinary speech."[36]

Caught in the pincers of his own novel usage, his inability

---

[34] Thomas' first efficient cause, that included voluntary or freely-chosen behavior, was influenced by Aristotle: When the materialists "had their day,... men were again forced by the truth itself... to inquire into the next kind of cause [*Met.* 984b]."

[35] See C. Adams and P. Tannery, Eds., *Oeuvres de Descartes III* (Paris: CNRS and Vrin, 1964-76), p. 298, and J. Cottngham et al, Trs., *The Philosophical Writings of Descartes III* (Cambridge University Press, 1931), p. 173. From Rozemond, "The Role of the Intellect," p. 112, fn. 27.

[36] For example, compare St. Augustine's *Confessions* (XIII, 11) and Descartes' *Meditations*, p. 39.

to articulate how mind and body 'met' in a pituitary gland influenced the everyday speech over which he puzzled. In distinguishing mind from body, he dogmatically imposed *concepts* on his *experiential awareness* of their composing one person. From a 'little person in one's head' to a 'ghost in the machine,' thought was not reconciled with our bodies. And bodies could exhaustively compose persons only by persons not ascribing 'truth' to their thought: 'Thought' would be a corporeal thing and 'truth' is not ascribed to such things. Rather it is ascribed to statements, which express thoughts, about bodies.

§

Paradoxically, scientists who reject conceptual distinctions of body and mind will tend to speak of thinking as a phenomenon and of that phenomenon in terms of their own thoughts *about* it.

§

Scientists inextricably *experience* themselves as unities of mind and bodies when they operate experimental setups. Yet, they must *conceptually* acknowledge an immaterial nature of their mind for intelligible scientific 'truth'— notwithstanding truth in physics being related conceptually to a materialistic determinism for their limited purpose.

The determinism is supposed by exactly measured phenomena in classical physics and inexact measurements in quantum mechanics. The mechanic's equations determine probabilities without admitting that microphysical phenomena either think or freely choose. Paradoxically, scientists who reject a conceptual distinction of body and mind will tend to speak of thinking as a phenomenon and of the phenomenon in terms of their own thoughts *about* it.

In arguing that the mind is a mere matter of bodily neural circuitry, for instance, the paradox attaches to everyday language when scientists use the Cartesian language in question:

> It seems odd that in... debunking Cartesianism, we find
> nearly as many references to mind as... to the brain and neural
> circuits... [If the scientist means] to cash out Cartesian

38

language into neural-bodily state language, then he should do so! Why continue to deploy Cartesian terminology...?[37]

Having noted problems that played into the hands of Hume and influenced Kant, it is important to note that Descartes, at least, did not argue for certain extremes. He did not reduce *thought* to a 'species of sensation' as would be done by Hume or, as Kant, to a mere possible noumenal reality — along with our free choice of will.

Idea of a Perfect God

If there was any question of Descartes' realism in which indubitably real thoughts are held to represent other realities, despite his dualism, it is erased by his arguments for God. Without being oxymoronic, one of the arguments reflects something akin to a cosmologico-ontological proof in which efficient and formal causes are employed for a clear and distinct idea of a perfect God.

In order to causally establish this God's existence, Descartes thinks that there must be a certainty that his idea of the existence is not caused by something other than God. Interestingly, he refers to a 'natural light' which brings to mind, epistemologically, his first indubitable idea as the basis for other clear and distinct ones.

Thus in virtue of a natural light which reveals truth such as "inasmuch as I doubt, it follows that I am, and the like...",[38] he affirms that "there must be at least as much reality in the efficient and total cause as in its effect" and not only that "something *cannot* proceed from nothing... but... that what is more perfect, i.e., contains more reality, cannot proceed from what is less perfect."[39] Also, the light reveals not only the same for "effects the reality of which philosophers term

---

[37] See P. Tibbitts review of *Descartes' Error: Emotion, Reason, and the Human Brain* (NY: G. P. Putnam's Sons, 1994), by A. R. Damasio, in the *American Scientist* 84 (1996) 91.

[38] Descartes, *Meditations*, pp. 43-44. For challenges to there being a 'Cartesian circularity' of "I can know *p* only if I first know *q*" and "I can know *q* only if I know *p*," see Dicker, *Descartes*, pp. 119-146.

[39] *Ibid.*, p. 45, emphasis added. Note the modal term '*cannot*'. Efficient causes are agencies of production wherein, for example, it is *impossible* to produce marble when there are not geomorphic processes.

actual or formal, but... ideas the reality of which is viewed as being what they term objective [*i.e.*, representational]."[40] And hence since he has the clear and distinct idea of a perfect God, nothing less could cause his idea since nothing else could be equally representational or perfect. Surely, he is not perfect since he doubts and a religious influence of society is ruled out since, besides his doubting other existing things, society is not perfect either.

§

Could Descartes have made explicit a mode of necessity, in his causal reasoning, which would have challenged Hume's idea that there is no 'necessary connexion' between events?

§

Intriguingly, while Thomas' clear-cut cosmological proofs began with the senses for inferring God, both he and Descartes view *thought* as a cause. Words such as 'impossible,' 'cannot' and 'must' suggest reasoning in a context of modal logic. Thus although Descartes untenably bifurcates bodily and mental causes in contrast to the medieval tradition, he notes that "there *must* be at least as much reality in the efficient and total cause as in its effect." This modality can be recast as a necessity and impossibility.

'It is impossible there is an ideational effect of a certain degree when there is no cause with an equal degree of reality': 'Necessarily if there is no cause with a given reality $(\sim C)$, there is no ideational effect $(\sim E)$'. This reasoning lends itself to a modal analog of *modus tollens*:

Necessarily if $\sim C$ then $\sim E$, and E, therefore C

Compare $N(\sim C \to \sim E)$ to 'If there is not a disease causing one to forget ideas $(\sim D)$, one does not forget ideas $(\sim F)$': F

---

[40] *Ibid.*, p. 45. V*ia* an Aristotelian-Thomistic understanding, 'formal causes' refer to either *(i)* what essentially things *are*, as the cause of marble *is* essentially C_aCO_3 and as a blueprint denotes what *is* essentially a house, or *(ii)* 'actualities' that cause things to strive to be (*entelechy*) what they are only 'potentially', as the form 'man' causes the male child to desire to be a man and as the 'acorn tree' causes the acorn to be a tree.

when ~*D* may obtain by a material implication ~*D* → ~*F* since N(~*C* → ~*E)* is not contravened. In virtue of truth that seems clear and distinct modally, the modality N(~*C* → ~*E)* is not merely a contingent truth if as a *matter of fact* it is not the case that '~*C*' is true and '~*E*' is false. It may set epistemic parameters for what are admitted scientifically as reasonable contingent truths. That is, the truth that one may forget *(F)* when there is not a disease causing it *(~D)* admits of other mental or physical causes.

N(~*C* → ~*E)* is part of an argument which seems onto-logical *and* cosmological. While it involves a cosmological modality that 'something *cannot* come from nothing,' it begins with an idea of 'God.' The argument is not further pursued here. Besides Descartes' divorce of spiritual and ideational causes from physical ones, other arguments would be of more interest to scientists oriented to sense experience. In beginning with it, for instance, Thomas suggests a modal argument which bears on modern physics. His assertion that since "it is *not possible* that the same thing should be at once in actuality and potentiality..., whatever is in motion *must* be put in motion by another" is related uncannily to a law of thermodynamics: "it is *impossible* to construct... a period-ically functioning machine that would do more work than the energy supplied... from outside."[41]

Idea of an External World
Could Descartes have made explicit a modal necessity, in his causal reasoning, which would have challenged Hume's idea that any 'necessary connexion' between events is merely supposed psychologically? Kant also suggested that there were psychologically certain judgments. They tended to be *synthetic* ones which, since they were supposed *a priori*, were confused with *analytic* or logically necessary judgments. An assumption that the rationalists were guilty of this confusion led to a notion that the causal principle, supposed *a priori* by scientific inquiry, has a truth-valueless metaphysical status. This status resulted in anti-metaphysical philosophies which sought 'truth' without metaphysics.

---

[41] *Cf.* Thomas' *Summa* (I, 2, 3) and Yavorsky's *Physics*, p. 165.

Having made these points about a 'cosmic cause' based on sense experience, it is important to note that Descartes relates his idea of God to sensations of an external reality. And this Cartesian reality, which pertains to ordinary experience, will relate to recent insights on science.

§

Descartes' idea of freedom was inconsistent with Hume's empiricism and transposed by Kant from certainty, in a Cartesian sense, to a questionable judgment 'All persons are free agents.'

§

Descartes denies that a perfect God who is without any defect, morally or any otherwise, is consistent with an omnipotent evil god. This god had only been a possibility, anyway, and the former was an inferred certainty. The certainty of a perfect God is inconsistent with His deceiving Descartes about what he is overwhelming inclined to believe. Thus, since he is warranted in believing that he has sensations, God would also be less than perfect if he was deceived about the existence of either his body, in which sensations occur, or an external world that causes them. And hence, he is not only able to *generally* rely on his senses, notwithstanding possible error, but to "conclude that corporeal things do indeed exist."[42]

A question posed by modern secular philosophers is how God "can allow evil if he is supremely good [?]".[43] Typically, there is no reference to any medieval philosophies whose present-day remnants are dismissed as the 'confused philosophy' of seminarians.[44] From the fifth century of Augustine to the thirteenth century of Aquinas, there were various

---

[42] Descartes, *Meditations*, p. 72.

[43] See Dicker's *Descartes: An Analytical and Historical Introduction*, p. 143, which, though excellent in many respects, poses the question as if it were simply unanswerable when there are many modern as well as medieval religio-philosophical answers.

[44] See A. Kenny's reference to exactly this smug attitude, in A. Kenny, ed., *The Oxford History of Western Philosophy* (Oxford: Oxford University Press, 1994), p. 367-368.

responses. For example, our moral dignity as human beings had no intelligibility apart from our ability to freely choose good or evil.[45] Though evil is now often viewed as a left-over religious superstition, a specter of superstition clouds deeper difficulties for modern philosophy. Before addressing this difficulty, Cartesian levels of downward doubts and upward certainties are noted:

1) THE SENSES	3) EXTERNAL WORLD
2) DREAMING	2) A PERFECT GOD
3) EVIL GENIUS	1) EXISTING SELF

COGITO ERGO SUM

Three levels of Doubt & Certainty

Empirical/Theoretical Challenges

Though Descartes situated free will in the intellect,[46] the idea of 'freedom' was both inconsistent with Hume's empiricism and transposed by Kant from certainty, in a Cartesian sense, to a questionable judgment 'all persons are free agents'. Stemming from the medieval idea of persons as voluntary efficient causes, the judgment was presupposed by moral inquiry and became a metaphysical counterpart of the causal principle.

The principle's post-Kantian relegation to a *synthetic a priori* pseudo-statement to which 'truth' is not ascribed, by logical positivists, led to the disregard of a metaphysics of freedom. But moral concerns and the ideal of physics, as a paradigm epistemic enterprise, inevitably continued. Hence, there also continued talk about 'free will' in moral theorizing, without explicating it philosophically, and acknowledgment of 'causes' in the human and natural sciences without reference to knotty epistemological problems which threatened a rationality of physics.

---

[45] See St. Augustine, *On Free Choice of the Will*, Tr. A. Benjamin et al (London: Collier Macmillan Publishers, 1986), pp. 85-88, 125-126 etc.

[46] This is the case, however much at other times Descartes intimates an idea of 'mind' which is restrictive in comparison to Thomistic concepts. These concepts begot a complementariness of natural and voluntary causes, including a first-cause free choice of will, as opposed to their distinctness.

For example, a formalized physics per se made no reference to causes. But its application to predictions of physical systems involved a metaphysical presupposition that future phenomena are related to past ones in virtue of causal regularities. And the regularities were expressed by a causal principle. Concluding that the principle is true, because true predictions involve the regularities, would amount to a question-begging argument *petitio principii*. At the same time, this dilemma was related to another, not anticipated by Descartes, to which there may be a viable Cartesian response. There emerged an anomaly of how ordinary scientific perceptions could be true when Einsteinian physics and quantum mechanics portrayed a world at odds with an everyday way it is perceived.

§

In a world where ideas would be displaced from a morally relevant experience of our nature and Nature's God, it would be a short step from 'I think, therefore I am' to a nihilistic inference 'I *am* but might *not be.*'

§

Since most perception virtually smacks of a Cartesian reality in which perceptual truth is related to appearance, the new theories posed a serious challenge. Despite distinctions of naked-eye from instrument-aided observation, one response is that the theories are corroborated by predictions that still rely on physical eyes as opposed to 'eyes of a theoretical mind'. Cartesian data are still the phenomena which are interpreted as theoretical state descriptions of physical systems at given times that, taken with theories by which theoretical terms are understood and rules of inference, imply states of the systems for future theoretical descriptions. And these are themselves identified with empirical state descriptions, understood as predictions, which beg for perceptual corroboration.

For example, Einstein's theory was corroborated *inter alia* by observing that a measured distance between two stars differs in night and day. And De Broglie's quantum-physics hypothesis was supported by appearances of diffraction when

44

beams of particles, interpreted as electrons, interacted with a substance. But by emphasizing a 'theoretical seeing' over an ordinary one, scientists such as Duhem appealed paradoxically, even if covertly, to predicted phenomena as they appear to support theories which show that the appearance is erroneous![47]

To avoid the error, A. Fine posits the other extreme. He rejects Einstein's claim that theoretical entities, in his general theory, are real. For "if we grant his claim," despite the theory's predictions, "not only do space and time cease to be real but... the usual dynamical quantities."[48] Yet, their reality may still hold in a Newtonian domain which is nested between phenomena approaching the speed of light and ones where Planck's constant obtains.

Further, a Cartesian denial of the error, either way, was presaged by St. Augustine: Nothing is wrong with a perception of oars appearing bent in the water. That is how they should appear. *Judgments* are wrong that they really are bent. The job of a scientific theory, say one of optics, is precisely to explicate and predict the appearance.

Newton-Smith strengthens these points by noting that we can "reject particular reports involving *O*-[observation] terms only if we have strong evidence (which rely on other observation reports) for a theory..."[49] The point would be missed by objecting that persons before modern astronomy would have been wrong to think that stars are white since, by our theory and instrument-aided study of stars, we reject those reports. The point is not that the reports should be rejected but rather that they reflect how stars still appear. And the appearance begs for theories which also explain our perceptions.

Unhappily, there ensued Hume disavowal of an external world and incorporeal self, much more of God. Whether Descartes could have strengthened his position by a medieval

---

[47] *Cf.* P. Duhem, *La theorie physique* (Paris, 1914), p. 218.

[48] *Cf.* D. Papineau, ed., *The Philosophy of Science* (NY: Oxford University Press, 1996), p. .31.

[49] W. H. Newton-Smith, *The Rationality of Science* (London: Routledge & Kegan Paul, 1981), p. 28.

modal-logic reasoning,[50] there was a general view, following Hume, that he assumed uncritically that existence was a predicate or that there were 'necessary connexions' between cause and effect.

§

Political ideology arose to fill a vacuum with the substantive truth of being alive and to give meaning to life. Paradoxically, there arose a culture of death.

§

In a world where ideas would be displaced from a morally relevant experience of our nature and Nature's God, it would be a short step from 'I think, therefore I am' to a nihilistic inference 'I *am* but might *not be*': In restricting 'truth' to the logically trivial and empirically contingent — whatever *is* might *not be*, the 'I' is faced with the specter of an existential *angst* of nothingness.

University of Paris Professor B. Stora notes a political nihilism, regarding modern terrorism in Algeria, the rationale for which is an ideological "I kill, therefore I am."[51] Certainty about one's physical existence is expressed negatively, though concretely, by a power to cause the nonexistence of another's mind and body. In view of a disembodied Cartesian doubt, certainty is sought by silencing objections about what others say is true. A rationale for political suppression is that 'truth' cannot even be ascribed objectively to scientific theories, let alone to theories of ethics and politics.

Political ideology arose to fill a vacuum with a substantive truth of being alive and to give meaning to life. Paradoxically, there arose a culture of death. In order to appreciate how such consequences of philosophy cannot be glibly dismissed, Hume's rejection of metaphysical truth is now considered.

---

[50] See, A. E. Moody, *Studies in Medieval Philosophy, Science, and Logic* (Berkeley: University of California Press, 1975), p. 376.

[51] See also M. Hennad of the University of Algiers, and A. Rouadjia on ideological mass murder: "To exercise terror is a way to show one exists," in E. Ganley's Paris Report "I Kill, Therefore I am," *The Associated Press* 30 August 1997.

A Metaphysical Rationalism

The rejection, exacerbated by Kant, induced both the question 'Whence comes *truth* if not from metaphysics' and ideological answers which posit political power.

Chapter 3

An Empiricist Metaphysics of Skepticism

A nineteenth-century lure of political power, as odd as it may seem, was catalyzed by the earlier British Empiricists. In reply to Continental Rationalism, they held that rationalistic ideas led to dogmatic impositions of *a priori* metaphysical biases on sense experience. Empiricism was alluring since it stressed experience about which persons might agree. It did not appeal to a metaphysics about which there seemed to be either little agreement or an agreement which, in any event, was empirically unverifiable.

Among the Empiricists, David Hume (1711-1776) was the most rigorously consistent. Locke and Berkeley held that ideas derived from experience showed how little was known to be strictly true. But they accepted a common-sense truth about issues of the day that Hume revealed to be inconsistent with an exacting empiricist view of 'truth.'

Epistemology is the study of 'truth.' The study, herein, indicates that Hume proclaimed various truths on the basis of an induction and medieval mode of reasoning he eschewed. Had the eschewed reasoning been appreciated by Kant, he might not have tried to mediate between rationalism and Hume's 'critical thought' for a critical account of knowledge. Rather than denying knowledge of a causal principle presupposed by scientific inquiry, which induced skepticism and led to politicization of 'truth,' a truth might have been ascribed to the principle which was stronger epistemologically than an empirically contingent truth suggested by Hume.

Before considering how Hume may have actually assumed a uniquely strong 'truth' in his own skeptical reasoning, we exam *(i)* why the reasoning led to attacks on religion, *(ii)* his radical theory of knowledge, and *(iii)* how a dubious *knowledge* of knowledge impacted notable contemporary philosophers of science.

§

Despite the fact that Hume rendered incoherent a concept of 'truth' in science, his orientation to the scientific revolution led to his belief that the greatest obstacle to enlightenment was religious 'superstition.'

§

Hume's attack on religion followed his skeptical reasoning. The reasoning even resulted in his denial that a causal principle is known *a priori*. Kant rooted its *a priori* status in our cognition. This gambit lessened skepticism only temporarily because the cognition thesis was itself metaphysical. Immediate doubt was cast on scientific truth, until the time of Kant, since it rested on an unknown truth of the principle. But doubt about the principle was paled by that about a religious metaphysics.

Though 'critical thinking' resulted in an unequaled modern skepticism, the skepticism shaped Hume's anti-metaphysical quest for new grounds of truth. Despite his failure to even articulate a theoretical truth of science, his orientation to the scientific Enlightenment led to a supposition that the greatest obstacle was religious 'superstition.' And hence his writings were peppered with incautious criticisms of religion in general, and of Roman Catholicism in particular, because Catholicism was "the most zealous of any sect..."[1]

---

[1] David Hume, *A Treatise of Human Nature*, Ed. by L. A. Selby-Bigge (Oxford: Clarendon Press, 1967), p. 115. Notwithstanding a deletion of his anti-Christian remarks in secondary textbooks, Hume's works are still often used by philosophers 'sensitive' to *not* imposing religious views on their students. Besides often failing to be equally sensitive to students who are believers, important insights for philosophy are often disregarded as well. As considered later, the insights include modalities of philosophical theology which Hume also neglected.

In using his empiricism to explain Catholicism's superstitious "mummeries,"[2] Hume may have initially strengthened the Reformation only to have its ideas consigned, by most secular academics, "to a limbo of subjectivity and second-class importance."[3] In order to appreciate his influential pessimism about 'truth,' three levels skepticism are considered.

First-Level Skepticism: Sensations *vs.* Reality

Though Hume disavowed parts of his *Treatise* in favor of the later *Enquiries Concerning Human Understanding* which alone contain "his philosophical... principles," the *Enquiries* retained an initial skepticism deepened by others: knowing the truth of a causal principle and inferring truth by induction.[4] The latter are addressed after dealing with his divorce of reality from sense impressions. Internal impressions and an external reality tend to be treated as the same thing under a rubric of 'sense experience'.

Hume was optimistic that experience is not only the basis for "all the sciences" but for a moral philosophy not "inferior in certainty... to any other of human comprehension."[5] But his analysis led to a skepticism about our comprehension since all ideas are mere "copies of our impressions."[6] That is, more lively impressions are the source of less vivid ideas that are not known to correspond to an external reality but rather to mere sense impressions.

---

2 D. Hume, *Enquiries Concerning Human Understanding and Concerning the Principles of Morals*, Intro. by L. A. Selby-Bigge, 3rd Ed. (Oxford: Clarendon Press, 1975), p. 51. In discussing the quality in ideas of "resemblance," Hume states that "The ceremonies of the Roman Catholic religion may be considered as instances... The devotees of that superstition usually plead in excuse for the mummeries [pretentious ceremonies],... that they feel the good effect of those external motions, and postures..."

3 T. O'dea et al, "Religion in the Year 2000," *Philosophy Looks to the Future*, Ed. by P. Richter and W. Fogg (Ill: Waveland Press, 1985), p. 545.

4 Hume, *Enquiries*, p. 2. Selby-Begge notes that this work's omission of Bk. I in the *Treatise* cannot be due to Hume's "discontent with the positions" but rather to a "desire to make the *Enquiries* readable" (xii).

5 Hume, *Treatise*, pp. xxii, xxiii.

6 *Ibid.*, p.19.

Impressions are like after-images when we close our eyes after looking at bright lights. Images and not external lights, by this analogy, yield our idea of 'lights.' Hume laments that even Locke confused ideas with "perceptions,...sensations and passions, as well as thoughts," though, adds Hume, he was led into the confusion by "the [Catholic] schoolmen, who... draw out their disputes to a tedious length, without ever touching the point in question." [7]

§

In supposing theories to be true in virtue of mirroring physical reality, scientists are said to assume a metaphysical realism. Bizarrely, Hume's *realism* would have 'truth' ascribed to ideas only when they reflect our internal sensations.

§

Now one might assume that a piece of chalk in one's hand both exists and *is* as it appears to be. This assumption brings to mind Descartes' high-quality experiences which are so vivid that, apart from dreaming, some ideas induced by the senses seem to be virtually indubitable. Consequently, one might say that the idea of the chalk's existence as well as its being white and brittle is patently true.

However, by analogy to a psychologist's ink-blot test in which patients report what they see, one's descriptions of the alleged chalk tell us much about one's internal sensations and nothing about the thing *per se*. Hume does not say that there are not external realities which resemble our impressions but rather that we cannot strictly know that this is so.

Scientific Truth: Correspondence to Sensations?
There can be no doubt that Hume's antagonism to religious superstition was alternatively expressed by his sympathy with science. In supposing scientific theories to be true in virtue of reflecting an approximate nature of physical reality, scientists assume what is said to be a metaphysical realism. Bizarrely, however, Hume's *realism* would have 'truth' ascribed to ideas

---

[7] *Ibid.*, p. 22, fn. 1.

only when they reflect our internal sensations. How are sensations related to observation?

The observation term 'water,' which refers to an extra-sensory phenomenon, would be related to an internal sense impression. But there could be no correlation of the impression to either the phenomenon or theoretical idea H_2O. Indeed, Hume states that "we need but enquire, from what *impression* is that supposed idea derived?"[8]

He holds that ideas derived from anything other than internal impressions are metaphysical. This would transpose physics, that does exactly this, into a species of metaphysics. That the transposition is not spurious is revealed by F. Suppe who, noting the conclusions of a national symposium on the philosophy of science at Chicago Circle, criticizes a radical Humean empiricism of physicist Paul Feyerabend.

In holding that scientific ideas are derived from sensations, Feyerabend's "realism is an empty one wherein the correspondence of a theory with reality plays no role in its... truth" since his "position commits him to a view of 'knowledge' where the truth of ϕ has no bearing on whether one knows that ϕ... carrying Hume's skeptical program to its logical limits."[9] The limits reflect a view in which 'truth' is relative to possibly inconsistent theories used to interpret truthless sensorial sentences. And intriguingly, a connection of our Enlightenment to one of sophistic Greece, with its scientific Atomism, is clear in Plato's *Theaetetus* (161^d): "If what every man believes as a result of perception [*qua* sensation] is indeed true for him... where is the wisdom of Protagoras... and testing one another's notions [?]."

Importantly, 'truth' is ascribed to ideas or statements *about* phenomena. It is as senseless to assert that sensations

---

[8] *Ibid.*, p. 22. Emphasis is not added.

[9] See *The Structure of Scientific Theories*, Ed. F. Suppe (Chicago: University of Illinois Press, 1977), pp. 640, 641, 641n. Feyerabend and Thomas Kuhn became the epistemic inspiration, beginning in American universities in the 1970s, for relativistic radical feminists, deconstructionists, and others who denounced any objective truth in a manner reminiscent of Greek Sophism (which enjoyed some revitalized defenses among philosophers).

or phenomena are true as to ascribe 'truth' to statements which describe sensations. To speak of sensory descriptions as being true is to speak of 'truth' only trivially. Thus it is difficult to see how there could be any coherent idea of empirical 'truth,' on the Humean account, as it is conceived in physics, if not metaphysics.

§

With due respect to Hume's scathing criticism of religion, can it be said that he and his progeny could see 'philosophical specks' in the eyes of others but not 'logs' in their own?

§

Hume's attention to traditional metaphysics does not erase the difficulties. For example, he speaks of a metaphysical idea of God which cannot be traced back to an impression since, in being a physical sensation, the impression could not give rise to the idea of a nonphysical spiritual Being. An idea of this Being "arises from reflecting on the operations of our own mind, and augmenting, without limit, those qualities of goodness and wisdom."[10] But Hume's own claim that his empiricism would banish "all that jargon, which has so long taken possession of metaphysical reasonings"[11] belies this fact: His own empiricist anti-metaphysics is itself composed paradoxically of metaphysical ideas. From what impression is derived his *own* idea that legitimate ideas are derived from sense impressions?

In bringing to mind a future verification principle of logical positivists whose epistemic ideal was physics and whose ultimate philosophical 'father' was Hume, are Hume's anti-metaphysical principles also self-refuting? Ironically, he especially sought to refute the 'superstitions' of religion. But the religious dictum that sins of the father are visited on three generations takes on a novel spin. The verification principle was a self-refuting metaphysical sentence. For it specified that 'meaningfulness' was ascribed to sentences if and only if they

---

10 Hume, *Enquiries*, p. 19.
11 *Ibid.*, p. 21.

were empirically or logically true (false) and it was not itself true or false. By the same token, Hume's idea of legitimate ideas, which was a paradigm idea for the principle, was a self-refuting meaningless idea because it was not itself either analytically true or true in virtue of being derived from sensations.

With due respect to Hume's scathing criticism of religion, can it be said that he and his progeny could see the 'philosophical specks' in the eyes of others but not the 'logs' in their own? That philosophers with vastly different backgrounds are concerned with his mischievous influence is clear — from a phenomenology of Merleau-Ponty to W. H. Newton-Smith's analytic approach to philosophy.

The approach of Newton-Smith is enlightening. He admits that the assertions "I see a red patch" and "I'm having a blue after-image" express truths with which many Positivists mistakenly associated the language of observation or sense-data. At the same time, he notes that reporting on "inner sensory experience and not making any claims... about the external world play no role whatsoever in the practice of, say, physics or chemistry."[12] Merleau-Ponty views it from another angle. After noting that "red and green are not sensations, they are the sensed (sensibles), and that quality is not an element of consciousness, but a property of the object," he states that Hume's analysis of experienced objects "went on to dissect and emasculate this [very] experience."[13]

Sensations and 'Phenomena Themselves'

Despite Hume's denial of any rational basis for induction, his followers tirelessly contrast the 'fool' who does not assume the future will behave as the past to Hume's famous defense of common sense. But in addition to a schism between common sense and philosophy, he puts to rest his philosophical defense by asking even his defenders what evidence "assures us of any real existence and matter of fact, beyond the present

---

12 W. H. Newton-Smith, *The Rationality of Science* (London: Routledge & Kegan Paul, 1981), p. 26

13 M. Merleau-Ponty, *Phenomenology of Perception* (London: Routledge & Kegan Paul, 1978), pp. 4, 220.

testimony of our senses..."[14] Hume's skepticism holds even if the senses are *lively*.

The *lively* sense impressions, not things sensed, would be the only source for the defenders' relatively *dim* ideas on the matter. In precisely this sense, the notion of a 'thing per se' draws attention to an ignored influence on Kant's idea of a thing-in-itself (*ding an sich*). The latter is a noumenal reality in contrast to reality as it appears.

§

Unless we are consciousness of both sensations and ideas, the very idea of 'sensation' would be senseless since it could not be distinguished from the thing sensed.

§

Before noting further skepticism, a question is posed in light of the philosophical theology attacked by Hume. Long before him, was there not a tenable response to the problem of the senses? The senses were not considered apart from the objects sensed. And the response did not lean on an argument which relied circularly on them. St. Augustine used a logic of modal reasoning, perhaps confused with metaphysics, wherein some behavior is experienced as being modally impossible. He pioneered relevant insights usually credited to modern existentialists who also tend to underestimate logic.

In virtue of a modal logic of physical impossibilities, developed by Aristotle,[15] Augustine appealed to our self-conscious experience for submitting that it cannot be false that our rear feet are not raised until the first are put down when it is true we walk.[16] A patency of his insight on walking should not obscure Hume's disingenuousness appeal to immediate sensations. By this appeal, he rejected even quaint ideas such as one walking wherein it is *more* than reasonable,

[14] Hume, *Treatise*, p. 26.

[15] See R. Trundle, *Medieval Modal Logic and Modern Science* (Lanham, MD: UP of America, 1999), pp. 18-26.

[16] St. Augustine, *On Christian Doctrine*, Tr. by D. W. Robertson, Jr. (NY:: Macmillan Publishing Co., 1988), p. 71.

given our physical nature, to expect any future behavior to resemble our past behavior.[17]

Augustine's insights include those in *On Free Choice of the Will* and the *Confessions*. They range from even "a beast is aware... it sees when it sees," with a suggestion that it is phenomenologically impossible to see and not be conscious of both seeing and the thing seen,[18] to "men who count... are aware of what they count."[19] They are aware of what is counted and not of mere sensations of counting.

Coupled to St. Thomas' appeal to our experience of ourselves as voluntary causes of external events — as first causes who freely choose them,[20] these insights render tenable public reports of sensations. They also presage the existentialism of, among others, Jean-Paul Sartre. When we are aware of either internal sensations or external objects, we are also incontrovertibly aware of our consciousness of them. In not being either an idea derived from a sensation or a sensation per se, consciousness does not skew that of which we are conscious. Unless we are consciousness of both sensations and ideas, the very idea of 'sensation' would be senseless since it could not be distinguished from the thing sensed. Nor does it make any sense to speak of sensations if one is not conscious of both them and a person to whom they may be reported.

Second-Level Skepticism: Cause and Effect

Presumably presupposed by scientific inquiry, which leads to truth claims about physical reality, is the assumption that all events have causes. If the assumption is made *a priori* — prior to experience, and if it is not either derived from experience

---

[17] *Ibid.*, pp. 69, 72.

[18] St. Augustine, *On Free Choice of the Will*, Tr. by A.S. Benjamin and L.H. Hackstaff (NY: Macmillan Publishing Co., 1985), p 45.

[19] St. Augustine, *Confessions*, Tr. by R. S. Pine-Coffin (Middlesex, England: Penguin Books Ltd., 1984), p. 94.

[20] St. Thomas Aquinas, *Summa Theologica*, I, 46, 2 and 83,3. For a tie between Aquinas and our being consciousness of ourselves as well as things external to us, see R. Trundle's "Twentieth-Century Despair & Thomas' Sound Argument for God," *Laval Theologique et Philosophique* 52 (1996) 101-125.

or known to be true, there is a serious question about the epistemic integrity of a scientific truth that supposes the truth of a causal principle. Hume's critique of the principle is a central reason for his being celebrated as the 'Father of Critical Thinking.'

§

A question ensues of how Hume can viably refer to a 'wound' as opposed to its 'sensation.' The sensation from which is derived the idea 'wound' cannot be pain since it is the effect.

§

Thus for example, in an *Introduction to Logic & Critical Thinking*, M. H. Salmon soft pedals theoretical problems about a causal principle's truth. He stresses Hume's anticipation of pragmatism and practical psychology. Hume, was "*NOT* recommending that we cease making causal investigations...," since "this would not only be foolish but also psychologically impossible." Here, there is an emphasis on the psychological over the logical which so influenced Kant. The book adds that "philosophers and scientists have adopted the... pragmatic stand in view of Hume's analysis."[21] How the analysis actually deepened skepticism begs for a look at his underlying idea of 'thinking' as an association of ideas. Ideas were related by, among other things, a principle of causality.

Causality as a Principle of Association
If ideas were not associated, they would be isolated without any relation between them by which there could be a process of thinking. In order to explain thinking, Hume held that ideas are related by principles of association. Evidently, the principles refer to qualities in ideas which include *resemblance, contiguity,* and *cause or effect.* In particular, *resemblance* is the quality in terms of which, for instance, a "picture naturally leads our thoughts to the original";[22]

---

21 M. H. Salmon, *Introduction to Logic and Critical Thinking*, 2nd Ed. (NY: Harcourt Brace Jovanovich, Publishers, 1989), p.132.
22 Hume, *Enquiries*, p. 24.

contiguity means closeness in time or place whereby, for example, "mention of one apartment in a building naturally introduces an enquiry... concerning the others";[23] and *cause or effect* is the quality by which, for instance, "if we think of a wound, we can scarcely forbear reflecting on the pain which follows it."[24]

A question ensues of how Hume can viably refer to a 'wound' as opposed to its 'sensation.' The sensation from which is derived the idea 'wound' cannot be pain since it is the effect. Does the idea come from looking at either our own injuries or those of others? But what can be meant by the phrase 'looking at injuries'? We are *not* to speak of seeing injuries, since they are external things, but rather of internal sensations. As previously noted, such questions reveal odd ways of speaking. At the same time, the oddity is exacerbated by a problem of causality even if there could be tenable reference to external things.

Skepticism can be momentarily suspended about whether qualities other than *cause or effect* are derived from the senses. Hume claims that his principles "will not... be much doubted."[25] Two other claims are considered. These include his provision for causality with one hand, only to take it back with the other, and an anomalous logic of causality.

Causality With One hand; Taking it Back . . .
Causality is not merely the most important idea of association since it affords discoveries of some things causing others, such as elasticity causing phenomena to return to an initial state after deformation. In addition, by *"reasonings from analogy, experience, and observation,"*[26] the idea is exploited for reducing "the principles, productive of natural phenomena, to a greater simplicity, and to resolve the many particular effects into a few general causes..."[27] After noting that these causes are "probably the ultimate... principles which we shall ever

23 *Ibid.,* p. 24.
24 *Ibid.,* p. 24.
25 *Ibid.,* p. 24.
26 *Ibid.,* p. 43, emphasis added.
27 *Ibid.,* p. 30.

discover in nature," that may have influenced a complacency of later physicists,[28] he adds that the causal principles include "Elasticity, gravity, cohesion of parts, communication of motion by impulse..."[29]

§

Hume gives with one hand of common sense what he takes back with another. Laws owe "merely to experience." But even after experiencing "cause and effect, our conclusions... are *not* founded on... any process of understanding."

§

An ignored contribution may be the recognition of causal reasoning from *observation* to theory. Today, theorizing is often held to begin with bold conjectures. The latter are like 'buildings piles' lowered on 'observational swamps' wherein observation plays no role in theory formation but only in falsifying predictions.[30] Under an influence of Hume's anti-inductivism, Karl Popper worsened the skepticism he sought to soften by accepting that universal theoretical truth is not be obtained inductively: The truth is not only *not* inducted from observation but *not* verified by predictions since their truth does not imply true theories.

New theories may involve modified theoretical concepts. For example, Einsteinian 'mass' is indebted to Newton's idea. Yet the notion that theories are only theoretical conjectures may not just overlook, say, J. J. Thomson's reasoning from observations of cathode-ray tube phenomena to electrons as their causes. The notion may ignore reasoning from experiences such as 'pressure brought to bear' to kinematic ideas of 'force' which, as causes of motion, come to be understood as a function of mass times acceleration ($f = ma$).

---

28 See Stanley Jaki's "The Last Word in Physics," *Philosophy in Science* 5 (1993) 9-32. Jaki notes that Planck, Rutherford, Schrodinger, and Bohr believed "they had formulated the last word in physics...".

29 *Ibid.*, p. 30.

30 K. Popper, *The Logic of Scientific Discovery* (London: Hutchinson, 1968), p. 111. But a probable 'truth' allegedly holds for conjectures when they yield highly improbable true predictions.

This is not to say that modern equations refer to causes, much less to medieval ones as 'explanations.' Rather it brings to mind a proverbial apple that falls on Newton's head. A phenomenon may come to be conceived theoretically in a reference frame associated with earth, as caused by a gravity force 'P' directly proportional to a mass m times the acceleration of free fall g ($P = mg$).[31] And gravity as a cause may, in turn, lead to consideration of an inverse square law. Some scientists may shift from speaking of 'gravity as a cause' to holding that the law,

$$F_{gr} = G m_1 m_2/r^2,$$

reflects gravity's force; not its cause as criticized by Hume.[32] Why the latent criticism?

Shifting from the idea of 'gravity as a cause' to an idea that there need be no 'cause of gravity' was a convenient stratagem. But there was no incentive to interpret modern laws so that gravity and other properties or processes did not pertain to 'causes' until certain problems were made poignantly clear. Theoretical truth involved a notion of 'causality' presupposed *a priori* but only known, if at all, by immediate sense experience.

In the end, Hume gives with one hand of common sense what he takes back with another skeptical one. Discovering a law owes "merely to experience." And even after experiencing "cause and effect, our conclusions... are *not* founded on... any process of understanding."[33] But this understanding reveals an anomalous logic of causality.

An Anomalous Logic of Causality
The idea of 'cause' leads to skepticism because it involves only three other limited ideas derived from sensations. Where A and B are events, and '$\rightarrow$' denotes 'If... then...' for

---

[31] *Cf.* B. Yavorsky and Yu. Seleznev, *Physics*, Tr. from the Russian by G. Leib with contributions by N. A. Boguslavskaya (Moscow: MIR Publishers, 1979), p.65.

[32] For example, see M. B. Evans, "Newton and the cause of Gravity," *The American Journal of Physics* 26 (1958) 619-624.

[33] Hume, *Enquiries*, pp. 31, 32.

a causal relationship between them, the relationship may be
schematized as follows:

$$A \to B$$

(i) *A* is prior to *B* (*priority*).
(ii) *B* follows *A* (*constant conjunction*).
(iii) *A* and *B* are close together (*contiguity*).

Event A causes B

Priority, constant conjunction, and contiguity are *legitimate* ideas. But there is a habit of association that leads to a
metaphysical idea of a 'necessary connexion' between causes
"attained by reasoning *a priori*."[34] Hume denies that *prior* to
events, such as a falling apple, there is any legitimate idea of a
cause such as gravity. A central problem was set for Kant who
exalted Newton's laws. In addition to 'gravity as a cause'
being an applied instance of a causal principle, the principle is
presupposed *a priori* by scientific inquiry. The inquiry could
not result in true laws since the principle would have to follow
from experience *a posteriori*.

§

**Hume says that there is no stronger understanding
of $A \to B$ where it is impossible that ~B when A.
This may ignore an ordinary language which
analytic philosophers, whose tradition is
rooted in Hume, are loathe to accept.**

§

Hume seeks to show that, because of repeated experiences,
we come to misguidedly think that causal relations are
logically necessary. Negatively put, we tend to suppose an
impossibility that certain things occur when others do not.
Our inference would be stronger, epistemologically, than a
material implication of propositional logic.

But to say this logic does not always permit an impossibility of consequents not obtaining when antecedents do is
not to say that implication does not permit the impossibility
or that there are not degrees of more epistemological strength

---

[34] *Ibid.*, p. 27.

than that granted by Hume. Where 'events' are expressed by propositions, $A \rightarrow B$ may even express the relatively weak ordinary inference "*if* its antecedent is true... its consequent is true" in terms of which, accordingly, the extraordinary in the second row below is the *exception*: [35]

A	$\rightarrow$	B
t	**T**	t
t	**F**	f
f	**T**	t
f	**T**	f

Truth Table: A Humean Anomaly

Yet Hume says *without exception* that there is no stronger understanding of $A \rightarrow B$ where, for instance, it is impossible that $\sim B$ when A. This may ignore an ordinary language that analytic philosophers, whose tradition is rooted in Hume, are loathe to accept. And this holds even if, until recently, they largely followed Hume's disregard of modal ideas. While the ideas do today "pertain to the philosophy of language," notes J. Holt, "their deeper source is in [medieval] modal logic, the formal study of the different modes of truth — necessity and possibility..."[36]

One philosopher suggests that we may speak of a possibility that 'Persons do not see a given object *(~S)*' when 'They are looking at it *(L)*.' But although '$\sim S$ when L' is not logically impossible, it may be impossible in view of our sentient nature.[37] Or, we ordinarily assert an impossibility that 'One doesn't feel pain when one's toe is broken': Necessarily if one's toe is broken, one feels pain. Given our experience of pain-enduring athletes, however, such claims may contrast to one at a soccer game: 'If a player's toe is broken, then he doesn't run.' That is, 'He doesn't run' may well be false when 'His toe is broken' is true.

---

[35] I. M. Copi, *Symbolic Logic* (NY: The Macmillan Co., 1972), p. 15.

[36] J. Holt, "Whose Idea is It Anyway: Philosophers Feud," *Lingua Franca* (Jan/Feb 1996) 32.

[37] *Cf.* F. I. Dretske's ordinary-language analysis of seeing in *Seeing and Knowing* (Chicago: University of Chicago Press, 1969), pp. 18-35.

Further, Hume holds that an empirical truth of $A \rightarrow B$, where A and B are true, is strictly known if known at all (since sensations are not known to reflect external reality), only by immediate experience. The word 'experience' enjoys a more liberal interpretation only by usurping what is unique to his empiricism: its idea of a psychological habit with no basis in "reasoning, or... understanding."[38]

Either there is this understanding or the one of Hume is self-refuting. Is there no such understanding of causality which underlies his thought that all ideas, derived from sensations, are associated? Associations of priority, constant conjunction, and contiguity bring to mind Hume's denial of a causal relation between ideas by a 'necessary connexion'. Either there is or is not such a connection.

§

Hume asserted that all "reasonings may be divided into... [logically necessary] relations of ideas"or "matter of fact and existence." But unless there is another 'truth,' Hume's own assertion is not only metaphysical but self-refuting.

§

Given there is no connection, when Hume specifies a connection "among ideas, namely *Resemblance, Contiguity* in time or place, and *Cause* or *Effect*,"[39] it cannot lead to any reasoning *a priori*. Prior to each immediate experience of himself, as opposed to others for whom he speaks, he cannot know if those ideas will hold for the associated ideas that he specifies *a priori*. And given such an *a priori* connection, his reasoning exceeds a material implication of propositional logic largely developed by the positivists he influenced. These considerations, as soon amplified, bear on strict implications of modally necessary connections.

One need not assert that Hume's own idea of how 'ideas are associated' necessitates a causal reasoning, warranting

---

38 Hume, *Treatise*, p. 32.
39 *Ibid.*, p. 24.

another idea that 'ideas are associated necessarily,' to assert that he and his followers seem to miss the point (*ignoratio elenchi*) of their own critical thinking. The latter led Hume to assert that all "reasonings may be divided into... [logically necessary] relations of ideas... or... [empirical] matter of fact and existence."[40] But unless there is another 'truth' other than necessary and empirical truth, Hume's assertion is not only metaphysical but self-refuting.

In the first place, is not his universal assertion uttered *a priori*? In the second, is it not the case that the assertion cannot be said to be true as either an empirical "matter of fact" or as a logically necessary "relation of ideas"? At the same time, he may illustrate an important sort of reasoning *a priori* that is not logically necessary. He may draw attention to an underlying reasoning necessary for the scientific truth which presupposes a true causal principle.

The problem of saying that the principle is both necessary and true, where the 'truth' has a basis in experience and is in some sense known *a priori*, cannot have a solution posed by Kant. He rooted the *a priori* in an *a priori* cognition. Appeal to the cognition, as soon discussed, amounted to a question-begging psychological response to a logical difficulty.

Third-Level Skepticism: Problem of Induction

The difficulty of knowing that events have causes is related to that of induction. Hume's central concern with induction was reasoning from past to future causes and from experiences to a conclusion which goes beyond them. That the two sorts of induction are connected is evidenced by his questions. How could we know future effects of objects "without consulting past observation... ?"[41] Is the process of reasoning from one instance to a conclusion "so different from that... [of] a hundred instances?"[42] Before exploring the questions in more

---

[40] *Ibid.*, p. 35.

[41] *Ibid.*, p. 29. Consider inducting a law for electrons by an intuitive induction (*epagoge*), and being able to use the law for predictions of a microphysical system in virtue of causal relations to its present state.

[42] *Ibid.*, p. 36.

depth, there is attention to causal regularities and induction as they bear on Nature's uniformity.

Induction and Uniformity of Nature
The notion of a 'uniformity of Nature' generally means that nature is characterized by a future which behaves as the past in terms of causal regularities. Such regularities are presupposed by scientists when, for example, they seek to corroborate previous research by duplicating its experiments. This notion of a 'uniformity of Nature' is implicitly criticized by Hume when he notes: Should we say that "from a number of uniform experiments, we *infer* a connexion between the sensible qualities..., [the] question still recurs, on what process of argument... this inference is founded?"[43]

§

Do future results reflect a *certainty* which Hume admits to be psychological? This begs a question of whether the psychological is unrelated to the logical.

§

He adds that it cannot be founded in past instances because when the scientist asserts that they *"will always be conjoined...* he is not guilty of a tautology."[44] That is, to assert that certain instances will be *conjoined* is not to assert, tautologously or redundantly, that this was the case with past ones. Can two similar assertions be formulated as an argument for reasoning to the future from past instances?

Even when the instances are concluded to invariably hold in the future from a premise that properly specifies associations such as 'priority,' Hume responds that the scientists's argument is not a deductive one in which a conclusion follows with logical necessity. Rather the argument is inductive. Though having a supposed conclusion that is probable, it simply appeals to experiment. But, says Hume, appealing to experiment "is begging the question."[45] The question remains

---

43 *Ibid.*, pp. 36, 37.
44 *Ibid.*, p. 37
45 *Ibid.*, p. 37.

after the conclusion of why associated qualities will necessarily hold in the future.

The scientist's argument is no better than our everyday culinary reasoning that from "a body of like colour... with bread we *expect* like nourishment and support."[46] Ordinary persons make no pretension to a rational justification which justifies their expectation. But in supposing that the scientific enterprise is thoroughly rational, largely because of a leftover metaphysics of medieval scholastics, thinks Hume, scientists burden themselves with an illogical circularity. This amounts to arguing that past instances will obtain since the future has behaved *as* the past *in* the past.

Hume's rejection of appeals to the past has been forcefully challenged. While his argument that induction is "correct in assuming that reasonable men make inductions... and in showing that induction is not deduction," says Korner, he is wrong in replacing surreptitiously a notion of justification by "justifiable justification."[47] A justification is an expectation which does not need to be justified.

In sum, unjustifiable justifications warrant no skepticism. Reasoning from past successes to expected future ones, on the whole, is not discreditable.[48] The reasoning is not discountable by relating 'discreditable' to such things as 'unverifiable' or 'unfalsifiable.' To object that it is not falsifiable because not discreditable, for instance, is to confuse a physical thesis with one of metaphysics *'ta meta ta phusika'* (things after physics). Demands on metaphysics are different from those on physics since theories of physics permit, if not verification or falsification, empirical evidence to count for or against them. But this difference per se is no more reason to reject the metaphysical reasoning of Korner than of Hume.

If Hume reasons that inductive justifications beg for question-begging justifications and his reasoning is itself a 'process' for or against which no future evidence counts, the

---

46 *Ibid.*, p. 37. Emphasis added.
47 S. Korner, *Experience and Theory: An Essay in the Philosophy of Science* (London: Routledge & Kegan Paul, 1966), p. 194.
48 *Ibid.*, p. 193.

question ensues of how his reasoning eludes metaphysics and which — the metaphysics or his reasoning — has more merit. The merit is not on Hume's side if he employs an induction he refutes. That he refutes his own reasoning seems evident by his assertions. For instance, he says "It is *certain* that the most ignorant and stupid peasants... improve by experience, and learn the qualities of natural objects, by observing the effects which result from them."[49]

§

Thus there is not merely a problem of inducting laws which are empirical: There is one of coordinating empirical terms such as "weight of book" with theoretical ones like "F_{ik}" (force exerted on an *i*-th particle by the *k*-th one).

§

Do future results reflect a *certainty* which Hume admits to be psychological? This begs a question of whether the psychological is unrelated to the logical. Korner's insight is strengthened by noting that logic is inextricably related to a philosophy of logic wherein logicians have philosophized perennially about similar problems.

For example, Aristotle influenced Thomas' psychology, founded psychology and formal logic, and first saw a relation. He defended scientists who believe that principles reflect unchanging natures of phenomena. His *De Anima* specified that sensations apprehend individuals, while knowledge grasps universals" (417^b), and that the mind "is not at one time knowing and at another not" (430^b).

And by a logic in his Square of Opposition, Aristotle argued philosophically that universal scientific principles *(archai)* sprang inductively from particular observations. Finding expression as empirical propositions, the observations led to the principles by an intuitive intellection called an

---

[49] Hume, *Treatise*, p. 39. Emphasis added. Hume indulges in an induction he rejects when *he abstractly reasons*: "Nature will always... prevail... over any abstract reasoning whatsoever" (40). How could he know about Nature in the future apart from its past?

'epagoge.'[50] How may this bear on universal past and future truth? Consider 'inductive deductions.'

Nature of 'Inductive Deductions'

The Humean dilemma of reasoning to timeless universal truth would especially pertain to physics. Simply stated, the universal laws of physics might be taken with descriptions of observed phenomena in order to either draw conclusions or make predictions, relevant to deductive arguments, of the following abbreviated sort:

1. All interacting forces $(F_{ik}$ and $F_{ki})$ of two point particles ('i' and 'k') in an inertial reference frame are equal in magnitude and opposite in direction.
2. Hume holds a book which weighs 1 kilogram.

∴ He exerts an upward force of 1 kilogram.

Empirico-Theoretical Deduction

A caveat is, of course, that the above may disregard such things as other relevant interacting forces and beg for an observation-theoretical distinction, *e.g.* "book" from "i-th particle." Having noted these things, the conclusion "He exerts..." is deduced from a description "Hume holds..." and an interpretation of Newton's third law:[51]

$$F_{ik} = -F_{ki}$$

Thus there is a problem of coordinating empirical terminology such as "weight of book" with theoretical ones like

---

[50] See R. Trundle's connection of Aristotle's Square to physics, as well as to Hume and Popper, in "Applied Logic: An Aristotelian Organon for Critical Thinking," *Philosophy in Science V* (1993) 117-140.

[51] Empirico-theoretical reasoning, in a formalized science, might be recast as follows (though it is itself a simplification):

$$[e_1 \wedge (e_1 \approx t_1) \wedge (t_1 \wedge L_o \vdash_L t_2) \wedge (t_2 \approx e_2)] \rightarrow e_2$$

An empircal state description (e_1) is treated *as if* it is equivalent to a theoretical description t_1 $(e_1 \approx t_1)$ of a *system at a given time*. Then, t_1 is taken with a law L_o and rules of logical deducibility '$\vdash_L$' to yield t_2 with $(t_2 \approx e_2)$, to imply $(\rightarrow)$ an empirical state description e_2 of the *system at a future time*.

"F_{ik}" (force exerted on an i-th particle by the k-th one). But a Humean dilemma at hand is how we can affirm universal theoretical truths or even true empirical generalizations. How can '*All* experienced bodies...'— much less a theoretical one by which experienced bodies are understood — be obtained inductively from '*Some...*'?

Ironically, Hume's criticism of inductively reasoning to *all* bodies further influenced a twentieth-century Humeanism of Sir Karl Popper. In order to sidestep induction and ascribe 'truth' to either laws or theories, the latter were initially construed as 'bold conjectures.' That is, 'truth' is not reached by empirical induction from a 'swampy ground up' but rather by a 'theory-downward process of testing.' He pioneered a transition from verifying a theory or testing for a its verifiable truth to its 'falsification' by a *modus-tollens* reasoning. However, he no less than Hume fell into a questionable, if not self-refuting, philosophy of logic.

§

So certain is Hume of the 'conjunction' by which we incorrectly ascribe truth to statements about *all* of anything that, paradoxically, he formulates his empiricist ideas as a universal law about *all* operations of the mind!

§

Before elaborating on the logic's problems, it is important to note a Popperian *modus-tollens* reasoning. The latter can be represented $L \rightarrow P \,/\, {\sim}P \,//\, {\sim}L$, for purposes of simplicity, where 'L' denotes a law *qua* conjecture and 'P' a prediction which turned out to be false and falsifies L.

On one hand, many philosophers of science and scientists acknowledge this reasoning. Physicist Kurt Hubner notes that, from confirmed predictions, we "can only conclude that nature has not expressly said no to the... theory — but neither has it said yes" and that "Falsification... is simply another word for 'Popperianism'."[52] On the other, this Popperianism evolved into a more optimistic position. Popper sought to

---

[52] K. Hubner, *Critique of Scientific Reason*, Tr. by P. R. and H. M. Dixon (Chicago: The University of Chicago Press, 1985), pp. 140, 162.

ameliorate a pessimism, in which theories are not known to be true, by a truth that is probable.

History repeats itself. Hume no less affirmed a probabilistic inductivism he denied than Popper. Popper concluded that when a theory's highly improbable predictions are true, it is "probable that the theory has both a truth content and higher degree of verisimilitude than those of its competitors which led to predictions that were less successful..."[53] Hume concluded that in terms of an "operation of the mind, by which we infer like effects from like causes,... it is not probable, that it could be trusted to the fallacious deductions of our reason."[54] Whereas Popper needed to affirm the likelihood of a theory's truth in order to accommodate an obvious increasing 'truth' in the history of science (*verisimilitude*), Hume needed to affirm some likelihood about our reason in order for his empiricism to say anything substantial.

Indeed, one of Hume's conclusions does not use a mere inductive terminology of the likelihood of 'many' or 'most' cases of our unjustified beliefs. In asking "What, then, is the conclusion of the whole matter?," he responds in the language of categorical deductions that "*All* belief of matter of fact or real existence is derived merely from... the memory or senses, and a customary conjunction."[55] And so certain is he of the 'conjunction' by which persons incorrectly ascribe truth to statements about *'all'* of anything that, paradoxically, he formulates his empiricist ideas as a universal law about *all* operations of the mind![56]

> Does it happen, in *all* these relations, that, when one of the objects is presented to the senses or memory, the mind... reaches a steadier and stronger conception of it than what otherwise it would have been able to obtain? This seems to be the case... And if the case be the same with the other

---

[53] See Popper's response to his critics in *The Philosophy of Karl Popper*, P. A. Schlipp, Ed., (La Salle, Ill: Open Court, 1974), pp. 1192-93.

[54] Hume, *Treatise*, p. 55.

[55] *Ibid.*, p. 46. Emphasis added.

[56] *Ibid.*, p. 51. Emphasis added.

relations or principles of association, this may be established as a *general law*, which takes place in *all the operations of the mind*.

These remarks are not those of the common sense everyday Hume. They are those of the strictly philosophical Hume. He was unable to yield any definitive conclusions about anything without the deductions or inductions he rejects.

From Self-Refuting Inductions to Skepticism

As soon expanded on, Aristotelian-Thomistic inductions and deductions afford insights to which Hume appealed, if surreptitiously, in terms of which things have an essential nature. For example, despite recent biomedical developments, persons have perennially reasoned *ceteris peribus* that we have a reproductive nature whereby all persons must have two biological parents. Though having them is not logically necessary, would we not say it is *impossible* for persons to exist when they have no male and female parents? Or, *necessarily* if there are not the parents, they cannot come into the world?

§

Hume's identity with a dogmatic Enlightenment is apparent in his universal a priori claims such as that "as we advance nearer the *enlightened ages*, we soon learn that there is nothing mysterious or supernatural..."

§

Expanded on later, this sort of truth is weaker epistemologically than a logically necessary truth, say Hume's father either did or did not die before he was born, but stronger than an ordinary empirical truth such as his father did not die before he was born. Called 'modal truth,' the truth illustrates fundamental sorts of inferences from biology to physics which is echoed by an Aristotelian-Thomistic process of reasoning to essential natures of things.

The nature of things is not enumerated literally Rather, the reasoning involves grasping things such as our mind, by our own incontrovertible consciousness, and our reproductive

72

system by experiencing sexual activity and births of children. Apart from the reasoning, how could Hume speak about our reasoning or mind per se? And if he did not conduct scientific inquiries to draw his conclusions, it may be supposed that they were based on his own experience.

In view of these points, an Aristotelian-Thomistic experience of ages and intuitively known scientific 'first principles' have a tenability which cannot be dismissed cavalierly. The tenability is augmented by considering a Humean alternative. True principles for deductions will presuppose prior deductive knowledge and it other knowledge *ad infinitum*, as suggested in Aristotle's *Analytica Posteriora* II, 19, 100^{a-b} and Thomas' *Summa Theologica* I, 14, 5. It is unfortunate, then, that in Hume's *Treatise* there is scarcely a disguised contempt for, and hardly any attempt to wrestle with, central epistemological insights in the history of philosophy, much less those of Thomas or Aristotle. This is a trend which continued with the modern anti-metaphysical philosophies he inspired.

Moreover, the inspired philosophies also tended to disparage religion. As we may ask how Hume can say "It is experience only... which assures us of the laws of nature,"[57] we may question how he appeals to Nature to "establish it as a maxim, that no human testimony can ever have such force as to prove a miracle, and make it a just foundation for any system of religion."[58] His identity with a dogmatic Enlightenment, in this regard, is apparent in his further assertions that "It forms a strong presumption against all supernatural... relations, that they... abound among ignorant and barbarous nations" and that "as we advance nearer the *enlightened ages*, we soon learn that there is nothing mysterious or supernatural..."[59]

Hume did not merely commit a straw-man fallacy in regard to the Church. No Church Father either held that miracles could be proved or confused faith with reason. In inconsistency with his own empiricism, he posited universal

[57] *Ibid.*, p. 127.
[58] *Ibid.*, p. 127.
[59] *Ibid.*, p. 119, emphasis added.

maxims which were themselves metaphysical with no rational assurance in true laws of Nature.

Finally, it is not so much Nature to which Hume appeals in his rejections of proofs of God. Since proofs which admit of God's possible existence admit that the existence is doubtful, it is the case, historically, both that the proofs tend to posit His necessary existence and that such an existence is one subject to particular criticism by Hume.

§

Everything is causally dependent, as Hume's own existence was on his parents and they on theirs and so on. Precisely, this dependence reflects the thought of late medieval philosophers whose thought Hume relegates to metaphysics.

§

Hume notes that the idea of 'necessity' either comes from an "impression... convey'd by our senses"[60] or is of the sort that "makes two times two equal four."[61] Given that 'four' means 'two times two,' the latter necessity is trivial. And the former is illegitimate since any idea of something is derived is conceivable apart from that thing's necessary existence. In light of Hume's notion of existence, one of his arguments against belief in God is criticized by J. P. van Bendegem. The argument is formulated initially with the premise 'No being exists necessarily' (P_1). Where x = God (G) and 'If God exists, he exists necessarily' is the second premise (P_2), 'God's existence is not necessary' is concluded (C):[62]

$$P_1: \quad (\forall) \sim NE\ (x)$$
$$P_2: \quad E\ (\,G\,) \rightarrow NE\ (\,G\,)$$
$$C: \quad \sim N\ (G)$$

It is noted that Hume's argument assumes the existence of at

---

60 *Ibid.*, p. 165.

61 Ibid., p. 166.

62 *Ibid.* Pages 159-166 are particularly relevant. Professor Van Bendegem, Chair, Department of Philosophy at Vrije Universiteit Brussel in Belgium, suggested this argument to me in a letter on March 2, 1996.

least one necessary being, namely Hume himself.[63] Thus in inferring that no being's existence is necessary, something else must be necessary. In conceding the necessity of Hume's existence, there also ensue various questions: Is his existence necessary in the sense of being a necessary condition? Is the condition necessary?[64]

The necessary condition of Hume's existence is not the only problem. Hume denies that universal truth can be derived from sense experience, in terms of premises with the words 'all' and 'no.' There is no *a priori* nontrivial knowledge and he rejects question-begging inductions to universal premises. Yet his own premise 'No being exists necessarily' is universal. And in the universal premise $(\forall)\sim NE$ (x), 'x' is God and God is not an object of sense experience.

But let us permit the universal premises and note that they nonetheless beg for experienced-based reasons. Hume may provide them. For example, he says that "reason [per se], *as distinguish'd from experience*, can never make us conclude, that a cause... is absolutely requisite to every beginning of existence," from which we might infer that "*experience* can... make us conclude, that a cause... is absolutely requisite to every beginning of existence."[65]

Pari passu existing beings are causally dependent on other dependent things, as Hume's own existence was dependent on his parents and they on theirs and so on. Precisely, this dependence reflects the thought of late medieval philosophers whose thought Hume relegates to metaphysics. They held that it is modally, not logically, impossible for causally dependent beings to exist when there is not an uncaused Being whose existence is that on which they depend: 'Necessarily (N) if there is not an uncaused Being $(\sim B)$, there are not causally dependent beings $(\sim D)$': $N(\sim B \rightarrow \sim D)$. Taken with 'There are the dependent beings' (D) and the definition $N(\sim p \rightarrow \sim q) =_{df}$ $(\sim p \Rightarrow \sim q)$, there is:$(\sim B \Rightarrow \sim D) \wedge D \therefore B$.

---

[63] Prof. Van Bendegem's insight, adding "A strange conclusion, indeed!"
[64] My initial response to Van Bendegem.
[65] Hume, *Treatise*, p. 157, emphasis added.

The modal conditional $\sim B \Rightarrow \sim D$ is not a material implication which is true if *as a matter of fact* it is not the case that
$\sim B$ is true when $\sim D$ is false. Rather it reflects an impossibility
of the falsity when $\sim B$ is true. And the truth is modal. A
modally necessary truth does not posit logically necessary
connections between ideas.

The truth sets parameters for what would be reasonably
admitted as empirical truth — including the truth that we not
only think of experienced things without thinking of their
necessary existence but of their existence as being dependent
and merely possible. The impossibility that there can be any
dependent thing when there is no thing that is not dependent
$(\sim B \Rightarrow \sim D)$, might be understood as a modally necessary
principle of causality 'writ large.'

§

**Kant worsened Hume's skepticism by confirming
that the presuppositions of moral and scientific
inquiries did not have known truth-values. In
not having the values, there were ideological answers to 'Whence comes
truth if not from metaphysics?'**

§

In conclusion, Hume may have tacitly acknowledged an
inference to a necessity which brings to mind Aristotle's *Prior
Analytics* 43^{b} and Thomas' *Summa* (I, 2, 3). Perhaps, given
Hume's own empiricism, he reasoned from experienced beings
who have an existence which is merely possible to an
impossibility: The idea that 'Experienced beings do not have a
necessary existence $(\sim N)$' *cannot be* false when it is true that
'Thinking about their existence does not evoke an idea of
their necessity $(\sim I)$': Necessarily if thinking about experienced
beings does not evoke the idea of their necessary existence
$(\sim I)$, their existence is not necessary $(\sim N)$: $\sim I \Rightarrow \sim N$.[66] But,

---

[66] This modality brings to mind ontological arguments that begin, not
with experience, but with ideas of necessary Being. See R. B. Marcus'
Modalities (NY: Oxford University Press, 1993), p. 166. She criticizes some
ontologico-modal arguments but not cosmological ones.

clearly, the necessity is not logical but modal. There might be a *reductio* which supports $\sim\!I \Rightarrow \sim\!N$: To suppose experienced beings have a necessary existence is to suppose they *cannot* 'not be.' That is, it is impossible that they either came into or will go out of existence.

But this supposition conflicts with the experience at hand as well as with what is necessary for an intelligibility of scientific inquiry. The supposition is not a logical absurdity but a modal one. At the same time, it is modest in contrast to Hume's own reference to *all* beings, including those of which there are not sensations.

Hume did not distinguish logical from modal senses of the word 'necessity.' A modal sense bears on that which is more than reasonable, if not what it makes sense, to say about experienced things — a point also missed by Kant to whom we turn shortly. He accepted Hume's dichotomy of empirical and logically necessary truth wherein there was no known truth of the causal principle. Since the principle is presupposed by scientific inquiry, truth afforded by the inquiry rested on what is not either an *analytic* or *a posteriori* judgment. Thus there ensued skepticism.

Far from resolving skepticism, Kant positively worsened it by holding that the presuppositions of moral and scientific inquiries did not have known truth-values. In not having the values, the presuppositions invited ideological answers to Whence comes 'truth' if not from metaphysics? The question led to substitutes for metaphysics of a dialectical determinism, as manifest in political classes, and to the unfettered free will of a will-to-power of fascist supermen. Absurdly, power was pursued by persons who became virtual conditions of truth for truth-claims about human nature and Nature.[67] Precisely, Peter Redpath refers, in his Foreword, to dominating classs who are the new substitutes for metaphysics! Also, if persons are truth-conditions, does this not explain the ideological appeals to *ad hominem* arguments (arguments against the person)?

---

[67] *Cf.* D. Livingston, *Philosophical Melancholy & Delirium: Hume's Pathology of Philosophy* (U. of Chicago Press, 1998), This work's exaltation of Hume's methods for assessing politics and limits of interpretation, even if correct, does not avert the thesis herein of Hume's pejorative influence.

Chapter 4

Kantian Shift: From an Ideal of Physics to Politics

The politicization of 'truth' was an unintended consequence of Immanuel Kant's Copernican Revolution. This Revolution joined Rationalism's allowance for knowledge to Empiricism's critical thought. In mediating between the latter's skepticism and the former's dogmatism in his *Critique of Pure Reason*,[1] Kant (1724-1804) is credited with avoiding inconsistent views of the two schools.

One school rooted 'truth' in reason apart from experience and the other in experience with no reasoning *a priori*. Kant conceded to the Rationalists a necessity of reasoning *a priori* and to the Empiricists a substantive truth which is *synthetic*. Today, there is recognition that *synthetic a priori* judgments are not known to be true. Ignored, however, is that their lack of truth made way for a later political correctness by excluding ascriptions of truth to truth-claims afforded by scientific and moral inquiries.

Did not Kant do for philosophy what Copernicus had done for modern science, so that truth in the paradigm science of physics was never really in doubt? There seems to be an assumption that the doubt will be overcome and that an enlightened revolution in philosophy compares to that of science. Science and philosophy alike have truly forged ahead! Coupled with admiration for Kant's articulation of how

---

[1] Herein, there is used Kant's *Critique of Pure Reason*, Tr. by N. K. Smith, Unabridged Edition (NY: Macmillan & Co., 1965). In regard to 1st and 2nd Editions, denoted by 'A' and 'B', the latter is generally used.

synthetic a priori judgments clarify the nature of an archaic metaphysics, modern philosophers have tended to ignore that key metaphysical ideas may have reflected a metaphysico-modal truth; one pertaining to morality and religion as well as to science. If scientific and religio-moral truth does rely on true modal ideas and if their abandonment has had tragic societal consequences, there should be some sense of urgency in reexamining Kant's revolution.

§

Moral and scientific inquiries came to be viewed as addressing radically different worlds.

§

Otherwise, let us be frank about what is at stake. Mainstream philosophy will continue to provide the seeds for its own suppression. And its adherents will play philosophical fiddle as a present-day Rome burns with ideology and global conflict.[2] Americans need only recall one of their least philosophical presidents to see how what is evidently enigmatic to many modern philosophers seems obvious in terms of common sense. President Harry Truman[3] lamented the relative ease of

---

[2] See R. Trundle's "Cold-War Ideology: An Apologetics for Global Ethnic Conflict?," *Res Publica* 37 (1996) 61-84. Kant's attention to presuppositions of determined and freely choosing behavior illuminates later ideologies whose behavioral extremes became entangled. Whereas fascism affirmed the radical freedom of superior men and races to create 'truth,' Marxism embraced a radical determinism and class warfare to explain its political origin. In open societies after World War Two, their virulent assimilation arose as a species of the New Left. Its *ad hominem* attacks on those who based 'truth' on human nature and Nature, as racist elite white classes, encouraged ethnic *Weltanschauungen* and global ethnic conflict.

[3] H. S. Truman, *Years of Decisions*, Vol. I (NY: Doubleday, 1955), p. 411. In *The New York Times Book Review*, Allan Nevins states that "we have seldom had a leader of more unphilosophical mind..." Truman's recognition that the Nazis and Marxists were equally evil bears on Anthony Kenny's assertion that, after the 1989 worldwide collapse of communism, the remaining Marxist sympathizers were "devotees in the universities of the West." Surely, Western philosophers have *not* been prominent among those who, since the 1960s, have resisted the political correctness of a New Left — imposed from *within* the university. See A. Kenny, Ed., *The Oxford History of Western Philosophy*, (Oxford University Press, 1994), p. 368.

80

killing the dictators who started World War II — their having 'only' left over sixty million persons dead — in comparison to *'killing' the philosophical ideas* which made them possible. Let the reexamination begin, then, with the central problem for a philosophical revolution which was the thought that preceded the nefarious deeds of our time.

The Shift in Response to a Problem

Kant's problem was to articulate knowledge in the physical and religio-moral realms. Knowledge in either realm was formulated in terms of principles or laws about *all* things. In exceeding what is sensed empirically, the laws were not empirically true. In having denials which were not self-contradictory, they were not logically true. Nonetheless, the scientific revolution fostered inordinate optimism because formalized laws made unparalleled predictions. The predictions presupposed that the future behaves as the past. And a coordination of past to future meant that everything is caused deterministically.

Determinism led to another problem since it did not seem compatible with freedom. The judgment that 'All persons are free agents' was presupposed by religio-moral inquiry and 'All events are caused' by scientific inquiry. The inquiries came to be viewed as addressing radically different worlds. Importantly, Kant's notion of noumenal and phenomenal worlds flourished not only in a context of scientific revolution but in that of the Enlightenment and Reformation.

Enlightenment and Reformation
Without ignoring excesses of Catholic practices or theological insights of Protestantism, it needs to be said that a solution to the problems was exacerbated by the Protestant Reformation and the Enlightenment's naive celebration of science. One need only consider an ensuing rise of 'scientific Marxism'. Marx's remark that as "the revolution... began in the brain of the *monk*, now it begins in the... *philosopher*,"[4] underscores

---

[4] K. Marx, *Toward a Critique of Hegel's Philosophy of Right*, Tr. by L. Easton and K. Guddat, in A. Wood, Ed., *Marx Selections* (NY: Macmillan Publishing Co., 1988), p. 29.

how the philosopher's revolution was related to the sixteenth-century Reformation. The latter broke with a millennial philosophical tradition as well as a theological one. And this break begot a theological 'house' divided against itself and a lack of any coordinated philosophical theology to challenge either pseudo-scientific claims or claims which confused metaphysics with physics.

Beyond the promise of modern physics, a largely secularized Kantianism had to deal also with the mounting inertia of the Enlightenment. Encoded in Baron d'Holbach's *Systeme de la nature* (1770), it found expression in the scientific world view that "Man is unhappy because he is ignorant of nature." Mastering Nature through science, not worshiping Nature's God, was the key to human happiness as viewed by a progressive secular Enlightenment.

§

Kant embraced a deterministic metaphysics of physics. It not only excluded scientific truth and free will: We were no longer voluntary causes, analogous to a First Cause, who could reason to Nature's God.

§

Kant was not duped by the Enlightenment's aversion to religion even if his religious allegiance was to the Reformation. But he was diverted from consequential insights of medieval philosophical theology. He ignored that reducing a liberal principle of efficient causality to an invariable sequence of physical (natural) events, as a metaphysics of the new physics which disavowed free will, proceeded *pari passu* with a denial both that persons were voluntary efficient causes and that they could reason causally to God. Pope John Paul II aptly notes Kant's departure from a millennial reasoning that "God is a knowable object... of the visible world."[5]

Though holding that this world is not a truth-condition for religious and moral truth claims, Kant tried to show that

---

5 Pope John Paul II, *Crossing the Threshold of Hope*, Tr. V. Messori (NY: Alfred A. Knopf, 1994), p. 34.

the claims were not excluded by science: To say there is sense experience only of physical reality is not to say there is no reality which is not sensed empirically. A nonempirical reality would come to be discerned from one known theoretically in virtue of theoretical terms of science which were coordinated with observation. Differences between an observed reality known theoretically and a religio-moral reality, assumed merely for practical purposes, led to the *Critique of Practical Reason*. That is, the limits of practical reason are determined by reason known theoretically. Theoretically, a problem was how the causal principle can be known prior to experience for the coherence of scientific truth.

Turning to a Scientific Paradigm
The scientific paradigm to which Kant turned, that would be joined to physics for a new field of astrophysics, was the Copernican revolution. Copernicus had revolutionized astronomy by assuming that the earth was 'active', in the sense of revolving around a 'passive' sun. This assumption ameliorated Ptolemaic anomalies. By analogy, anomalies in philosophy were noted for Kant's purpose: The Empiricists viewed the mind a passive 'blank tablet' on which sense impressions were made. And the Rationalists viewed it as something akin to a passive container of ideas from which information about the world was deduced. Thus, as Copernicus assumed that the earth was active, an activity of the mind was assumed for acquiring knowledge. Knowledge of a phenomenal world involves an active cognition that interpreted *a priori* a raw material of experience.

Prior to any experiential ideas of the reality that concerns scientists, an external material such as sound and light enter a structure of mind. As a prism processes light, the mind has an *a priori* cognition which processes or interprets a material of experience. Besides being active in this manner, our cognition mediates between the previous notions of mind: *(i)* The mind is not initially 'empty' of sense impressions as held by the Empiricists. Nor is it 'full' of innate ideas prior to experience as it was for the Rationalists. And *(ii)* there is not a pristine knowledge of the Rationalists with indubitable ideas of reality without interpretation. Nor is there an Empiricist skepticism.

Ideas were not derived from sensations divorced from external reality. Addressed by the prism analogy, a material reality is the source of interpreted judgments.

§

Hume questioned how the causal principle could be known a priori. Kant's attempt to root the *a priori* in an *a priori structure of mind* amounted to a psychological response to a logical problem.

§

A denial that judgments are known *a priori* led Kant to ground the *a priori* in human cognition. Our cognition does not afford scientific knowledge based on pure reason, in agreement with Empiricism, since empirical and theoretical ideas are skewed by an interpretation of experience. But experience is synthesized *a priori*. This seemed to permit *a priori* knowledge in accord with Rationalism. A Rationalist dogmatism is avoided by a critical account of knowledge. And the same knowledge excludes an Empiricist skepticism. Kant's view of knowledge distinguished psychological from logical certainties about ideas such as 'all events are caused' or, in the terms of Rationalism, 'nothing occurs without a reason.'

Practical and Theoretical Consequences

A synthesized raw material means that *different* materials of experience are, in effect, related psychologically. Here, we recall that relationships of different experienced materials is consistent with Hume's denial that there is any 'necessary connexion' between our ideas of 'events' and 'causes' since they are different. That is, a proposition that 'A causes B' is not a logically necessary truth. Importantly, one mode of synthesis for science is relating events causally.

Formulated as a universal judgment, causal relations may be expressed 'All events are caused.' The latter is a causal principle generated by an a priori structure of mind; that is, by the mind's *a priori cognition*. For example, an event can be experienced in terms of an external reality. The reality might emanate a raw material of what, in physics, is called 'radiant energy.' This is energy transferred by radiations of things such as visible light and heat. Our cognition would relate, *a priori* or automatically, a hot or lighted thing to a cause. And the lighted thing which may itself come to be interpreted as a cause of our being hot or illuminated.

Hume realized that the causal principle is not logically necessary. He denied a 'necessary connexion' between ideas because 'cause' does not refer to the same thing as 'event.' But the lack of such a necessary connection does not counter the fact that the principle has an 'a priori status.' At the level of interpreted ideas, there *would* be a 'reasoning *a priori*.' Surely, the causal principle does not follow inductively from *some* experienced events since it refers to *all* past and future ones. But an empiricist criticism that ideas are based on particular experiences, so that the universal principle cannot be inducted literally, would presumably miss Kant's point. The point would be that the principle expresses how our cognitive structure interprets all events *prior* to ideas which are based, indirectly at least, on experience. Is there, then, a question about our ideas in terms of 'reasoning *a priori*'?

The answer is 'yes' because Hume's criticism of reasoning *a priori* meant, among other things, that there was no knowledge *a priori* of a causal principle. Kant did not establish that there is knowledge of the principle's truth. Rather, he showed that the principle merely expresses how our psyche interprets physical reality. Consequently, his attempt to root the '*a priori*' in an *a priori* cognition did itself, in a way which brings to mind his own critique of rationalism, amount to a psychological response to a logical problem. And in terms of Kant's own subsequent articulation of metaphysical judgments, as later expanded on, his judgment that all persons have an *a priori* cognition would itself be metaphysical.

Since these points are virtually ignored by most modern philosophers, they need to be stressed because they already reveal a 'crack' at the very foundation of Kant's Copernican Revolution. The Revolution has a flaw that does not bode well for Kant's critique of pure reason. Attention to the crack may explain why the thesis of an *a priori* cognition was abandoned in later philosophical movements. This does not mean that their proponents came to appreciate, much less articulate, why the thesis of an a priori cognition was disregarded.

Practical Import: 'Critical Thinking' a Euphemism

Empirically or logically, there was no reason to accept Kant's thesis of an a priori cognition. Also, his thesis amounted to a psychological response to a logical problem posed by Hume. Kant's response had all the hallmarks of a *lack* of Hume's 'critical thinking.' But was not Hume as uncritical as Kant? The question of whether they were critical is not intended to express contempt. Rather, the question indicates that the much trumpeted 'critical thought,' which supposedly shows how modern philosophy differs from a dogmatism of previous millennia, is more a euphemism for logic textbooks than an accurate description.

§

An immaterial free will, 'good,' and God were only *noumena* which were possibly real. But there was no doubt about a reality of material things interpreted scientifically as *phenomena*. The seeds were sown for a rabid secularism of modern society.

§

Typically, textbooks teach that there is only empirical or logically necessary truth. But a sentence which expresses this claim would not itself be true. One widely used textbook states that 'truth' is ascribed to either logically true statements that "do not make any genuine assertions about the world" or to empirically true ones such as "It is raining..."[6]

In addition to the question of what students are to surmise about sentences of ethics and theoretical ones of science, what are they to think of textbook truth-claims which permit only such truth? To ponder whether the claim is itself true would, indeed, be to critically think and to ask another question: Can logic be properly taught apart from some history of philo-

---

6 P. J. Hurley, *A Concise Introduction to Logic* (CA: Wadsworth Publishing Co., 1991), p. 307.

86

sophy and the philosophy of logic? Clearly, Hume and Kant influenced claims about 'truth,' which were not known to be true, and ignored a truthlessness of their own metaphysical claims. In virtue of an esteem for these philosophers and for logic, as a study which underlies a rationality of all others, a question ensues about whether generations of students — if not their teachers — can think critically.

Further questions are raised. In lamenting that a self-refuting verification principle is institutionalized by modern society, Hilary Putnam notes that permitting only empirical and logically necessary truth, which arose from a Humean-Kantian-Positivist tradition, was a "philosophical gambit [which] was a great mistake."[7] Wittgenstein suggested that there was an overlooked truth, recognized surreptitiously by ordinary persons, whose necessity bordered an epistemological strength between a necessity of logical truth and truth deemed empirically reasonable.[8]

But before Wittgenstein and Putnam, as well as between them, lie generations of students who had to struggle with uncritical curricula of higher education by their own common sense. One upshot was that many students and citizens were not merely alarmed by the epistemological mischief, from self-refuting radical relativisms to politicized agenda, long before many scholars and university administrators. Students were often resisted, by many administrators and scholars, in their attempt to avoid a wholesale flight from reason which began paradoxically by its *critique*.

Having noted serious problems at the root of Kant's *Critique* which shaped general philosophy, the philosophy of science, and science itself, attention is turned to how his thesis of an *a priori* cognition led to a distinction of phenomenal from noumenal realities with notable consequences. Whereas an immaterial free will, 'good,' and God are noumena — things-in-themselves (*ding an sich*) which are only possibly

---

[7] H. Putnam, "Philosophers and Human Understanding," *Scientific Explanation: Papers Based on Herbert Spencer Lectures*, Ed. by A. F. Heath (Oxford: Clarendon Press, 1981, p. 100.

[8] L. Wittgenstein, *On Certainty* (NY: Harper & Row Publishers, 1972), pp. 42e (#335), 59e (#454).

real, there is no doubt about a reality of material things which are interpreted cognitively as phenomena.

Phenomena were the subject of science. Thus science and its notion of causal determinism enjoyed a greater ontological status than realities which bore on morality and religion. The weakened status of religion and strengthened one of science proceeded *pari passu* with an increasing theoretical shift to a political left. As society became more scientific and science was associated with rationality, there arose a specter of human perfectibility. It was increasingly sought deterministically by a science which can progressively shape our nature.

§

On the one hand, there is a lesson in the *Critique*. An irrational relativism *begins* with interpretations of reality. Man is the measure, as Protagoras said, of 'what is.' Kant's a priori structure of mind was the new Protagorean measure.

§

Subsequently, a nineteenth-century approach to politics was influenced by Kant. In the words of one political scientist, this approach was "fundamentally rationalist, whether Marxist or liberal democratic. It saw... problems that could be solved by... reason and science."[9] At the same time, a liberal epistemology ensued in general science by allowances for various theoretical interpretations of phenomena.

Theoretical Import: Rational and Irrational Interpretations
Physicists began to speak increasingly of 'phenomena' in terms of a new nuance. The word denoted a modesty in their reluctance to ascribe unqualified truth to theoretical *interpretations* of empirical data. And this epistemic humility was appropriate in light of subsequent dilemmas such as the Underdetermination-of-Theory-by-Data (UTD) Thesis. On this Thesis, any empirical datum is underdetermined due to a logical possibility that logically inconsistent theories may be

---

[9] L. T. Sargent, *Contemporary Political Ideologies*, 7th Ed. (Ill: The Dorsey Press, 1987), p.116.

empirically equivalent in their explications, manipulations, or predictions of phenomena.

As a backdrop to the Thesis, consider a datum of light. Light is subject to particle *(p)* and nonparticle *(λ)* interpretations. This holds despite, if not in view of, de Broglie's eventual wave-particle equation. Where h = Planck's constant and $p = mv$ = magnitude of the momentum of a moving particle, there is the equation:

$$\lambda = h/mv = h/p$$

The equation illustrates that phenomena may in principle be underdetermined with empirical properties whose theoretical interpretations are inconsistent. Physicist Saul Youssef notes that the two-slit experiment still forces us to conclude that the light is "both a particle and a wave."[10]

In suggesting that knowledge of physical reality involves interpretation, Kant may have contributed unwittingly to a theoretical modesty in which scientists should be open in principle to different theories. Contrary to a post-Kantian received view, the theoretical modesty is not undercut by either Karl Popper's criticism of de Broglian-like equations or the W. H. Newton-Smith's discussion of a UTD Thesis. Before discussing the Thesis, there needs to be attention to some apparent confusion on the part of Popper. Many of his important insights are disregarded for present purposes.

Given the previously noted relativism in higher education, persons who are not biased ideologically would be sympathetic to Popper's alarm about quantum equations which contribute to a "general anti-rationalist atmosphere which has become a major menace of our time..."[11] But his alarm in this instance is confused. For the anti-rationalism does not obtain when, on the basis of physical reality, physicists posit the truth that light is both a particle and a wave. There is no irrational

---

[10] Saul Youssef, "Is Quantum Mechanics An Exotic Probability Theory?," in *Fundamental Problems in Quantum Theory* (NY: New York Academy of Sciences, 1995), p. 904.

[11] K. Popper, *Quantum Theory and the Schism in Physics*. From *Post-script to the Logic of Scientific Discovery*, Ed. by W. Bartley, III (NJ: Row-man and Littlefield, 1982), p. 142.

relativism in holding that light, being a wave, is relative to an experimental context.

Popper's alarm stems from his incorrect assumption that there is a *sophistic* relativism. The latter begins with truth-claims to determine truth about reality, such as Protagoras' thesis that 'man is the measure,' rather than with reality as the condition for truth.

Rational interpretation The wave-particle equation's truth, or other de Broglian-like ones, is based on an experimental setup whose results are objectively duplicated. Thus although there is a relativism, it is rational and in agreement with scientific realism. Though there are weak and strong realisms, reality is the condition for truth where 'truth' means that truth-claims about either the existence of theoretical entities or a veracity of theories are checked against objectively measured domains of reality. And hence the worry over inconsistent interpretations is, in this case, unwarranted.

§

On the other hand, Kant contributed to a critique of reason. We do not even demand that phenomena abide by the Principle of Noncontradiction. And there is no self-contradiction in saying that reality need not abide by it.

§

There is a lesson in the *Critique*. An irrational relativism *begins* with interpretations of reality. Man is the measure, as Protagoras said, of 'what is' and 'that it is'. Popper's measure of what is the case is similar to theoretical piles lowered on a virtual reality-in-itself of a swamp. Is the swamp, apart from theoretical interpretation, ever observed? No, because any observation of the swamp is always obscured by theoretical piles.[12] His realism is not merely in question but, given his fame before Feyerabend and Kuhn, his influence on their theory-dependent relativisms. A falsification of theories by

---

12 K. Popper, *The Logic of Scientific Discovery* (London: Hutchinson, 1968), p. 111.

falsely predicted observations may seem to support a realism despite his analogy. But his *Conjectures and Refutations* makes clear that observation is underlaid by theory and that theoretical 'piles' never reach observational 'swamps.'[13]

A rational relativism which is a species of realism, by contrast, does not impose either theory or conceptions of rationality on reality in an *a priori* way, say in terms of a rationalism of Aristotle, Descartes, or Popper. The relativism is rational in the sense that it begins, in accord with scientific methodology, with our experience of reality and proceeds to concepts. How can concepts be used to specify *a priori* that reality must conform to various norms of reason? One of Kant's contributions, in this regard, is a critique of pure reason by way of antinomies such as 'The world has a beginning' and it 'has no beginning'.

We do not begin inquiries by demanding that phenomena abide by the Principle of Noncontradiction. And there is no self-contradiction in saying that reality need not abide by it. The Principle's limits beg for attention to Newton-Smith's criticism of the UTD Thesis since he views it as a threat to a scientific realism which is rational.

Newton-Smith's impressive defense of rationality in *The Rationality of Science* should not obscure an irrelevant and failed attempt to weaken the Thesis: One of two rival theories T_1 and $\sim T_1$ may be "integrated into a total theory of nature" in terms of which there are "evidential reasons for selecting that theory."[14] In letting the selected theory be $\sim T_1$ and the total theory be T_2, it seems easy to see that $\sim T_2$ may obtain with the specter of another global theory T_3 and so on. Also, he seems headed for a red herring in trying to save a rational realism by "restricting from the set of sentences... a realist construal [of] any undecidable sentence" and regarding truth to involve some "common part of the two theories."[15]

---

[13] K. Popper, *Conjectures and Refutations* (London: Routledge & Kegan Paul, 1963), p. 387.

[14] W. H. Newton-Smith, *The Rationality of Science* (London: Routledge & Kegan Paul, 1981), p. 41.

[15] *Ibid.*, p. 42.

Besides begging a question of why theories need common elements, it seems wrong to conclude that "If there were nothing in common except the observational consequences, realism... would be implausible."[16] Plausibility does not include a commonness of theories. Precisely, a question ensues: Is it modally possible, as opposed to logically possible, for theories to be false when they have systematically true observational consequences?

How could the consequences be true when the theories are false in the sense of not reflecting reality? And whether addressed by the same or different theories, reality not only need not abide by the Principle of Noncontradiction but, in principle, may have inconsistent properties. These include such things as particles and waves and, even at a mundane level, human behavior subject to interpretations of being both freely chosen and determined.

§

Kant's analysis of the mind's interpretation of experience does not erase his psychological response to a logical problem. But it does reveal that invalid arguments may sometimes have provocatively true conclusions.

§

For example, conflicting interpretations are typical in courts of law. Prosecutors often hold that criminals freely choose to violate laws and defending lawyers argue that the laws were violated involuntarily. The involuntariness may be supported by psychiatrists who stress internal physiological causes and by psychologists who point to environmental ones. Though behavior may sometimes be understood in terms of conditioning, distinctions of it from causal determinism are moot in the absence of a free choice of will which might be ignored for purposes of scientific inquiry.

This is not to say that behavior may be *exhaustively* both determined and not determined any more than to say microscopic phenomena are completely particles and nonparticles.

---

16 *Ibid.*, p. 43.

It is to say that in seeking to make reality conform to reason, some philosophers of science have disregarded inconsistent interpretations which may be both relatively true.

Kant's contribution to 'truth' in regard to interpreted phenomena does not erase his psychological response to a logical problem. But it does indicate, by analogy, that invalid arguments may still have provocatively true conclusions. Significant insights on truth and reality may flow out of troubled epistemic waters. At the same time the waters also stirred up an irrationalism that transposed the notion of *a priori* cognitive interpretations into *Weltanschauungen*.

Irrational interpretation Grave concerns with neo-Kantian ideas of 'interpretation' are better focused on Weltanschauung Analyses. Finding influential expression in the views of physicists Thomas Kuhn and Paul Feyerabend, the Analyses have provided an irrational apologetics for radical feminism, *e.g.* a gender one, which is infused with a Nietzschean-Marxist relativism. In Kathryn Parsons' pioneering "Nietzsche and Moral Change," for example, Kuhn, Feyerabend, and Engles' Marxism are enlisted to support a worldview of women for the women's liberation movement.[17]

In noting that the relativism is often concealed under a rubric of science, the purpose at hand is not to expound on Feyerabend or Kuhn *per se*. It is to underscore that Kant's thesis of the mind's active interpretation has helped to fuel a politicized science. Before tying science to political ideology, there is brief consideration of Kuhn.

The very title's of Kuhn's *The Copernican Revolution* and *The Structure of Scientific Revolutions*[18] leads one to expect a neo-Kantian theme of revolutionary interpretation. There are general themes that whatever is true in a paradigmatic weltanschauung of Aristotle may be false in one of Newton. And without discriminating between falsities of the

---

[17] K. P. Parsons, "Nietzsche and Moral Change," *Nietzsche*, Ed. by R. C. Solomon (NY: Anchor Press, 1980), pp. 169-193. Engles is praised and Aristotle criticized.

[18] Cf. T. Kuhn's *The Copernican Revolution* (NY: Random House, 1959) and *Structure of Scientific Revolutions* (Chicago, Ill: University of Chicago Press, 1970).

one and truths of the other, historically succeeding paradigms do not yield increasing truth. In a fashion similar to differently colored Kantian lenses, the paradigms differently determine *a priori* how the world is viewed.

By contrast, Feyerabend's anarchistic *Against Method*, published by New Left Books, holds that 'truth' is relative to possibly inconsistent theories in any historical period.[19] Their interpretive 'statements' are imposed *a priori* on Humean-like sensations, expressed as sentences, which have no truth-value. Values of 'true' or 'false' arise when sensorial sentences are interpreted as statements in the contexts of theories.

§

Wittgenstein triggered "a second Copernican Revolution; *i.e.***, an extension of the critical philosophy to... a 'Critique of Language'." Since he is the most esteemed thinker in the West, there are attempts to conform his critique to a trendy post-Kantian relativism.**

§

And though a theory's statement may be coherently true and false if theories are incomparable, there is still an evident irrationality of the scientific enterprise. For a point of the enterprise is to pursue truth by evidence. But evidence is understood circularly by sensorial sentences interpreted *a priori* by theories. Thus theories are similar to ideologies since theoretical interpretations guarantee that evidence has only truth-values consistent with theories!

Theories based on relativistic ideologies, influenced by Feyerabend, must be kept from the public at all costs:

> if the radical feminists, counterculturists, and others were to acknowledge in the public arena their theoretical convictions, they would... lose any public following *and deservedly so....*
> such convictions as that texts and statements have no

---

19 *Cf.* Paul Feyerabend's *Against Method* (London: New Left Books, 1975) and "Against Method," *Minnesota Studies in Philosophy of Science*, Vol. I, Ed. by M. Radner et al (University of Minnesota Press, 1970), pp. 17-130.

determinate meaning, that no hypotheses... are any better supported than their denials, or that claims... [of] fact reflect nothing about the facts. [20]

Interpretations relevant to science, ideological or otherwise, would intrigue philosophers who are influenced by the 'later' Wittgenstein. Nicholas Gier notes that Wittgenstein was "involved in a second Copernican Revolution; *i.e.*, an extension of the critical philosophy to a fourth Critique, a 'Critique of Language'..."[21] Regrettably, since Wittgenstein is the most esteemed thinker in Anglo-American philosophy, some of his followers have sought to conform his critique to a trendy post-Kantian relativism.

Predictably, the relativism often begins with linguistic conventions as kinds of Kuhnian meanings of 'truth.' Stephen Toulmin did not merely appeal in his *Human Understanding* to procedure *per se*, rather than to a theory's truth, for explaining its predictive or manipulative success.[22] He tied 'truth' to 'rationality': What is rational or true at one time may be irrational or false at another where 'falsity' and 'irrationality' are relative to linguistic conventions at the same or different times in history.[23]

Is history merely a matter of linguistic conventions with conflicting truths about the world? And is the world, viewed this way, any less enigmatic than one with either inconsistent Kuhnian paradigms or self-confirming theories which, being shaped politically, are as blind to facts as political ideologies? Whereas Nazi intellectuals interpreted *a priori* Einstein's theory as 'Jewish physics,' Soviet intellectuals relegated his physics to a false one of the 'bourgeois class.'

---

[20] L. Lauden, *Science and Relativism* (Chicago: University of Chicago Press, 1990), p. 163. It is important to note the degree in which Feyerabend and Kuhn have influenced textbooks in higher education.

[21] Cf. N. Gier, *Wittgenstein and Phenomenology* (NY: SUNY Press, 1981), p. 34. From a quote of R. Mandel in "Heidegger and Wittgenstein: A Second Kantian Revolution?," in M. Murray, Ed., *Heidegger and Modern Philosophy* (New Haven, CT: Yale University Press, 1978).

[22] S. Toulmin, *Human Understanding*, V. I (NJ: Princeton University Press, 1972). pp. 172-173.

[23] *Ibid.*, p. 134.

To say that Kuhn or Toulmin never intended this use of language is as irrelevant as Nietzsche's defenders who say he never intended fascist interpretations of history by his goal to "mold facts... [by] active interpretation."[24] A Nietzschean apologetics for fascism and Marxian dominating classes can as easily embrace interpretations or paradigms as conventions for how the world is viewed differently — as if different views beget different worlds.[25]

§

The idea of a *Weltanschauung* is "heir to the philosophical tradition which includes *Nietzsche*... Accordingly, it conveniently can be viewed as a sort of *neo-Kantian* pragmatic position [without the categories]..."

§

A troubling aspect of relativistic worldviews, characteristic of a New Left in American Universities, is its encouragement of racial and gender identities for interpreting the world in order to counter dominating-class views of dead white males.[26] In noting an absurdity, philosopher of science and physicist Alan Chalmers states in *Science and Its Fabrication* :

> The natural world does not behave in one way for capitalists and in another way for socialists, in one way for males and another for females, in one way for Western cultures and another for Eastern Cultures. A large-scale nuclear war... would destroy us all, whatever our class, sex or culture.[27]

---

24 F. Nietzsche, *The Will to Power*, Tr. by W. Kaufmann and R. Holindale (NY: Random House, 1968), p. 327.

25 See O. Schutte, "Nietzsche, Mariategui, and Socialism: A Case of Nietzschean Marxism in Peru?," *Social Theory & Change* 14 (1988) 71-72: Marxism was enriched by Nietzschean ideas by socialists who, however, do not credit him since he is "associated with fascism." Also, see R. Trundle's "Nietzschean Politics and Marxian Science," *Review Journal of Philosophy & Social Science* 17 (1992) 96-127.

26 See R. Trundle, "Has Global Ethnic Conflict Superseded Cold War Ideology?," *Conflict and Terrorism* 19 RAND CORP. (1996) 93-107.

27 A. Chalmers, *Science and Its Fabrication* (Minneapolis: University of Minnesota Press, 1990), p. 112.

Swan Song of Copernican Interpretations

That irrational interpretations are tied to Kant by way of a Nietzschean epistemology, if not one of Marx, is evidenced by a statement about which there was no controversy among philosophers of science at an international symposium on science's theoretical structure. The statement specified that the idea of a '*Weltanschauung*' is:

> heir to the philosophical tradition which includes *Nietzsche* ... Accordingly it conveniently can be viewed as a sort of *neo-Kantian* pragmatic position [without categories]...[28]

The theoretical consequences remind us of practical ones. Had there been attention to Kant's psychological response to a logical problem, which led to his idea of the mind's interpretation, irrational interpretations may not have been ignored or confused with rational relativisms by many mainstream philosophers who exalted critical thinking. Thinking at a theoretical level should precede a practical one as Kant's theoretical *Critique* is prior to practical reason and Newton's theory to an applied engineering physics.

Here, a point needs to be made. Practicality was stressed over theoretical scholarship by both communist and fascist intellectuals whenever possible. The emphasis held especially for philosophy because they sought to suppress scholarly criticism of their interpretive shenanigans.

Whereas the communist hammer and sickle symbolized that scholarship is mere labor for ideological ends of the state, Hitler used the taxable labor of ordinary citizens to fund Nietzschean research which supported intellectually his Nazi program. The "PROGRAM OF THE NATIONAL SOCIALIST WORKERS' PARTY" specified that all educational institutions "shall be adapted to *practical* life. The conception of the State Idea (science of citizenship) must be *taught* in the schools from the very beginning."[29]

---

[28] F. Suppe, Ed., *The Structure of Scientific Theories* (Chicago: University of Illinois Press, 1977), pp. 126-127, fn. 258, emphasis added.

[29] R. Payne, *The Life and Death of Adolf Hitler* (NY: Praeger Publishers, 1971), p. 144, emphasis added.

Having noted how morally relevant scholarship should be based on scientific assessments of how *is* human nature and not on *a priori* interpretations of political ideology, scholarly interpretations are now considered in terms of the mind's *a priori* categories. In virtue of joining two judgments which were generated by the categories, there arose a disingenuous idea of metaphysics: Metaphysical claims are not known to be true but are still presupposed by truth-claims of physics.

Interpretive Categories From a False Judgment?

Though the mind's interpretations stem from an *a priori* cognition, the latter has cognitive categories which more rigorously determine interpretations of phenomena. Phenomenal ideas have specific sources in categories that organize and synthesize *a priori* a raw material of experience.

§

Kant held that 'truth' is empirically possible, without concepts related necessarily, or logical in virtue of necessary relations. Ignored are truths which, in different senses, express necessities or impossibilities.

§

Hume's problem that experience amounted to internal sensations which alone are known was to be resolved by categories which were translucent structures. The latter are similar to lenses. In allowing stimuli of external reality to 'pass through', they were denoted as categories of *quantity, quality, relation* and *modality*.[30] Having said this, what follows is not intended as a fullfledged exposition but rather as a format to illustrate ensuing metaphysical judgments.

Whereas *quantity* means that the mind interprets a raw material of experience in terms of one or many phenomena, *quality* means that phenomena are understood positively or negatively. Where 'ϕ' denotes a phenomenon, quantity and

---

30 Cf. Kant's *Critique of Pure Reason*, pp. 112-114, where he says unqualifiedly that "the list of all original pure concepts of synthesis that the understanding contains within itself *a priori*."

quality would be a categorial basis for asserting that 'Two ϕs are moving with increasing velocity.' The latter involves a quantity of two and something which positively occurred. By contrast, the assertion 'Two ϕs are not moving...' denotes the same quantity but something negative. And while *relation* is a categorial basis for ϕ's causal relation to another phenomenon φ as well as for subject and predicate concepts synthesized in judgments, *modality* is the basis for phenomenal notions of possibility or impossibility, existence or nonexistence, and necessity or contingency.

These sets of modalities are both interrelated and related to truth-claims. For example, *modality* is the basis for what is conceivable one way or another: a contingent truth that 'Two ϕs are causes of φ,' which means a denial that φ was caused by ϕ is conceivable in virtue of not being self-contradictory or logically impossible. And *modality* is also a categorial basis for what is necessary for intelligibility such as 'Two ϕs either are or are not causes of φ,' which reflects the Principle of Excluded Middle *(p ∨ ~p)*.

But what is necessary for intelligibility leaves open the question of whether reality must conform to the Laws of Thought. We do not demand that reality abide by the Laws. Rather we seek for our ideas, judgments, and statements about reality to abide by them. Whether or not they do, may depend on a given domain of reality,

All four categories may be illustrated by $p ∨ ~p$ in terms of 'Two ϕs either are or are not causes of φ.' The latter does not merely express positive and negative quantities of ϕ. Also, there is the possible empirical truth that they are related causally and a necessary truth that they are or are not related causally. And as will become clear by considering Kant's logically necessary analytic judgments and logically possible synthetic ones, *modalities* of necessity and possibility are the categorial basis for assertions which are not either logically necessary or empirically true in a usual sense.

In reflecting Hume's supposed critical thought, Kant held that 'truth' is empirically possible, with no synthesized ideas related necessarily, or necessary in virtue of concepts related analytically. Ignored are truths which, in these senses, express impossibilities or necessities. Did Kant confuse a truth-valueless metaphysics with metaphysico-modalities whose truth is known?

Indeed, Kant prefaces his discussion of the categories by saying that the truth of a "hypothetical judgment *(antecedens et consequens)*" involves forms "one and all problematic only."[31] In being problematic, they regard what "is possible to assume... and may therefore be obviously false." This means that when there are *antecedens* such as 'There is a hypothetical judgment about the categories' *(C)* and a *consequens* 'It is problematic only' *(O)*, Kant's own judgment $C \rightarrow O$ may itself be false.

§

Kant's judgment about the categories, *which is possibly false by his own admission*, is the shaky foundation for his notion of metaphysics which shaped all modern mainstream philosophies.

§

For the only impossible falsity is an inference rule such as hypothetical syllogism. He says that in a "syllogism $[p \rightarrow q / p // q]$ the antecedent $[p]$ is in the major premise problematic" and only "shows... that the consequence $[q]$ follows in accordance with the laws of understanding." Consequently, the only understanding that is not possibly false — as is his own judgment about the categories, is a rule of inference such one of *modus ponens*:[32]

$$p \ (C) \rightarrow q \ (O)$$
$$p \ (C)$$
$$\therefore$$
$$q \ (O)$$

An Apodeitic Law of Understanding
(Rule of Inference: MP)

---

31 *Ibid.*, p. 110. The next two quotes are from the same source.

32 *Ibid.*, pp. 109-110. There are either *apodeitic* judgments that are logically true or *assertoric* judgments that are empirically (contingently or problematically) true. Does this not reflect a Humean dichotomy of 'truth'?

Given that Kant's judgment about the categories is not logically necessary, whether expressed as 'If there is a hypothetical judgment about the categories, it is problematic only' or as 'All hypothetical judgments about them are problematic only,'[33] the only understanding which admits of not being possibly false is a rule of inference.

Casting into question all judgments, as examined shortly, Kant's own judgment about the nature of *a priori* categories is nonetheless his foundation for articulating four kinds of judgments. For they are composed of concepts and the categories contain "all the elementary concepts of the understanding in their completeness, nay, even the form of a system of them in human understanding..."[34] Whereas a modern understanding is ostensibly aided by metaphysics since it consists of two judgments — the *synthetic* and *a priori*,[35] the understanding is enriched by physics since it involves all four judgments. Also, in addition to the judgments of empirical physics, others are related to a "permanence in the quantity of matter, to inertia, to the quality of action and reaction, etc..." which "constitute a *physica pura*, or *rationalis*, which well deserves, as an independent science, to be separately dealt with..."[36]

Possibly False Judgment Underlying Physics?

In recalling that physics is rooted in categorial interpretations of reality, we note that Kant named four categorial judgments: *synthetic, analytic, a priori*, and *a posteriori*. The *a priori* and *synthetic* can be joined for a judgment that, beyond the one about the categories, cannot even in principle be known to be true or false. Yet it is presupposed for the intelligibility of scientific inquiries — again, by Kant's own admittance.

---

[33] *Ibid.*, p. 159. In the judgment 'All bodies are heavy,' says Kant, "I do not here assert that these representations *necessarily* belong *to one another* in the empirical intuition, but... *in virtue of the necessary unity* of apperception in the synthesis of intuitions..." But intuitive judgments do not have self-contradictory denials even if, presumably, having 'a priori necessity.'

[34] *Ibid.*, p. 116. See footnotes in *Metaphysical First Principles of Science*.

[35] *Ibid.*, pp. 55. "Propositions" is used here: "Thus metaphysics consists, at least in intention, entirely of *a priori* synthetic propositions."

[36] *Ibid.*, p. 56.

The following introduces the categorial judgments in an Aristotelian propositional form. This form is convenient for clarifying categories of subject and predicate concepts, *e.g.* 'All *Ss* are *Ps*' or 'Some *Ss* are not *Ps*,' as well as truth-claims with knowable truth-values. The clarified values disclose how restricted is Kant's notion of 'truth.' Moreover, this form reveals how experience is coordinated to theory in the later philosophy of science.

§

Judgments which follow from particular experience may 'inspire' universal laws. The best kept secret since the Manhattan Project, however, is that laws treated as if they are known *a priori* are learned only *a posteriori* "from nature."

§

Synthetic judgments have predicates that add information to subjects such as 'All events are caused phenomena' and 'All bodies are phenomena having weight.' Since the predicate 'phenomena having weight' does not mean the same thing as the subject 'bodies' and 'caused phenomena' is different from 'events,' the judgments are not logically true. One can think of events apart from causes and of bodies independently of weight. Consequently, denials of the judgments are not self-contradictory. And thus the contradictories 'Some events are not caused phenomena' and 'Some bodies are not phenomena having weight' are conceivable.

Analytic judgments lack predicates which add information to subjects since to think of the subjects is, at least implicitly, to think of the predicates. This point is illustrated by the judgment 'All bodies are phenomena with extension.' The latter does not seem to be excluded by 'extension' arising from nonscientific phenomenological experience or by the idea of an 'extentionless body' as a point particle.[37] 'Particle' is not an observation term but rather a theoretical term. And

---

37 E.g. see John Compton's "Phenomenology and the Philosophy of Nature" in *Man and World* 21 (1988) 65-89 and R. Trundle's "Physics and Existential Phenomenology" in *New Horizons in Philosophy of Science*, Ed. by David Lamb (London: Ashgate Publishing Ltd., 1992), pp. 66-86.

to say that 'extension' is rooted in experience is not to say that experience is a test of the meaning. Since the concepts 'extension' and 'bodies' are related analytically, the contradictory 'Some bodies are not phenomena with extension' amounts to 'Some bodies are not bodies.' In being logically necessary, a hallmark of analytic judgments is that their truth can be affirmed by mere analysis of the meanings of subjects and predicates.

A priori judgments are easily confused with analytic ones because both are characterized by necessity and universality. But although universality holds for 'All bodies are phenomena with extension' and 'All events are caused phenomena,' for example, they have different sorts of necessities. Scientists necessarily assume *a priori*, as expanded on shortly, that all events are caused. Whereas this assumption is necessary for an intelligibility of scientific inquiries without being logically necessary, the 'necessity' of all bodies being extended is of a logical or analytic sort. Both judgments are *a priori* since they are affirmed necessarily *prior* to experience. But the one for causality has a denial which is not logically false and the other a denial which is. In short, a priori judgments are necessary in the sense of being either analytic or presupposed necessarily for a coherence of various inquiries.

A posteriori judgments follow from our experience, as phenomena having weight follows from experiencing specific instances of the weight. And these judgments may lead to empirical laws. For example, although Kant refers to laws applied *a priori* in physics, he speaks of their being learned *a posteriori* "only from nature."[38] In virtue of Nature being experienced, various laws arose on an experiential basis in the history of science. These, said Kant, bore on a determination of the weights of balls being caused by Galileo "to roll down an inclined plane," air-supported weight which Torricelli had "calculated beforehand to be equal to that of a definitive volume of water," and metals being changed into oxide by Stahl who also changed "oxides back into metal."[39]

---

[38] Kant, *Critique of Pure Reason*, p. 20.
[39] *Ibid.*, p. 20.

Whether considered in terms of Stahl's publicized phlo-giston theory of combustion or Newtonian laws to which he refers,[40] Kant suggested that there is a 'transcendental unity of apperception' whereby the mind transforms raw data into related sets of elements which are conceptualized empirically and theoretically. In order to indicate how theory might evolve from sets of conceptualized empirical elements in Kantian judgments, consider a phenomenal or observational judgment which relates 'bodies restoring their shape' to a theoretical term 'elasticity.'[41]

§

One of Kant's studiously ignored admissions is that In "the practical knowledge of reason, data may... be found sufficient to determine... knowledge that is possible *a priori*, though only from a *practical* point of view..."

§

The *synthetic* proposition 'All bodies restoring their shape after deformation are bodies having elasticity' was viewed as an entry-level proposition for an incorporation of experience into theory by early twentieth-century philosophers of science. But since the proposition had epistemological defects such as elasticity being a possible property for a larger class of bodies in the predicate, it was recast as: 'If a body x is deformed by an external force at time t, x will restore its shape at t if and only if x has elasticity':

$$(x)(t) \, [Dxt \rightarrow (Rxt \equiv Ex)]$$

Here, the symbol (x) reads 'for every x,' (t) specifies 'for every t,' D reads 'is deformed at time,' R designates 'restores its shape at time', E denotes 'elasticity,' the arrow $\rightarrow$ means 'if... then...,' and the symbol $\equiv$ reads 'if and only if.'

However, experience has been related uneasily to theory. Typically, theoretical reasoning begins with coordinations of empirical and theoretical descriptions, say 'a body at time t...'

---

[40] *Ibid.*, p. 25.
[41] Cf. Suppe, *The Structure of Scientific Theories*, p. 21.

and 'the particles of a solid s_o at $t...$,' in terms of an empiricio-theoretical inference which may be expressed in a simplified logico-mathematical schema:

$$[e_1 \wedge (e_1 \approx t_1) \wedge (t_1 \wedge L_o \vdash_L t_2) \wedge (t_2 \approx e_2)] \rightarrow e_2$$
$$[e_1 \wedge (e_1 \approx t_1)... \wedge (t_2 \approx e_2)]$$
$$\therefore$$
$$e_2$$

'$(e_1 \equiv t_1)$' is not used since, by a UTD Thesis, an empirical state description e_1 is subject to logically inconsistent but empirically equivalent theoretical interpretations.[42] Rather, an interpretation is understood wherein e_1 is treated *as if* it is identical to a theoretical description t_1 $(e_1 \approx t_1)$. Then, t_1 is taken with law L_o, say $\sigma = \Delta Fel/\Delta S$ where 'σ' is mechanical stress equal to elastic force (Fel) per unit of cross-sectional area S of a body, in terms of a theory 'T_o.' And with rules of logical deducibility $\vdash_L$, $t_1 \wedge L_o$ afford deductions of t_2 and e_2 by treating them *as if* they are identical $(\approx)$.

On the one hand e_2, if not its truth, follows *a priori* ($\therefore$) by a reasoning of modus ponens in accord with Descartes' hypothetico-deduction. On the other, a Humean skepticism arises, that Kant does not escape, of a material implication ($\rightarrow$) in the first premise. The truth of the consequent e_2 is understood as a prediction which is related by causal regularities to a prior state of the system. At the same time, e_2 does not imply the truth of a law L_o and $\sim e_2$ falsifies it.

Given that the meanings of L_o, t_1, and t_2 begin 'downward' in the context of a theory T_o and not inductively upward from an experience of physical reality, reality does not establish their truth. As truth about either God or freedom is not known 'theoretically' but treated *as if* it is in practical reason, the truth of scientific theories is not known theoretically but treated *as if* it is in practice. Thus Kant says of the practical:

[In] the practical knowledge of reason, data may... be found sufficient to determine... knowledge that is possible *a priori*,

---

42 Cf. S. Korner, *Experience and Theory* (London: Routledge & Kegan Paul, 1966), p. 185. Such a schema is discussed but not the problem at hand.

though only from a practical point of view, to pass beyond... all possible experience.[43]

What does not follow from experience can be *synthetic a priori* but not *a posteriori*. Despite a later view that ~e_2 alone afforded any knowledge, *e.g.* that L_o is false — challenged by Imre Lakatos who still agreed that the truth of L_o could not be inferred from e_2, Kant was obliged to understand theories of physics as having a metaphysical truth-valueless status of being *synthetic a priori*.

§

A Humean schism between what is not known theoretically but is assumed by practical common sense got a novel spin with Kant's *Critique of Practical Reason*.

§

The *synthetic a priori* judgment all events have causes, by comparison, is not analytic since mere analysis cannot certify its logically necessary truth. And understood as a causal principle, its truth is not known empirically because it is presupposed *a priori* by scientific inquiry. In contrast to laws of physics which are fruits of the inquiry, the principle finds its immediate source in an a priori category of relation. A category of *mind* alone relates events causally for a possibility of experience. And thus the experience cannot be taken to reflect how reality really is. Thus says Kant:

> go back to our proof of the principle of causality... observe that we were able to prove it only of objects of possible experience; and even so, not from pure concepts [analytically], *but only as a principle of the possibility of experience...*[44]

Though a causal principle is presupposed by scientific inquiries which result in ostensive truths, the principle is not itself known to be true. In possibly not reflecting how reality is, the principle is both possibly false and assumed paradoxically for truth in science. Again, Kant responded to Hume's criticism that the principle is not known *a priori* by

---

43 Kant, *Critique of Pure Reason,* p. 25.
44 *Ibid.*, p. 253, emphasis added.

grounding the 'a priori' in an *a priori* cognition. This gambit amounted to a question-begging psychological response to a logical question. Precisely, a question ensued of whether the principle corresponds to reality.

Physics Without Metaphysics

Despite a Copernican ideal, Kant's categorial judgments were similar to Newton's development of the calculus. Both developed technical languages for advancing their revolutions. While the revolution in physics yielded stunning new truths, however, 'truth' in philosophy was undercut by a truthless metaphysics. A metaphysics of determinism and freedom was *synthetic*. And freedom was as presupposed *a priori* by a religious or moral inquiry as causal determinism by a scientific one. In not following from experience, a metaphysics of either inquiry was not empirically true. Since religio-moral inquiries were overshadowed by those of physics, there was a search for truth in physics without metaphysics.

Kant thought that to accept a metaphysics of physics was to accept one of morality and religion. He was, afterall, a self-avowed Protestant.[45] Did he strengthen religion or morality? Actually, like a person with one crippled hand who prays for both hands to be the same and is answered by two crippled hands, Kant simply brought down truth-claims in physics to the same paltry level as those in religion and morality. Why, then, was metaphysics not devasting to science?

Whereas scientists enjoyed a metaphysics related in both theory and practice to phenomena about whose material reality there was no doubt, in the *Critique of Pure Reason*, ethicists and theologians suffered a metaphysics related only for practical purposes to noumena about whose immaterial reality there was doubt. Though a Humean schism between what is not known theoretically but is assumed by common sense got a novel spin in the *Critique of Practical Reason*, the latter was thought to bear merely on ethics. But the schism also bore on theoretical problems of knowledge in science.

---

[45] See Kant, *Critique*, p. 29, and R. McLaren's *Christian Ethics* (Prentice-Hall, 1994), p. 60, on Kant's Protestant individualism.

Were the practical and theoretical ever reintegrated? The answer that what is known theoretically led to applied philosophies, such as business ethics or women's studies to take paradigm examples, simply raises questions about their underlying theoretical scholarship.

§

There was an epistemological *equality* of noumena and phenomena since there was no known truth. But there was an ontological *inequality* since phenomena alone referred to an experienced reality.

§

Qualms about the scholarship are evident in a plethora of works.[46] Claire Fulenwider, in *Feminism in American Politics*, for instance, uses a standard social-science methodology for empirically testing radical, reform, and social feminisms. They gave clear evidence of functioning as political ideology. And former women's studies professors Daphne Patai and Noretta Koertge, in *Professing Feminism*, lament that the studies tend to subjugate scholarship to indoctrination. Their criticism is noted by Susan Bourque:[47]

> Make no mistake, this is a disquieting volume. Many readers will take exception... Nevertheless, many feminist scholars will also recognize the concerns Patai and Koertge raise. This is penetrating, trenchant criticism written by women who are sympathetic former participants in women's studies programs.

Further, Richard de George's practical ethics, in the *Journal of Business Ethics*,[48] admits that it was religious universities which pioneered business ethics by a millennial philosophical theology until it was dominated by an applied philosophy in secular institutions. In terms of the latter, theology is relevant in virtue of ignoring the revelation which makes it unique. Or,

---

[46] See Claire Fulenwider's *Feminism in American Politics* (NY: Praeger, 1980), p. 56, and Patai and Koertge's, *Professing Feminism: Cautionary Tales from the Strange World of Women's Studies* (NY: Basic Bks, 1995).

[47] Susan Bourque, "Book Reviews," *Signs: Women in Culture* 22 (1997) 454.

[48] See Richard de George, "The Status of Business Ethics" *Journal of Business Ethics* 6 (1987) 201-11.

it is irrelevant since it includes faith, besides sense experience and reason. But practical reason, even in the secular domain, was not fortified theoretically by pure reason. This reason relegated the 'good' and God to mere regulative concepts. Their practical application presupposed free will and they were necessary for coherent experience. But the necessity was expressed synthetically, assumed *a priori*, and not known to be empirically or logically true.

'Truth' is problematic when it regards realities to which mere regulative moral concepts refer. The problem holds even if we assume that the realities are necessary for practical endeavors. The endeavors presuppose what is necessary for comprehension and not what is true. This fact evidently resulted in a peculiar twist of logic. There was an *epistemological equality* of a metaphysics of noumena and phenomena since the there was no known truth. But there was an *ontological inequality* since phenomena referred to an experienced reality and the reality of immaterial noumena was in question. This inequality of different realities was taken surreptitiously to make a difference about 'truth.'

Noumenal realities of 'good' and God were insufficient truth-conditions for ascribing 'truth' to moral and religious claims. The claims do not refer to verifiable realities which count for or against them. Scientific theories, at least in principle, had a truth content. Their referents were real even if they involved theoretical interpretations *of* observational interpretations *of* a raw material of experience. Observational predictions did at least count for or against theoretical truth. Even if the truth was not verifiable—though in practice it was so construed, there was a supposition that scientific theories were stronger epistemologically than theories of ethics and theology. The latter, if entertained at all, were either modeled on or compared to the paradigm of science.

A. Edel's "Romanell Lecture" bases changing conceptions in ethics on changing scientific theories and laments that theories of morality are "not much further advanced than the Pre-Socratics were in physics."[49] Physicist M. A. Rothman

---

[49] A. Edel, "Romanell Lecture," *Proceedings of the APA* (1987) 823-40.

asserts that the Judeo-Christian explanation of God as Creator is "not even an empirical statement."[50] And E. M. Adams makes religious talk accountable to science by a "tolerant" verification principle wherein religious truth-claims are false if not "metaphorical."[51]

Finally, Thomas O'dea's "Religion in the Year 2000" approves of the fact that science tends to both "mathematize thought" and consign ideas "which cannot be thus refracted to a limbo of subjectivity and second-class importance."[52] And academic journals often suggest a rational primacy of science for truth about either ethics or religion. *The Journal for the Scientific Study of Religion*, for instance, states as its purpose "To publish studies of religion using scientific methodology and... theories, critiques, etc., of a scientific (objectively falsifiable) study of religion."[53]

§

'Voluntary causes,' from Aristotle to Thomas, include an agency of free will. The latter is still necessary for coherent *scientific* as well as moral truth.

§

Taken with skepticism about religion and ethics, a zealous acceptance of truth in science, as a patent fact, begs for sober responses to troubling questions. How can there be truth apart from inductions rejected by Hume? More to the point, how can truth come from scientific inquiry if it presupposes a causal principle not known to be true? A disregard of the questions belies an epistemological insecurity. The insecurity is belied by impatience with 'quibbling.' Attempts will be made to quickly educate us on how modern physics has truly forged ahead. Physics describes physical systems with no reference to

---

50 M. A. Rothman, *A Physicists Guide to Skepticism* (NY: Promethius Books, 1988), p. 161.

51 E. M. Adams, "The Accountability of Religious Discourse," *International Journal of Religion* (1985) 3-17.

52 T. O'dea et al, "Religion in the Year 2000," *Philosophy Looks to the Future*, Ed. P. Richter and W. Fogg (Ill: Waveland Press, 1985), p. 545.

53 A. Bahm, Ed., "US Journals," *Directory of American Philosophers*, (Bowling Green, OH: Philosophy Documentation Center,1988-89), p. 196.

an archaic medieval causality. Thus it will be noted that Newton vainly sought to explain a cause of gravity. First, the explanation was attempted in terms of an ether's increasing density in proportion to the sun's distance which exerted a net force inward. And second, an explanation was sought by a failed causal hypothesis of active bodily powers.[54] But do we *not* know that along with his development of the calculus, his law $F_{gr} = G\ m_1m_2/r^2$ could be used successfully to calculate gravitational force and, by its assumption, to infer Kepler's law of elliptical motion?

In blurring scientific success and truth, this gloss abandons truth in the moral and religious realms as well as overlooks an intriguing historical fact. These realms were assaulted by the Greek Enlightenment's discredited relativism and deterministic metaphysics of physics. The realms were equally assailed by an ideal of physics in the modern Enlightenment which led to a similar relativistic metaphysics. This metaphysics along with that of science is tolerated amidst antagonism to religion and enthusiasm for a scientific revolution.

Among the four causes of medieval philosophical theology, only efficient causes were partially accepted by this revolution for viewing the cosmos as a composition of mass particles with purposeless deterministic interactions which obey mathematical laws. In applying to quantum and relativistic physics, the laws presuppose that 'All events have exactly or inexactly measurable causes.' The latter is no less metaphysical than a principle of efficient causality which has the advantage of including voluntary as well as material causes.

From Denying Metaphysics to Politics

The classical-medieval notion of 'voluntary causes' is tied to a human agency of free will which is necessary for coherent *scientific* as well as religio-moral truth. In modern societies which increasingly did not locate the 'good life' in traditional morality or religion but in a progress of science, the apparent reliance of scientific truth on a truth-valueless metaphysics led to 'articulations' of how physics did not presuppose meta-

---

[54] MacKinnon, *The Problem of Scientific Realism*, p. 14.

physics. Herein, the effort is to show that this was a mistake which led to politicized truth.

Before considering a shift to this 'truth,' a metaphysico-modal reasoning is considered which integrates freedom and causal determinism. Also, it affords a coherent understanding of the world. This understanding does not, as the Kantian tradition, divorce practical and theoretical reason.[55] In order to appreciate the modal reasoning, let us briefly consider attempts to reject metaphysics.

§

In the absence of free will, scientific truth-claims and counter claims are equally true because equally determined. Other claims include that all claims are and are not determined.

§

Typically, a metaphysics of causal determinism is said to be unrelated to modern physics in virtue of the fact that its laws, such as a dynamics of motion in terms of $f = ma$, make no immediate reference to a causal principle. Since it is often held that laws are mere generalized sketches or schematic forms which beg for interpreted applications, the disavowal pertains to the applications as well.[56]

In the case of $f = ma$, applications include $mg = md^2/sdt^2$ for free fall, $mg\mathrm{Sin}\phi = -md^2/sdt^2$ for simple pendulums, and $m_1 d^2 s_1/dt^2 + k_1 s_1 = k_2(d + s_2 - s_1)$ for coupled harmonic oscillators. Understood in terms of a general theory composed of laws, these applications involve theoretical state descriptions of physical systems at present times to predict the systems at future times. But when it is noted that a coordination of the times presupposes an invariable sequence of events, expressed precisely by a metaphysics of causal determinism which is not known to be true, there is a disingenuous shift of attention to a supposed indeterminism of quantum physics.

---

55 See Marcus' *Modalities*, p. 229, for her reference to "metaphysical modalities" relevant to "common as well as scientific discourse."

56 E.g. T. Kuhn, "Second Thoughts on Paradigms." From Suppe, *The Structure of Scientific Theories*, pp. 464-465.

Kantian Shift

This gambit of divorcing physics from a metaphysics of causal determinism has been related, since the Enlightenment, to 'saving truth' in physics and to viewing physics as a paradigm of truth in other disciplines. Yet as classical and relativistic equations are deterministic of exact measurement, equations of quantum physics are *not* indeterministic in the sense of relinquishing a causal principle. Rather they are deterministic of probabilities. In stating that "probability statements—like the uncertainty relation—are fundamentally unavoidable,"[57] both this point and an ensuing skepticism are underscored by physicist Kurt Hubner because the causal principle implies only:

> the *demand* to *presuppose* and to *seek after* the existent Y for every X. Thereby the causal principle becomes a *practical postulate (praktisches Postulat)*... according to what one wills (the end that is sought).[58]

Intriguingly, this assertion underscores in a single stroke that the presuppositions of causal determinism and free will are taken to be both inconsistent and devoid of any known truth. Overlooked is that a reality of freedom is needed for the coherence of scientific as well as religious and moral truth: In the absence of a truth that we have free will, there is not only undermined moral and religious truth but truth in science as well. Scientific truth-claims would themselves be determined with no way to assess which claims were true. Paradoxically, this dilemma includes the nonscientific truth-claim that all claims are causally determined.

The problem was worsened by a materialism of modern causality wherein "all bodies were treated as if they were nothing but a collection of material particles..."[59] 'Truth' is not ascribed to particles but to thoughts, expressed as statements, about them. Thus if statements and thoughts are reduced to material things, there is an epistemological vacuum in which there is no 'truth.' One might object that all truth-

---

[57] K. Hubner, *Critique of Scientific Reason*, Tr. by P. Dixon Jr. and H. Dixon (Chicago: University of Chicago Press, 1985), p. 17.

[58] *Ibid.*, p. 22. Emphasis *not* added.

[59] MacKinnon, *The Problem of Scientific Realism*, p. 16.

claims beg for proof, including the ones for a reality of freedom. However, human free will is needed for a coherence of 'truth' *per se* — including the claimed truth that all truth-claims are determined.[60]

§

There can be no intelligible talk of thinking without our being aware of it. This awareness involves our freedom to think or not to think, including paradoxically that all thoughts are determined.

§

In the positivist-analytic tradition influenced by Hume and Kant, there has been a studious disregard of existential and phenomenological approaches to affirming freedom. Our immediate and incontrovertible consciousness of certain realities has been overlooked. The icon of Anglo-American philosophy Bertrand Russell gave characteristic expression to this fact when he tempered his skepticism about a reality of free will by his caveat that "there may be very excellent arguments for free will [but]... I have never heard of."[61] Does not our consciousness of our behavior comprise our freedom to behave, or will to behave, in one way as opposed to another? Our consciousness of thinking cannot be reduced to thinking. And thinking that our thought is exhaustively

---

60 Besides the issue of freedom, does all 'truth' need proof? Aristotle noted that the Laws of Thought are not proven. Rather, thought itself pre-supposes the laws. The notion that all 'truth' needs proof means that proofs beg for prior ones *ad infinitum*. An objection that modern ethics admits of truth without proof in terms of 'intuition,' must wrestle with rejoinders. For example, Michael Philips notes that intuitions notoriously disagree: "moral argument... becomes *ad hominem* (my intuitions are less distorted than yours)," in "Weighing Moral Reasons," *Mind* (1987) 367-75. But he does not address freedom and, as a presupposition of religio-moral inquiry, it is largely ignored. The metaphysics of freedom tends to be no more addressed in Anglo-American journals than one of causality, though that presupposition has had more weight, surreptitiously, since the time of the scientific revolution and secularization of philosophy.

61 Bertrand Russell, *The Autobiography of Bertrand Russell* (MA: Little, Brown & Company, 1967), p. 70.

determined consists *paradoxically* in our freedom to think or not to think it.[62]

Freedom is limited. We are not free to not feel pain caused by an injury, for instance, but we are free to will that it cease being painful. Indeed, a diminishment of pain by our will is increasingly noted in medicine. And though the case at hand is not rooted in mere thought, it is based on what is necessary for a discursive intelligibility. There can be no intelligible talk of thinking without being aware of it. And this awareness involves our freedom to think or not to think, including paradoxically that all thoughts are determined. Indeed, thinking is a mode of behavior and our consciousness of it involves our freedom to either behave or not behave in given ways: Necessarily if we behave sentiently *(B)*, we are incontrovertibly conscious of our freedom to behave in given ways *(F)*. Where N denotes 'Necessarily,' there is: $N(B \rightarrow F)$. With a definition $N(p \rightarrow q) =_{df} (p \Rightarrow q)$, $B \Rightarrow F$ is taken with B for an analogue of modus ponens: *(B $\Rightarrow$ F) $\wedge$ B / $\therefore$ F*

There may be a rejoinder. To know that we have the free will to behave in given ways is to know we know that F in terms of the theorem *Kap $\rightarrow$ KaKap*, where *Kap* = 'person *a* knows that *p*' and *KaKap* = '*a* knows that *a* knows that *p*.'[63] But we note that *a* may know that *p*, as we know that *F*, by *a*'s immediate consciousness of thinking that *p* as we think that *B*. Thus the proof of our freedom actually gives expression to an undeniable certainty which is as immediately patent as the Principle of Noncontradiction *~(p $\wedge$ ~p)*. For us to

---

62 Though Sartre is an anti-metaphysical philosopher with problems of his own, a consciousness of freedom was a central theme his *Being and Nothingness* (1943). And while he was indebted to Heidegger whose ideas were construed by positivists as a paradigm of meaninglessness, the positivists' pioneering model was Wittgenstein. He praised Heidegger in "On Heidegger on Being and Dread." First published in the *Philosophical Review* in 1965, the latter was "sanitized" by deleting Heidegger's name to make it acceptable to Wittgentein's followers. It was republished without deletion in *Heidegger and Modern Philosophy*, ed. by M. Murray (New Haven: Yale University Press, 1978), pp. 80-83.

63 H. Kahane and P. Tidman, *Logic and Philosophy* (Belmont, CA: Wadsworth Publishing Co., 1995), p. 394.

know either the principle or that *F* is not to *know* that we know but rather to be either *intuitively* certain of the principle or *immediately* conscious of our free choice of will in terms of the proposition *F*.

This case for an immediate and incontrovertible awareness of our freedom proceeds *pari passu* with our being partly free from a deterministic spatio-temporal realm. Prima facie, the freedom is sufficient for scientific truth. The 'truth' would be incoherent if we are exhaustively a part of a reality which is determined. For logically inconsistent truth-claims would be equally true because equally caused. There would be no way to evaluate which claims were true since the evaluations themselves would be caused.

§

Principles of limited freedom and determinism are not only modally true but integrated: It is as impossible for the determinism to be false when scientific theories are true as to be unaware of our freedom to think or not to think it.

§

At the same time a causal principle is, as we have seen, presupposed for the intelligibility of scientific inquiries. Thus, if they yield truth, a dilemma of this truth presupposing a principle which is not known to be true is avoided if a modal truth is ascribed to the principle. Stated simply as 'All events are caused' and understood methodologically as holding for limited purposes of inquiry, the principle may be recast as 'Necessarily if there is an event, there is a cause'; that is, 'It is impossible that there is not a cause when there is an event.' This understanding affords the ascription of modal truth to the principle which might be defended by a common-sence experience manifest in ordinary language. Consider the event of a car suddenly ceasing to run. If one said that its ceasing to run had no cause, not only could there be no inquiry into what made it stop but its stopping for no reason would be taken as a joke or deemed impossible by ordinary persons.

To ascribe truth to the causal principle in virtue of its denial being modally impossible — not logically impossible, is to ameliorate the K-K Thesis which poses the dilemma of

116

how we know that we know. That is, knowledge afforded by an inquiry of physics presupposes metaphysical knowledge, namely knowing the truth of a causal principle which had been held in the Humean-Kantian tradition to be a truth-valueless synthetic a priori judgment. Given that this judgment is true, however, a knotty epistemological problem of the thesis is surmounted as well as shown to be phenomenologically and logically related to our freedom.

Accepting our limited free will and deterministic nature bears on a modern inability to ascribe 'truth' to theories. How could theories not reflect reality when they systematically predict its behavior in various domains? Unless the domains were truly reflected, phenomena could not be predicted: Necessarily if the phenomena are predicted, the theories are approximately true. Hence, besides establishing a truth of the causal principle in terms of the impossibility of an event when there is no cause, it is also impossible for the causal principle to be false when the theories are true. And it is impossible to think of these truths ($\sim T$) when we are not implicitly aware of our freedom to think of them ($\sim F$). That is, $\sim F \Rightarrow \sim T$. And thus even thinking of the interrelated truths of scientific theories and the causal principle are phenomenologically as well as logically related to our freedom.

Having been relegated to a metaphysics presupposed for coherent moral and scientific inquiries, the principles of freedom and causal determinism are not only modally true but integrated. However, the integration is insufficient for religious and moral truth. Though this truth presupposes freedom, for example, freedom does not imply the truth. This point explains part of a shift from metaphysics to substitutes for it in politics. The point was grasped by Nietzsche who responded to 'Whence comes truth if not from metaphysics?' by posing a will-to-power-to-truth of Supermen (*Uebermenschen*) to create it through their unfettered freedom. They ostensibly exercise such freedom through political and military exploitation. Echoing Nietzsche's *Beyond Good and Evil*, the exploitation results in either reshaping the nature of things in the world or creating a worldview (*Weltanschauung*) by which there are revolutionary interpretations.

117

Kantian Shift

In recalling also that this idea of interpretation influences the current philosophy of science, as aptly noted in *The Structure of Scientific Theories*, it needs to be added that this work reveals only half the story. Thus although the revolutionary positions of Kuhn and Feyerabend are lamented because they resemble Nietzsche's "neo-Kantian pragmatic position,"[64] another half of the story is that the positions are also similar to Marxian science.

This science specifies that 'truth' is relative to class-dominated worldviews in different historical epochs of a dialectically determined history. Whereas this history no less excludes free will than a mechanistic *determinism* of natural science, a neo-Kantian Nietzschean position holds that scientific as well as moral truth is relative to willful Supermen who *freely* create it. Before considering how a limited freedom and causal determinism beg for an element in human nature which renders intelligible moral truth, it is important to examine Kant's influence on irrational epistemologies. These begot an unparalleled apologetics for radical political views with roots in a falsely dichotomized notion of 'truth.'

---

[64] Suppe, *The Structure of Scientific Theories*, pp. 126, fn. 258, 127.

Chapter 5

Political Answers to 'Whence comes Truth?'

Kant's misguided dichotomy between empirical and logically necessary truth, in terms of which metaphysics was not known to be true, resulted in both radical and moderate conceptions of behavioral agencies. However, the agencies conceived moderately in open societies have been dangerously weakened because they were undercut epistemologically. This underscores that the 'practical' needs a basis in theoretical scholarship. The latter was, and still is, politicized by the political Left and Right.

In responding to whence comes 'truth' if not from metaphysics, Marx and Nietzsche provided answers that have impacted negatively on world affairs until the present time.[1] In order to reveal the continuing impact of their pernicious reasoning, a modal reasoning is temporarily disregarded that may ameliorate a still splintered conception of ourselves. We begin with how behavioral agencies were conceived in view of Kant's analysis of science and morality.

Whereas moral praise and blame presuppose a *freedom* related to one of Kant's agencies, science presupposes that human behavior is subject to a causal *determinism* of another agency. The agencies express behavior which is assumed, but undeniably experienced, by citizens in open societies. The societal assumptions are evident from judicial processes of weighing a morally relevant rationality against biological

---

[1] Cf. R. Trundle, "Cold-War Ideology," *Res Publica: Leuven Political Science Instituut* 37 (1996) 49-72.

drives to policies of pitting voluntary self-restraint against root causes of behavior.

Consequently, we work backwards to the influence of Nietzsche and Marx by exploring how conservative and liberal tensions, in giving way to only one of the agencies, may lead to closed societies. Since such societies are monolithic unities enforced by authoritarian means, ideas of human nature are themselves a means for justifying ends.

Since political ends are usurped by awkward ideas which slow decisions and pose moral concerns, the problem has tended to be resolved historically by one stroke: Politically affirm either a *freedom* of the superior man (*Uebermensch*) to willfully create truth by bursting the fetters of mythical conventions or a *determinism* wherein truth and 'new men' are molded progressively by a historical movement of Nature. Before relating such notions to Nietzsche and Marx, there are philosophical considerations of open societies.

Post-Kantian Backdrop to Open Societies

Since Kant's philosophy is conceded to be a 'Copernican Revolution' in its influence on modern thought, we may reasonably suppose he not only provided fertile seeds for future philosophical theorizing but liberal and conservative view points fostered by it. Since at least the time of Plato, with whom Kant is in concordance, a fruitful notion has pertained to political claims: To claim that political institutions are good is to be able to say what is 'good.' The response that a sentence about the 'good' is true in virtue of reflecting what it really *is* presupposes its reality as well as theories of reality (ontology) and truth (epistemology).

Thus theories of truth and reality are the basis for morality, as moral claims are for political ones. And hence politics does not determine morality and truth, and truth should not be politicized. Its politicization is tied to ideologies which have not traditionally affected open societies which promote the liberal arts and philosophical questions about 'truth.' It is disturbing, therefore, that Carol Iannone, Editor of *Academic Questions*, notes that 'truth' in America is under attack by liberationist educators who seek to "drain the curriculum of academic content... If you ever looked at recent furors over condom distribution and 'self-esteem' and wondered how on earth the schools had gotten involved in such things to begin with, this is the reason."[2]

Despite this reason, the content of academia has rested perennially on how truth about reality bears on human nature. And since we evolved from Nature, theories of our nature and Nature are a primary origin of reasoning from science to ethics to politics. But since the latter are rooted in seemingly pedantic theories, a relation of theory to the practical, *e.g.* to peace studies and studies of women, is often ignored. The danger kicks in precisely because these studies are often entangled with a politics which politicizes scholarship. At the same time, the practical studies can be no more tenable than the scholarly theories on which they lean.

§

The *bad news* was that metaphysics is presupposed by scientific inquiry. The *good news* was that if this inquiry permits metaphysics, it is also acceptable for moral inquiry.

§

Having noted Kant's scholarly influence, consider how its implications for practical politics have their origin in seemingly pedantic ideas. The ideas essentially involve his notion of the 'mind' and are briefly reiterated.

The mind is comparable to a prism. As a prism receives and diffuses white light, the mind has a structure that receives an undiffused raw material of experience—understood roughly as physical stimuli — and categorizes it 'prior to' our ideas. In this sense, the mind is an *a priori structure* that interprets phenomena. That is, the mind is active in the acquisition of knowledge and the word 'interpretation' would have central importance both politically and philosophically.

On the one hand, there was significant philosophical support for the Enlightenment's emphasis on science. This emphasis found expression in d'Holbach's *System de la Nature* (1770) in which unhappiness was held to stem from not

---

[2] C. Iannone, "They'll Never Learn," *Nat. Rev.* Vol. 52, No. 17, (2000), p. 57.

knowing Nature. Kant showed that it was part of our cognitive nature to know Nature by virtue of our mind 'automatically' interpreting physical events causally.[3] Here, we have an inevitable foundation for the social and political sciences which presuppose that all events are caused.

On the other hand, the causal judgment was inconsistent with moral evaluations and was not empirically or logically true. In being a function of the mind, the judgment was not empirically true because it was both universal and imposed *a prior* on experience. At the same time it was not logically true since its denial was not self-contradictory. In recalling that such judgments were now called 'metaphysics,' there was a mixed import: The 'bad news' was that a metaphysics without known truth is presupposed by truth-claims of science. And the 'good news' was that if metaphysics is accepted in science, then it should be acceptable for morality as well.

Metaphysics: Ontologically and Epistemologically

One need not expand on Kant's moral imperatives to note that moral truth-claims presuppose a metaphysical judgment that persons are free. Unless they enjoy free choice of will, it is senseless to say they ought never do one thing or always another. One can admit of scholarly disagreement over his moral-minded *Critique of Practical Reason* and theoretical *Critique of Pure Reason*. And one can still note that a criticism of pure reason weakened the case for a practical one which depended on the more rigorous theory. Theoretical reason specified that the mind's structure receives only stimuli of material things as well as that freedom is only a possible reality and not a thing on which other things act causally.

In terms of a theory of reality — that is, ontologically, a metaphysics of causal determinism was presupposed by liberal citizens who were oriented to science with its proverbial 'root causes.' A metaphysics of causal determinism seemed more solidly anchored than one of freedom because it bore on

---

3 Kant's metaphysical judgments, being *synthetic a priori*, have different concepts wherein the judgments cannot be logically true (*analytic*). And in being presupposed prior to experience, their universal truth cannot be derived empirically, i.e. they cannot be known *a posteriori*.

experienced phenomena. Surreptitiously, science enjoyed a prestige over morality and religion insofar as freedom, relevant to religion for a coherence of God's judgment, is not an experienced raw material but an immaterial reality—if it is real. Given that freedom is real, and this is a big 'given,' it is a reality-in-itself behind phenomenal appearances. In short, on the one hand, an inability to experience freedom does not necessarily mean it is not real. On the other hand, while an assumption of its reality is necessary for practical moral reasoning, the latter can be no more tenable than that of the theory on which it was based.

§

Open societies assume we have bodies subject to deterministic drives as well as a moral nature. In view of this nature, citizens may freely choose to abide by moral laws and are usually held responsible for doing so despite psychobiological drives.

§

In terms a theory of truth — that is, epistemologically, a deterministic metaphysics is as questionably true as one of freedom. This epistemological equality serves conservatives who emphasize responsibility as much as liberals who emphasize root causes of behavior. And though there seems to be more support for the behavioral causes when reality as well as truth is considered, a duality of human agency provides a theoretical backdrop for open societies.

Open societies assume that we have bodies subject to internal and external deterministic causes as well as moral natures in virtue of rational capacities. In view of the capacities, citizens may freely choose to abide by moral laws and are usually held responsible for doing so despite psycho-biological drives. And despite dilemmas of knowing where the drives 'end' and freely-choosing moral capacities 'begin,' the dual agency has tended to instill political moderation into citizens. This is not to say they have studied Kant. Rather, it is to say that a wisdom of moderation may be grounded in their ordinary experience of both themselves and others.

123

Overlapping Metaphysical Assumptions

Dual assumptions of human agencies may be schematized by overlapping circles. A black area of the political Left denotes causally determined behavior, a lighter area of the Right designates freely chosen behavior, and the area in the center represents an ambiguous common-sense agency of political moderation. This moderation assumes a limited freedom and determinism:

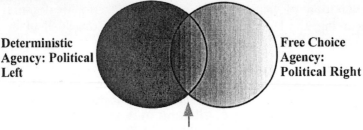

Deterministic
Agency: Political
Left

Free Choice
Agency:
Political Right

Center
Political Moderation

Overlapping Behavioral Agencies

In being mainly concerned with nurturing their families and pursuing careers — in getting on with the business of life, the common-sense experience of most citizens seems to suggest both sides of human nature. Parents may temper their anger, for example, in light of popular books on child psychology. But, they might sometimes spank their children for what they view as willful disobedience, notwithstanding psychologists who discourage spanking because it causes this or that behavioral pathology.

In the absence of acknowledging freedom, a distinction between causally determined behavior and, say, a Skinnerian operant conditioning is largely moot; being mostly a difference of exact and inexact measurement. Or, for instance, corporations may acknowledge that alcoholism is to some extent a disease in terms of which medical treatment is subsidized for employees. But employees may suffer blame for not willfully helping themselves as well. Though most citizens may identify themselves as either conservatives or liberals, a bit more to the right or left of an ambiguous political center,

124

they generally seem to seek a well warranted middle road in the social-political praxis.

Despite relatively extreme left and right-wing political groups in open societies, most decisions of citizens reflect a middle between those who emphasize our freely-choosing moral capacities and others the behavioral causes. Those of the *liberal to left* cannot wholly deny freedom when they morally blame the wealthy for being 'mean spirited.' And those of the *conservative to right* cannot ignore behavioral conditioning when they stress moral values in 'formative' childhood years. A danger to political institutions of over-stressing policies based on one or another behavioral agency surfaces in public debates. Aired in a news media which ties practice to theory, the debates reveal that institutions tend to respond to a moderate majority.

§

If a metaphysics of causality underlies science and science is increasingly viewed as ideal knowledge, the public will tend to drift leftward. Hilary Putnam notes that scientific forms of reasoning have been virtually *institutionalized* in society.

§

Having noted how news reports bear on political theory, we note that E. Bronner's "Liberals See Hope in Court" in the *Boston Globe* (July 7, 1991) illustrated an induced temperance of political-interest groups. In deference to a more moderate stance of the public, these groups addressed a controversy over Clarence Thomas' nomination to the Supreme Court. In reference to right and left-wing strategists, the report stated that "If a court... hands down opinions that are at one end of the ideological spectrum,... [it] thrusts its work into public debate." The debate attracts attention to decisions which allow "government power to encroach on personal lives." And this potential encroachment led the more extreme groups to defer to the public's "middle position." They did not relinquish their stronger political persuasions but tried to weaken their rival by appealing to public moderation.

125

Assumptions of Science and Politics

However, if a metaphysics of causality underlies science and science is increasingly viewed as ideal knowledge in our high-tech culture, we may reasonably suppose that the public's moderation might drift leftward. Harvard's Hilary Putnam notes that scientific forms of reasoning have been virtually *institutionalized* in society.[4] Also, perhaps the political pendulum has been tilted by activist movements, since the late 1960s, which lean on a Marxian 'science' such as radical feminism and a sex revolution influenced by it.

Revolutionary causes of feminists and the gay community have, in fact, fostered a 'raised consciousness' of white heterosexual businessmen who endorse controversial affirmative actions for public-relations purposes: "To stay out of court and cultivate public relations, white men in the boardroom were willing to sell out due process and equal-protection rights of white men on the assembly line and in the offices. It's an old story...," notes social scientist F. R. Lynch.[5]

Finally, a momentum for social-political uniformity is spread internationally by global organizations. The United Nations Summits at Rio in 1992 and Cairo in 1994 made a show of appealing to religious sentiments. But the Vatican's mainstream Christian input was not only uninvited but opposed. Ironically, most UN delegates loudly espoused a multicultural diversity. Yet the Vatican was the 'unofficial participant' which defended a genuine diversity of each country making its *own* final decision, about such things as families, in light of their cultural traditions. And its input at Cairo layed the foundation for preventing a feminist imposition of abortion agenda on Islamic and other religious countries at the UN Women's-Rights Summit in China.

The report "Chinese Rough Up Women," in the *New York Times* (September 7, 1995), is relevant. Given that many eminent feminists are members of the Left, it is ironic that

---

4 H. Putnam, "Philosophers and Human Understanding," *Scientific Explanation*, Ed. by A. F. Heath (NY: Macmillan Publishers, 1988), p. 100.

5 See F. Lynch's "Willy Loman, Angry White Guy," *Los Angeles Times*, 22 March 1995, A10. Visiting sociologist at Claremont McKenna College, Lynch also authored *Invisible Victims* (NY: Praeger Publishers, 1991).

feminist UN delegates experienced firsthand a gap in theory and practice. In trying to enter a theater amidst *securitate*, former Wisconsin University President Donna Shalala "pushed through like a fullback going for short yardage..." Another did not fare so well. "'What's going on here?' shouted Betty Friedan... who was slammed against a wall by Chinese police." Tending to admire communist ideals, many feminists identify themselves as socialists or Marxists of some sort — Simone de Beauvoir, Rowbotham, Firestone, Millett, MacKinnon, Sheila, Mitchell, Chodorow, Bleier, Steinem, Eli Zaretsky, Margaret Benston, Angela Davis, Evelyn Reed, Barb Ehrereich, Vivian Howe, and Rayna Rapp.[6]

§

When Stalin shrewdly suggested that killing one person is a tragedy and murdering millions an abstract number, he revealed how mathematized techno-scientific ways of thought may consign 'evil' to religious superstition.

§

In this vein, while the 1995 Copenhagen Summit urged a greater social conscience, its linkage of conscience to political activism and disregard of any Third-World responsibility was not as reminiscent of traditional Judeo-Christianity as of a liberation theology of the Left.[7] A difficulty influencing left-ward drifts of open societies is an apparent subjectivity of what *ought* to be the case as opposed to objective scientific descriptions of what either *is* or *will* be the case. Given a tendency to view things as caused phenomena with no question about their reality as opposed to freedom, the 'good' or God, Kant may explain why viewing things scientifically is more natural than understanding them morally.

Problems inherent in the human sciences, from sociology to psychiatry, pale before moral anomalies such as twentieth-

---

[6] M. Levin, *Feminism and Freedom* (NJ: Transaction Books, Rutgers-The State University, 1987), p. 26

[7] See W. Drozdiak's "$30 Million Social Summit Called Extravagant, Wasteful," *The Washington Post*, 12 March 1995, A14.

century 'mysteries of evil.' These mysteries range from Nazi death camps to Soviet gulags and Pol Pot's killing fields. When Stalin shrewdly suggested that killing one person is a tragedy and millions an abstract number, he revealed how mathematized techno-scientific ways of thought may consign 'evil' to religious superstition. In flirting with a scientifically determined progress of the Left, many Western intellectuals have rationalized its victims.

Victims include intellectuals in the West. Secret police files, after the Soviet Union collapsed, reveal that "hundreds of American leftists who had moved here... to help Josef Stalin build the *new worker's paradise,*... vanished, one by one, from the face of the earth."[8] Professor Julius Hecker, for example, taught at the University of Moscow and wrote books defending communism after earning his PhD in Philosophy at Columbia. After discovering in newly released files that "On April 28, 1938... the secret police informed him he would be shot in two hours," his daughter remarked "He was just an idealist." Official silence in the West on 14 to 20 million purged persons, which helped intellectuals delude themselves about the worker's paradise as opposed to the plain evils of fascism, was due to "The US government... courting the Soviet Union as an ally against Hitler."

Ideological Slide to Closed Societies

An intellectual slide to twentieth-century closed societies involved disregarding, not 'interpretation,' but a thesis of the mind's 'a priori structure.' Undoubtedly, this largely stemmed from its truth not resting on experience *(a posteriori)* or on logical analysis *(analytically)* so that the thesis seemed no less metaphysical than the metaphysics of determinism and freedom. But in being necessary *a priori* for the intelligibility of moral and scientific inquiries, freedom and determinism were retained as viable notions. Their ties to Nietzschean and Marxian-induced ideologies has been largely ignored. Before

---

8 A. Cullison, "Files Reveal Stalin's Secret Purge of American Leftists," *The Associated Press* 9 November 1997. Emphasis added. See this article for the following quotes.

considering these ignored ideologies, the nature of ideology is briefly addressed.

Nature of Ideology

Herein, 'ideology' refers to a system of social-political belief whose proponents, to various degrees, engage in the following behavior: *(i)* express either impatience or intolerance for anything less than fervent 'true believers'; *(ii)* pursue a *cause* deemed more important than common civility; *(iii)* tend to view civility itself as a reward for agreement and for achieving ideological ends; *(iv)* unabashedly ignore or suppress evidence counting against the belief; and *(v)* in open societies where there is limited power to suppress, silence disagreement and genuine critical thought by *ad hominem* attacks. These often involve calling opposition 'right wing' by the political Left and 'left wing' by the Right.

§

If causally determined behavior is stressed, a liberal to left-wing view prevails. It emphasizes little or no responsibility of citizens for 'criminality,' *e.g.* dysfunctional behavior; work or its lack being largely caused by economic forces...

§

For example, if conservative disagreement with the Left is due to moral concerns, these are politicized by being called 'right wing.' The name, of course, chills any dialogue. The same goes for labeling liberals 'left wing' by the Right. Using the word 'ideology' for all philosophical, scientific, moral and political views obliterates any distinction between them and the ideologies closed to argument and evidence. Ubiquitous use of the word 'ideology' may simply be careless speaking. However, it may also disguise a thinly veiled quest for power over reason as well as a cowardly avoidance of confronting one's own faults and thinking independently.

Having suffered firsthand both fascist and communist ideologies, the renowned philosopher Gustav Bergmenn said that an ideology-free society is desirable "if for no other reason than the humanity, the intelligence, and the courage it takes to bear life without support of ideological illusion."[9] And political scientist L. Baradat contrasts ideology to philosophy by noting that philosophy involves introspective analyses of political assumptions.[10] He renders poignant insights of Plato in his *Republic* 489^c that philosophy will be compared to ideology by ideologists: We can liken "our present political rulers to... sailors, and those whom these called... stargazing ideologists to the true pilots [philosophers]." This brings us back to how a moderate politics in open societies may slide into ideology. A conservative to Right is noted after a liberal to Left in terms of behavioral agencies.

Marxian Ideology and Determinism

If a deterministic agency is stressed, a liberal to left-wing view prevails. It emphasizes the following by degrees: little or no responsibility of citizens for 'criminality', *e.g.* dysfunctional and sociopathic behavior; work or its lack being largely caused by economic forces; capitalistic self-interest being that of an elite political class that causes or conditions dominated classes to accept its self-serving norms; class struggles increasingly liberating the oppressed from reactionary institutions; and a diminished or altogether abandoned role of traditional ethics and religion in influencing children, family, education, employment, and government institutions.

The institutions would generally be directed by educators, bureaucrats and government officials who have the requisite technical and scientific education. For example, in objecting to parental interference in elemenatry-school sex education, a liberal citizen states: "Imagine parents who are not skilled in the *latest educational techniques* wanting to dictate what their children are taught. Just because they pay tuition... does not give them the right to tell *professional educators* what to do."[11] (In regard to same sex-education programs on the same page, J. Spitzig takes a conservative to Right view: "Instead of

---

9 L. Addis' "Memorial Minutes" on Gustav Bergmenn, *Proceedings and Addresses of the American Philosophical Association* 61 (1987) 165.

10 L. P. Baradat, *Political Ideologies* (NJ: Prentice Hall, 1991), p. 10.

11 C. Griese,"No Right to Dictate," *The Cincinnati Enquirer (TCE)*, 1 April 1995, A7, emphasis added.

morality,... it serves up a gloppy melange of social psychology to engender a warm-and-fuzzy comfort level toward sexuality...The hell with making our kids comfortable with their sexuality... get them into heaven.") Ultimately, those holding a liberal to Left perspective lean toward directives of a scientific community.

§

Marx parlays Kant's notion of scientific determinism into one of morality. Thus, he ascribed a 'morality' to determinism *itself* by viewing it dialectically rather than mechanistically.

§

If there eventuates an acute view of a deterministic human agency, the political vision of a scientific community may itself be directed by a scientific visionary such as Marx. He equated himself to a scientist by proclaiming: "the physicist either observes natural processes... or, wherever possible, he makes experiments. What I have to examine in this work is the capitalist mode of production."[12] And it is imperative for his comparison of himself to the physicist to incorporate morality into science so that scientifically described change becomes morally desirable progress. But Peter Redpath reminds us that "While Newton's laws worked wonders... when applied to the material universe, when applied to personal behavior, fine arts, and literary studies, they often produced unenlightened despotism."[13]

In regard to despotism, Marx's indebtedness to Kant may illuminate a peculiar morality. The latter reflects ideological tendencies to cast extraordinary meanings on ordinary words for making acceptable what is heinous and senseless. Marx parlays Kant's notion of scientific determinism into one of morality. Thus, he ascribed a 'morality' to determinism *itself* by viewing it dialectically rather than mechanistically. A

---

[12] K. Marx, *Capital: A Critique of Political Economy*, Vol. I. From A. Wood, Ed., *Marx* (NY: Macmillan Publishing Co., 1988), p. 205.

[13] P. Redpath, *Masquerade of the Dream Walkers: Prophetic Theology from the Cartesians to Hegel* (GA: Rodopi Editions, BV, 1998), p. 104.

mechanististic determinism, critically expressed by Kant, led to a view of the material world as a purposeless mechanism. But if the mechanism were itself caused by a dialectically determined history, where history is a manifestation of matter unfolding progressively, then science and morality might be affirmed simultaneously in history.

Historical progress, grasped scientifically, even indicates that Marx's own idea of 'progressive history' is a determined and exactly measurable product at a historical moment. "From this moment," says Marx, "science, which is a product of... the historical movement... has become revolutionary."[14] Political revolution is the most dramatic way to change societies. As a political science that explains the very cause of itself and all other sciences, Marxian science is a '*science* of sciences' which supersedes a classical-medieval view of that *science* as metaphysics.

In a word, metaphysics becomes 'physics.' And since this new physics is political, there arises both politicized truth and relativism: What is true in one historical epoch, dominated by a political class, may be false in another as classes and epochs move historically through revolutions. 'Truth' is determined by epochal classes, radically separated by revolutions, which cause, condition, or socialize others to accept a conceptual framework. And 'truth' is not the fruit of a historical contin-uity of developing theories, based on experiment or corrobor-ated prediction, in a modern scientific tradition.

Many post-cold war intellectuals, with a liberal to Left sympathy, will object that 'truth' is not said to be relative but dialectically truer. If there is no truer 'truth,' what becomes of a progressive scientific vision? But consider an epoch of the Sophist Thrasymachus. His assertion that the just is unjust at different times, in virtue of who rules, brings to mind the Marxian idea that domination determines truth. For this reason, paradoxically, it will become clear that the same intellectuals tend to embrace relativism.

The relativism evoked Plato's response, in the *Republic* 337[b], that "twice six" may then absurdly become a false

---

14 K. Marx, *The Poverty of Philosophy*. From D. Mclellen, Ed. *Karl Marx: Selected Writings* (NY: Oxford University Press, 1987), p. 212.

answer to "how many are twelve?" These possibilities imply there is no truer 'truth.' Both this claim and its denial are, for the Marxist, equally determined so that the incoherence of each claim being both true and false is avoided only by another claim *sub specie aeternitatis* (relating to eternal things) where truth about changing 'truth' is from an extra-epochal standpoint. This point is soon strengthened.

A response that Thrasymachus was not a member of any dominating class ignores the fact that Sophism was related culturally to a dominant Greek Enlightenment. The reply also overlooks that Marx was not part of such a class. Precisely, at the same time, Marx adopted 'elitist' extra-epochal claims for himself. And in the late twentieth-century West, talk of a 'raised consciousness' was virtually ubiquitous — especially by his academics devotees in Anglo-American universities.

§

Ends are also achieved, not by political science, but, by sciences which are politicized. A prestige of science in postmodern culture is exploited for rejecting traditional morality and religion as well as for ignoring 'reactionary' facts which conflict with a mother science of Marxism.

§

Both the dialectic and relativism are ignominious. But the sophistic relativism, as noxious as it is, is less malignant than the dialectic because the latter begets a systematically sinister meaning of morality. Whatever furthers the utopian historical end is good (progressive) and whatever impedes the end is bad (reactionary). All human endeavors such as work, family life, science, morality, and art become an ideological or propagandistic means for achieving political ends. This politicization gives a radical spin to the 'ends justifying the means.'

The peasants' cries during the great leaps forward of Mao and Stalin come to mind since terror and mass murder are by definition, however unbelievable in our belief system, not only justified but positively good when they expedite the ends. The ends are also accomplished, not by political science, but, by sciences which are politicized. A prestige of science in post-modern culture is exploited for rejecting traditional morality and religion as well as for ignoring 'reactionary' facts of physics, biology, and psychology which conflict with a mother science of Marxism.

The ideogram of 'hammer and sickle' symbolized science as hard labor for ends of the state in communist countries. Dissidents, especially in the former USSR, either underwent *political* treatment in psychiatric hospitals for not grasping reality with a prescribed *correctness* or executed if a counter-conditioning reeducation was not effective. Centers for higher education, called 'technical' or 'scientific' institutes, also laud science and not either liberal arts or philosophy. The latter were, of course, the very disciplines that afforded Marx's chimerical creativity in the first place.

That Marxian dogma was still enforced in communist societies, even after their dissolution in the late 1980s, is evidenced by the *International Directory of Philosophy* (BG-SU Documentation Ctr., 1990-92). There was either absent any listings for the remaining societies or scholarship only on Marx. And that Marxian theory has practical consequences which still haunt Europe is illustrated by the statements of Marianne Birthler, Brandenburg's Minister of Education, in what was formerly communist East Germany. In an interview with *The Baltimore Sun* (June 30, 1991), she noted that rashes of youth violence, triggered by ideological intolerance, was a product of Marxism's empty "anti-fascism... part of the country's loathed authoritarian educational system that did not tolerate questions, doubts, or problems."

Youth violence is rife in open societies. Most statistics indicate a dramatic rise in the 1960s, however, when a counter culture of the Vietnam-War opposition evolved into splinter ideologies within a Marxian New Left. The war was portrayed by anti-establishment student activists as one waged on oppressed peoples by dominating capitalist classes. Radical feminists viewed similar classes as historically composed of males who tyrannize females. And Black militants decried the domination of Eurocentric elite white classes. Finally, a sex revolution was joined to criticism of white heterosexual males who, exploiting marriage for power, were part of a patriarchal political hierarchy. And a sex revolution not only prescribed extramarital sex, for undermining the religio-social status of traditional marriage, but lesbianism as well until chauvinistic male attitudes were liberated.

The liberation triggered an ideological apologetics for homosexuality and for—what had been traditionally called—'fornication.' Besides unparalleled sexual diseases worsened by a new anti-establishment drug culture for dropping out of the established one, there ensued a divorce epidemic, out-of-wedlock childbirths, nontraditional single-parent families, and escalating poverty and teen violence.

§

The 1960s still haunt the US armed forces. Dr. Gerald Atkinson, CDR USN (Ret.), whose PhD studies in Nuclear Physics exposed him to the New Left during his university days, warns that the military is still under attack for its political incorrectness.

§

The NY Population Council, composed mostly of women scholars, released a report that the "Western family model long idealized as the gold standard... is now clearly a myth... Children are at a greater risk of being poor and often are left to fend for themselves without adult supervision."[15] That the family dissolutions have spread globally is evidenced by a further statement that, starting in the 1970s in the West, the destruction of families is now "true whether... North America, Europe, South America or southern Africa."[16]

---

15 See F. Vrazo, "Breakup of Family is Global Problem," *Knight-Ridder News, TCE* (30 May 1995) A5. The Population Council's Social-Science Director, Cynthia Lloyd, noted that "with mothers working and fathers working or absent, children 'are roaming around on their own.' "

16 *Ibid*, p. A5. Also, USC Professor of Anthropology A. Moore explained a developing aggressiveness by noting that "Protests have gone from the gentle non-violence of Martin Luther King to the antics of ACT-UP and Queer Nation and others that use rudeness as a way of gaining attention" [*TCE*, 24 Nov 1994, H14].

Further, under a feminist influence in colleges, there was a rise of textbooks in which "costs of marriage, particularly to women, often are exaggerated" with "distortions of research, omissions of important data and misattributions of scholarship... influencing professionals who are advisors... of the family as an institution... [and students who naively accept the texts as authoritative]."[17] Finally, there was an influx into universities of, what some persons have coined, 'tenured radicals' who were either sympathetic with or part of a New-Left student movement.

The pioneering feminist Germaine Greer concedes that "the forging-house of most of the younger women's liberation groups was the university left-wing."[18] And political scientist L.T. Sargent notes that this wing consisted of liberal Marxists centered around the *New Left Review*. The name "New Left" was "appropriated by the growing world student movement and mass media in the mid1960s."[19]

Nor have 1960s been without effect on the U.S. armed forces. Dr. Gerald Atkinson, CDR USN (Ret.), who fought in Vietnam as Navy aviator and whose Ph.D. in Nuclear Physics exposed him to the New Left during his university studies, warns that the military is still under attack in the twenty-first century for its political incorrectness. The latter has led to a reeducation, at the Naval Academy, by an ethics curriculum "designed by Dr. Nancy Sherman who was brought to the Academy by the then-Superintendent, ADM Charles Larson, at the urging of SecNav John Dalton who in turn carried out the wishes of the Clinton administration..."[20]

---

17 See documentation of the Council on Families whose researchers include Judith Wallerstein and Barbara Whitehead: *Closed Hearts, Closed Minds: The Textbook Story of Marriage* (NY: IAV, 1997), quoted in "Marriage Bashing: College Textbooks Undermine a Building Block of Our Society," *TCE* 23 Sept. 1997, A6. The report anticipates academic *ad hominem* responses that these findings come from the "right wing."

18 G. Greer, *The Female Eunuch* (NY: McGraw-Hill Publishers, 1970), pp. 313-329.

19 L. T. Sargent, *Contemporary Political Ideologies*, 7th Ed. (Ill: The Dorsey Press, 1987), p. 149.

20 See Dr. G. Atkinson's "The Maguire Ethics Whitewash," 29 May 2000, *http://www.newtotalitarians.com/RebuttalToMaguire.html*, pp. 1-13.

Baby Boomers who "took over the administrative offices" and hated the military to a pathological degree which "was visceral," adds Atkinson, have penetrated the Naval Academy by the feminist canons of Ms. Sherman. Having replaced studies such as those of John Locke, the Founding Fathers, and implications of Nature's God for ethics in the Declaration of Independence by "Enlightenment philosophers... all with equal weight... [since] to prefer one over another would be judgmental'," she became an activist for New York's domestic partners' legislation which would give "unmarried couples living together, heterosexual or homosexual," the "same legal rights as husbands and wives."[21]

§

A feminist bedrock is that "gender itself is socially constructed." Ignoring biological differences permits truth about men and women to be relative to whoever controls education.

§

Downgrading traditional wives began much earlier with a medley of assumptions: construing heterosexuality as a norm of chauvinistic males, deriding as sexist a denial that women can do anything men can do, and extolling 'more important jobs' than wives being mothers who stay home to raise children during their formative years. The jobs included pursuits afforded by the military academy in 1976 and an inevitable slippery slope in 1993 with a boomer administration's allowance for women to serve in "Navy combat aviation and... surface ships."[22] And this allowance was supported by an academic feminism in which biological attractions of young men and women in close quarters were to be neutralized by the new studies and by a 'sensitivity training' which, theoretically, would cause or condition nonsexist behavior.

Professors Daphne Patai and Noretta Koertge note that a current bedrock of feminism is "that gender itself is socially constructed"—where disregarding "biological sex differences"[23]

---

21 *Ibid.*, Sherman on WNET-TV's "Religion & Ethics Weekly" 29 May 98.

22 *Ibid.* p. 1

23 Patai and Koertge, *Professing Feminism*, p. 138.

permits a truth about the differences to be relative to whoever controls education. The reeducation alarms many retired Naval officers such as Atkinson who quotes a dismayed cadet at West Point. The latter wrote him anonymously that "This military academy "marvels at the frequency of sexual misconduct... cases that occur (and the corresponding slide in discipline). I guess the brass assumed that a school full of virile young men would simply treat the women as 'brothers' and that the women were incapable of having a sex drive (much less be attracted to any of the men)."[24]

Given that cadets cannot speak out on their own behalf when they are subject to a discipline unimaginable to civilian students, a question arises of whether the public is simply uninformed or virtually treasonable in allowing their own children to be indoctrinated by an unnatural regimen which may have life threatening results in combat. It is reasonable to suppose that open societies are faced with serious problems if a New Left does influence society by an idea that political domination determines truth, where 'truth' is relative to a race or gender with power (though the quest for power is now reportedly augmented by "politically correct 'multicultural- ists'" for whom "Italian Marxist Antonio Gramsci" is all the rage "in American academic circles."[25]) Not the least problem would be an inflammation of ethnic conflicts. While not as deplorable as some global atrocities, there are philosophical assumptions which provide ideological support.

At the very apex of rising dissatisfaction in politicized communist societies in the 1980s, an eminent philosopher in an open society — Sidney Hook, himself a former Marxist scholar — warned that the greatest danger "to freedom of philosophical inquiry... [was] the growing politicization of the university."[26] These considerations are significant in view of Santayana's warning that not knowing history means we are doomed to relive it. And they bear on President Truman's 1945 speech when he lamented the relative ease of killing the

---

[24] From Atkinson, "The Maguire Ethics Whitewash," p. 11.

[25] See G.A. Geyer, "America Faces Ideological Strife," *TCE* 24 Dec 2000, E6.

[26] S. Hook, "Invited Address," *Proceedings Of The APA* 60 (1987) 511-12.

dictators who started World War II in comparison to killing the ideas that made them possible.[27]

And having endured the applied ideas of communism and Nazism in occupied Poland, an experience few academics in the West have suffered, Pope John Paul II was quoted by the *Associated Press* (16 May 1995) — fifty years after Truman's prediction — as warning that a "culture of war" threatens to destroy us since we failed to learn bitter lessons: "Sadly, the end of the war did not lead to the disappearance of... policies and ideologies which were its cause."

§

A conservative to Right stresses free choice of will for criminal behavior and successful employment. Pursuits of self-interest are coordinated ideally with the collective moral interests of society.

§

Nietzschean Ideology and Freedom

Causes of both Left and Right need reexamination in view of atrocious similarities in ideological behavior. The Nazi-Soviet pact reminds us of the Soviet Katyn-forest mass murder of Poles. Initially blamed on Nazis, the murder was only publicly admitted as a deed of Soviet troops in 1989. And while the Nazis modeled their feared Gestapo on the Soviet *Narodny Kommisariat Vnutrennikh Del* (NKVD prior to the KGB), Stalin ordered his troops to *not* help Poland fight the Nazis in 1945 since the Poles were a 'criminal people.' A Marxian idea that 'criminality' is a matter of causally conditioned behavior was not officially rejected. Stalin simply exploited allied talk of axis war crimes as a cover for not aiding the Polish people. He hoped that the people would have no resources left to resist communist occupation after fighting the fascists.

Understanding a fascist Right with roots in a Nietzschean apologetics, might begin with a 'conservative to Right' based on neo-Kantian assumptions of human freedom. Simply put, if the world is viewed in terms of a human agency in which freedom is stressed, there prevails a conservative to right-wing view which emphasizes: Responsibility for criminal behavior

---

[27] Harry S. Truman, *Years of Decisions* (NY: Doubleday, 1955), p. 411.

and successful employment; a pursuit of self-interest which is coordinated ideally with collective moral interests of society; and attempts to *conserve* traditional moral guidelines for family, education, and government. Though minimal government intervention is tolerated to ensure standards in education and industry, a conservative to Right tends to be a centrifugal force for both patriotism and the preservation of a society's cultural heritage. The notion of preserving such a heritage, if not the survival of a nation per se, is especially significant for understanding the rise of a more acute right-ward perspective which reinterprets morality.

This odd morality arises by political instability, by threats to individual autonomy, or by feeling that a nation's honor is demeaned. The latter are a short step to relinquishing individual will to a dictator who speaks as 'one for many' and whose power is amplified dramatically. While a dictator's power may be exercised initially for peacefully restoring stability, it may come to be harnessed for willfully shaping a *new world order* in a dictator's own 'image.' This may occur as increasing fear of a nation is held to enhance its honor. An idea of the 'will,' including a will-to-power, is related conceptually and existentially to 'freedom.'

On the one hand, Kant influenced the idea that a *practical idea of freedom* has a conceptual difficulty beyond its usual meaning as the liberty to exercise chosen behavior. For free choice of will is only a possible reality which is necessary for an intelligibility of morality. On the other hand, a practical idea could be strengthened by a *philosophical notion of freedom* in existentialism. Having roots in St. Augustine, existentialism includes modern contributors such as Nietzsche. While most existentialists view an incontrovertible consciousness of behavior as comprising the freedom to *choose* a given behavior even if it cannot be exercised, Nietzsche would not deny behavioral self-consciousness even as he goes beyond it. He understands inorganic as well as organic things as having a will-to-power to dominate everything else.

We are no more free to not will-to-power, given that our nature is part of Nature, than we are free to not feel pain when beaten. This turns a traditional naturalistic ethics on its

140

head. Possibly inconsistent moral laws are created in a willful way, by way of our power-seeking nature. This irrationalism contrasts to a perennial idea that our rational nature is the basis for moral and political laws (*lex naturalis*). Nietzsche's revolutionary spin on Kant's metaphysics of freedom sheds light on conservatives who, seeking to conserve traditions which have been fruitful over the ages, come under fire from both a Marxian Left and Nietzschean Right. The Right's bond to Nietzsche is addressed shortly.

§

Many conservatives may attempt to *conserve* traditional norms while recognizing an import- ance of science. But Kant's philosophy explains even here how there were nefarious practical consequences.

§

It is now noted that although moral praise and blame pre- suppose freedom, Nietzsche realized that freedom does not presuppose either morality or moral theories in terms of which praise and blame are understood. Traditional morality gave way to an unfettered freedom, as evident in *The Will to Power* and *Beyond Good and Evil*. Given that Kant's deter- ministic human agency led to rabid ideas of 'good' and 'evil' in one direction, it is reasonable to expect a radical agency of freedom to lead to zealous ideas in another.

Many conservatives may attempt to *conserve* traditional norms while recognizing an importance of science. But Kant's philosophy explains even here how there were nefarious practical consequences. The consequences stemmed partly from freedom being only a possible reality which did not imply any morality during both the Enlightenment's scientific revolution and the Reformation's challenge to the traditional Church. Reform and counter-reform weakened any theological responses to modern developments. But beyond a religious house divided against itself, Kant fostered an Anglo-European positivism for which religious and moral truth claims were 'meaningless' because they were not either *synthetic* (empirically verifiable) or *analytic* (logically true).

141

These events may not bode well for conservatism but they do for a slide to the Right. Since most conservatives do not know how classical-medieval notions may viably support their thought, much less how it was ignored by modern philosophy, they often appeal to mere tradition. One thinks of a reporter who interviewed truck drivers about gays and women in the military. When they responded simply that they had always believed it was wrong, the reporter turned smilingly toward the camera and signed-off smugly, "That's the news from here!," as if to confirm that they were unenlightened heterosexual white males. An inability to articulate reasons for traditions does not imply, of course, that there are not any.

Nevertheless, though traditional belief might make many conservatives feel anti-scienctific or anti-intellectual, if not homophobic or sexist or racist, conservative sympathies may be expected to shift rightward before leftward. And the shift will be facilitated if they feel humiliated. The humiliation brings to mind a nation's honor demeaned. Accordingly, it is reminiscent of angry citizens, whose belief is politicized by a demonization of their race or gender, and their being called 'right wing' anyway. In a Letter to the Editor, for example, one indignant citizen stated: "I do not want to go into what you would call a *right-wing tirade* on how I find homosexuality a sin... Instead... cancel my subscription." [28]

An actual right wing finds expression in Nietzsche, despite controversy over his link to fascism. Before discussing this evident link, the controversy is considered briefly in terms of attempts to preclude it after World War Two when the fruits of fascism were both plain and inexpiable. The attempts at 'damage control' were strengthened by Princeton's Walter Kaufmann who represented the trend. His commentaries and translations of Nietzsche's works into English were highly influential. Typical is his appeal to one of Nietzsche's drafts for a preface to *The Will to Power*. "I wish I had written it in French," he lamented, "so that it might not appear to be a confirmation of the aspirations of the German *Reich*..."[29]

---

[28] M. Kerkhop "I David, Take You, Mark," *TCE* 23 March 1995, emphasis.

[29] F. Nietzsche, *The Will to Power*, Ed. W. Kaufmann (NY: Random House, 1968), Preface.

First, however, with admiration for Kaufmann's scholarly translations, philosophical works are subject to interpretations apart from an author's intentions. Nietzschean research was not merely subsidized, under Hitler, by the German taxpayers. Recent scholarship, noted shortly, acknowledges the Left's reluctance to admit their indebtedness to his thought because it was associated with the Right.

Second, a pervading Nietzschean theme, beyond the work in question, is a celebration of unabashed conquests by bold leaders who, being supermen similar to gods (*Uebermenschen*), evoke fear and conform reality to their 'image' by power. Third, it has already been observed that many intellectuals after World War II, with a liberal to Left perspective, might, as does Kaufmann, irrationally defend Sophism.

§

Denials that Nietzsche provided an apologetics for fascism should be reconsidered. One might consider how its aggressive and egocentric tenor, which proves fatal in politics, stem from radical views of truth and reality.

§

Historians of philosophy have always acknowledged Nietzsche's indebtedness to a relativism of the Greek Sophists. Professor Norman Melchert notes, for instance, that "The Sophists produced a theory... picked up in the nineteenth century by... Nietzsche."[30] It is reasonable to suppose that a questionable defense of Nietzsche would incur one of the Sophists and vice versa. In point of fact, Kaufmann states in his classic textbook — at the very time that leftist ideology began to flourish in American universities in the late 1960s, that the Sophists' unpopularity "made it easy for Plato to picture the Sophists in the darkest colors." He adds that Plato's hostility to Sophism permits us to "portray him as a reactionary who sought... sanction in another world for convictions threatened by the Greek enlightenment."[31]

---

[30] N. Melchert *The Great Conversation* (Toronto: Mayfield, 1991) p. 45

[31] W. Kaufmann, Ed., *Philosophical Classics I* (NJ: Prentice-Hall, 1968), p. 53.

Kaufmann's writing ignores the merits of Plato's argument against the Sophists who held incoherently that truth is relative to power. Instead, there is reference to both politics and personal hostility. And since Plato's hostility is logically irrelevant to his argument against their relativism, Kaufmann's disregard of the relativism both reduces his criticism to an *ad hominem* attack and politicizes their quarrel by suggesting that the Sophists were progressive because Plato was "reactionary."

These points render problematical Kaufmann's influential interpretation of Nietzsche. Post-war views of his philosophy should be reconsidered. One might consider how its aggressive and egocentric tenor, which proves fatal in politics, stem from radical views of truth and reality. Specifically, both Nietzsche and Marx deny a reality lying behind appearances. Their answers of where truth comes from, if not from a true metaphysics, explain totalitarian events still suffered in the social-political arenas. Whereas Marx denied a reality of freedom behind the appearances of deterministic phenomena, Nietzsche disavowed the reality by affirming that phenomena were themselves the manifestation of a willful world-in-itself. The world-in-itself included a power-seeking creative behavior of individuals, races, and political bodies.

The philosophies of Marx and Nietzsche, in their essential applications, do not involve either an ambiguity or a metaphysical unknown which would diminish decisive ideological belief. For example, Nietzsche rejects Kant's thesis of a priori cognition, in terms of which phenomena are interpreted deterministically, as a mere metaphysical stratagem for the "expediency of a certain race."[32] It is a foregone conclusion that *racial* and *societal conflict* may be seen as conflicting 'wills-to-power.' Hence, philosophies may be understood as a mere ideological means for an end of power. That Nietzsche viewed free will as a necessary condition for the coherence of a 'will-to-power' is evident in his defense of our "right" to *choose* freedom. In addition to freedom being consistent with his choice of a metaphysics, "determinism is only a modus of

---

32 Nietzsche, *The Will to Power*, p. 278.

144

permitting ourselves to juggle our evaluations away once they have no place in a mechanistically conceived world."[33]

If not from Metaphysics, Truth from Dominating Classes or Supermen?

Let us briefly expand on the problem that a metaphysics of freedom and determinism have no known truth. If truth-claims yielded by scientific inquiry presuppose the truth-valueless notion that all events are caused, the 'truth' of the claims is undermined because they rest on what is not known to be true. The same dilemma, it is often ignored, holds for a metaphysics of freedom. If truth-claims afforded by moral inquiry presuppose the truthless notion that persons have free choice of will, the 'truth' of those claims is equally undercut since those claims also rest on a presupposition which has no known truth. Thus a question ensued: 'Whence comes truth if not from metaphysics?'

An avoidance of metaphysics, by virtually all subsequent philosophical movements in the West, was largely a response to this question. Pragmatism, positivism, analytic philosophy, and existentialism are the best known. Belatedly, philosophers of science also acknowledged a troubling K-K Thesis: "if skepticism is to be avoided [of *K*nowing one *K*nows], the exploitation of... 'causal' regularities in obtaining a posteriori knowledge must not require prior knowledge of those regularities."[34] But two radical answers veered off in opposite directions, outside mainstream philosophy, with Marx and Nietzsche. They held that truth comes from either dominating political classes or *Uebermenschen* who, in virtue of an unfettered free will, create truth by the will-to-power.

Self-Reinforcing Circular Reason

Ideologists who exploit the ideas of Nietzsche and Marx have much to fear from critical questions. Did Marx alone transcend a historico-material domain? He would have had to

---

[33] *Ibid.*, p. 416.

[34] See F. Suppe, *The Structure of Scientific Theories*, pp. 721-722.

know his ideas were true without their being both determined and possibly false in another historical epoch. Are Nietzsche's ideas a mere creation of his own will-to-power? Self-reinforcing circularities also arise: Changing the world by indoctrination and propaganda reinforce Marxian theory by preventing critical analyses of it and the theory reinforces propaganda by construing any criticism of it as a reactionary expression of class conflict.

§

Kant first raised the specter of interpretation with an 'a priori cognition.' Marx rooted interpretation in dominating classes and Nietzsche in a creative will-to-power. "Interpretation," he said, is "the introduction of meaning... there are no facts."

§

And though propaganda and indoctrination are applicable only to less than super-race masses, a Nietzschean apologetics for fascism interprets criticism as expressions of an inferior will-to-power; the will to undermine a 'copernican' freedom of creating truth by *Uebermenschen*.[35] Practical consequences of a radical Right and Left were poignantly expressed by an old Soviet woman who sighed despairingly that "In both Stalinism and fascism we see an insatiable thirst for power, a yearning to remake the world according to a particular design and the same contempt for human beings".[36]

The remaking of human beings begins with interpretation. Whereas Kant first raised the specter of interpretation with an 'a priori cognition,' Marx understands it in terms of dominating classes and Nietzsche by way of a creative will-to-power. "Interpretation," said Nietzsche, is "the introduction of meaning... there are no facts." He adds, "On a yet higher

---

35 Nietzsche, *The Will to Power*, p. 417. Nietzsche references Kant: "Our new 'freedom'... the pre-copernican prison and field of vision, would be something... regressive unless it is merely a bad joke".

36 See E. H. Methvin's "The Unquiet Ghosts of Stalin's Victims," *Nat. Rev.* 41 (1989) 24-52.

level [it] is to posit a goal and mold facts according to it; that is, *active interpretation*..."[37]

Both Nietzschean and Marxian interpretations are rooted in Kant's novel view of the mind. Its interpretive activity was likened, by analogy, to the earth revolving around the sun in Copernicus' revolutionary theory. This theory's analogy to a revolution in philosophy, however, had unintended consequences. Notwithstanding them, Kant at least distinguished his revolution from science and his idea of free will from a will to create truth. The distinction contrasts to Nietzsche and to a chimera of scientific Marxism.

One is updated by an anthology in America which praises a "Marxian Spirituality" years after a collapse of communist ideas in 1989. The *new* Marxian man will "make it his purpose to master his own feelings, to raise his instincts to the heights of consciousness,... to *create* a higher social biological type, or, if you please, a superman."[38]

The spirituality is disquietingly like a Nazi *Uebermensch*, its higher biological race of human beings, and a life-affirming positive Christianity. A National-Socialist fascism needs an affinity with fervent religious visions as does Marxism with its well-worn comparisons of Marx to the Savior and utopian end of history to heaven. An affinity between heaven and fascism does not need to be forced when one considers that Wagner's son-in-law likened himself to John the Baptist in his self-avowed discovery of Hitler as Savior. The Savior was a New Man, who replaced Adam, in Christianity.

While Christianity was openly relegated to myth by Nazi theorists, some social-science professors may ignore a greater applicability of myth to their own politicized beliefs than to traditional ones. Contrary to a standard social-science usage wherein historical truth is irrelevant to myth, traditional religious beliefs are sometimes treated as inexact unscientific stories. How could it be avoided if there is a pretension of the

---

[37] Nietzsche, *The Will to Power*, p. 327.

[38] L. Trotsky, "Socialism and the Human Future," *Marxism and Spirituality: An International Anthology*, Ed. B.B. Page (CT: Greenwood Publishing Group, 1993), p. 8. See R. Trundle's invited review of this book in *Canadian Philosophical Reviews* XIII (1993) 258-260.

social sciences to an exactness of either the natural sciences or Marxian ideology? Afro-American sociologist Clinton Jean notes *mainstream* liberal-Marxian analyses in social science of a class-structured Eurocentric history. He felt "uncomfortable," at Columbia and Brandeis, "about exactness... as liberal social science described it."[39] And social scientist Diana Deere notes how feminist ideology skews field work by ethnocentric assumptions. These include a "bond of sisterhood [which] was sufficient... to... interpret the experience of women in heterogeneous cultural settings" and "feminist conscious-raising among those whom we studied."[40]

§

Post-Kantian ideologies are strange bedfellows in our time. "A moral, social, and scientific paradigm... is not merely something through which we see the world. It... shapes the facts of the human world."

§

Ties of a pseudo-scientific liberal Marxism to Nietzsche are revealed by other feminist academics. Ofelia Schutte admits that Marxian doctrines are enriched by Nietzsche but that socialists do not credit him since he is "associated with fascism."[41] Coupled to Claire Fulenwider's empirical tests wherein virtually all feminist interpretation "gives clear evidence" of being "political ideology," the above does not bode well for objectivity in social science.[42]

Weltanschauungen for Shaping Truth

Kathryn Parson's pioneering feminism shows that the post-Kantian ideologies are strange bedfellows in our time. While exalting Engles' communist insights and creations of a "new human being," conflicting Nietzschean worldviews (*Weltan-*

---

39 C. Jean, *Beyond the Eurocentric Veil* (MA: UM Press, 1992) p. xvi.

40 C. D. Deere, "Forward," *Feminist Dilemmas in Fieldwork*, Ed. Diane Wolf (Boulder: Westview Press, 1996), p. vii.

41 O. Schutte, "Nietzsche, Mariategui, and Socialism: A Case of Nietzschean Marxism in Peru" *Social Theory and Change* 14 (1988) 71-2.

42 C. Fulenwider, *Feminism in American Politics* (NY: Praeger, 1980), p. 56.

schauungen) of different races and genders are joined to Kuhn's relativistic historical paradigms for shaping truth: "A moral, social, and scientific paradigm... is not merely something through which we see the world. It is something which shapes the facts of the human world."[43]

Academic ideologists in open societies must be cautious if they politicize truth by viewing education as indoctrination. Otherwise, they may add to an increasing chorus of public concern about political correctness. A subtle correctness in research may allay scholarly criticism of agenda celebrated uncritically in classrooms. Sociologist F. R. Lynch notes:

> In early April, 600 professional papers will be read at the Pacific Sociological Association Meetings... Though affirmative action is the hottest sociological topic in the United States, not a single paper title directly mentions the issue... Incredibly, sociologists have written few papers and fewer books on affirmative action: Political correctness dictates that the policies are to be applauded, not studied.[44]

This is not to say that those who avoid a study of the policies, for fear of being called 'racist' or 'sexist' or 'elitist,' are ideologists. It is to say that such politicized names are legitimatized by totalitarian theory for silencing a scientific inquiry which is needed for informed social decisions.

For example, Herbert Aptheker is a former University of California historian on Afro-Americans. After quoting Marx that theory grips "the masses when it demonstrates *ad hominem*," he let loose the *ad hominem* on those with whom he disagrees with words to which Western academics are now numb: These academics are accused of supporting "exploitative societies," and are "anti-scientific" and "elitist."[45] A Marxian strategy of academics who see themselves as an elite is to dismiss questions about their 'science'; to attack others by names which, arguably, are better suited to themselves. Part of the agenda is multiculturalism with links to Nietzsche.

---

43 K. Parsons, "Nietzsche and Moral Change," *Nietzsche*, Ed. R. Solomon (NY: Anchor Press, 1980), pp. 185 fn. 12, 186, 190.

44 F. R. Lynch, "Willy Loman, Angry White Guy," A10.

45 See H. Aptheker's quote of Marx (1844c, p. 182) in "The Spiritual in Marxism," *Marxism and Spirituality*, pp. 71, 73.

Whence Comes Truth?

Whereas Marx prompts ubiquitous reference to a 'raised consciousness' for uncritically accepting politicized agenda, Nietzsche fosters appeal to power over knowledge. J. Peacock noted in a lecture to the Japan-American Society that "Multiculturalism wants to celebrate... change, and it really does not have the patience to go through all this... analytical fieldwork."[46] He adds that "Knowledge may be a way to *power,* but multiculturalism often wants the *power* right away; as for knowledge, you can take it or leave it."[47]

§

Jean Kirkpatrick, former Ambassador to the UN, once noted that all ideological agenda must ultimately appeal to philosophy. In this respect, ties of Nietzsche to both fascism and Cold-War Marxism have been neglected or deliberately defused.

§

One can appreciate why Western academics exalt power and neglect 'knowledge' if the latter presupposes what is not known. A suspicion that many multiculturalists do not extol all cultures, but disparage the West, may be warranted by imagining their likely dismay at a prospect of the West being praised in the East. Turning to the East for meaning, a resistance to which would be deemed ethnocentric, makes sense if misunderstanding a central mode of reasoning in the West led to a societal *angst* and to an incoherent view of 'truth' in the sciences which were taken to be ideal enterprises.

The point is not that all forms of multiculturalism and affirmative action are bad. Some may be needed even if they need study. Nor is it that ideologies stem in all cases from literally reading Nietzsche and Marx even if radical feminists, called 'gender feminists' by more moderate equity ones, have unabashedly appealed to them. The point is that a proselytized ideology, during the Cold War, has been institutionalized

---

46 J. Peacock, "Multiculturalism in the USA," *AnArchaey Notes II* (Oct. 1994) 4. I am grateful to Professor Sharlotte Neely for this article.

47 *Ibid.,* p. 4.

in Western democracies with far-ranging influences on international attitudes and behavior.

Jean Kirkpatrick, former Ambassador to the UN, noted that all ideological agenda must ultimately appeal to philosophy. In this respect, ties of Nietzsche to fascism and Cold-War Marxism have been neglected or deliberately defused. A Nietzschean free will, for a coherent exercise of willful power, fosters a new boldness for taking 'responsibility' for various sorts of radical agenda which range from politicized teaching to terrorists who commit atrocities.

Taking responsibility for atrocities, which presupposes free will, conflicts with a Marxian determinism and offends any sense of decency in traditional morality. But as fascism personalizes morality for cults of Marxian prophets who willfully transcend history, Marxism makes them more than mythic *Hitlerian Uebermenschen* by viewing history as a scientific phenomenon. As Marx ties historical classes to conflicting worldviews, fascism transposes the views into ethnic Weltanschauungen which shape facts. As fascism incurs contempt for certain races, Marxists intellectualize racism by demonizing various groups as historical classes who resist a progressive egalitarianism. Einstein's physics was relegated to one of either an elitist class or the despised Jews.

Theoretical physicist J. Logan adds to these points. A central reason for a failure of the Nazis' fission project for the atomic bomb was a "certainty of their own superiority... The campaign against the Jews cost Germany many of the talented minds that were to shine so brightly on the Allied side."[48] With equally deadly assaults on race and reason, this kind of race-minded and class-conscious thinking now finds a peculiar synthesis in attacks on Einstein and other Western cultural figures as members of elite historical classes of 'dead white males.' They are the new scapegoat of ideology.

Ideological attacks on white males has filtered down from a political correctness in universities to secondary education. This is evidenced amidst controversy over multiculturalism.

---

[48] J. Logan, "The Critical Mass," *American Scientist* 84 (1996) 263-277. From declassified Farm-Hill transcripts of remarks by Heisenberg and other German scientists in reaction to the atomic bombing of Hiroshima.

Whence Comes Truth?

One student asks why he should "read all these dead white men... *The Odyssey*?" In belying his own anti-cultural racism, he added paradoxically "I think there is too much racism... because we don't understand one another."[49] Precisely, the very point of studying different racial contributions to culture has led, ideologically and irrationally, to an ethnocentrism which was supposedly to be eschewed by multiculturalism. How is this phenomenon pathological?

§

Western educators who relate increasing education to an increasing liberal to Left perspective beg a question: Is the perspective due to a *liberal education* or to a surreptitious *subjugation* of education to political ideology?

§

Like virulent germinations of a bacterial irrationalism, an adapting and mutating fascist Marxism both defies social-political antidotes and renders moot traditional distinctions between basic political perspectives. The confusion itself is fundamental to attempts at deconstructing our culture. A collapse of the perspectives is evident in the confusion of a political scientist who tries to retain them:

> Irrationalism permeates the approach of fascism... but, most importantly, irrationalism entails the rejection of the approach of the 19th century to social problems. This approach was... rationalist, whether Marxist or liberal democratic. It saw... problems that could be solved by... reason and science. In opposition... fascism and national socialism... appeal to the emotions and hate as tools for manipulating man.[50]

---

[49] See J. Guthrie, "Minority Authors Required," *TCE*, 21 March 1998, A6.

[50] Sargent, *Contemporary Political Ideologies*, p. 116. For further foreboding of an irrational fascism — but none of socialism or Marxism, see Renata Saleci's *The Spoils of Freedom* (NY: Routledge, 1995) and L. Birken's *Hitler as Philosophe*. Whereas Birken warns that our "failure to provide a postmodern substitute for [fascist] nationalism invites the reassertion of... obsessions of nation and race" in his own summary in *GPC Book News* (May 1995) 1, Saleci warns that the "rise of nationalist, racist, and anti-feminist ideologies is a frightening repercussion of the collapse of socialism" in Routledge's *Feminist Philosophy* (Spring 1995) 42013.

But it is perfectly clear that manipulative *ad hominem* attacks are shamelessly used by a current Left infused with old elements of fascism, or if one prefers, a mode of Nietzschean Marxism, for manipulating academics and ordinary citizens. This observation is not a defense of the Right which has been criticized with equal severity. That the Left may pose the greatest intellectual danger, seems born out by Anthony Kenny's *The Oxford History of Western Philosophy*:

> In the 1970s, paradoxically, Marxism in the East was universally taught and almost universally disbelieved, while Marxism in the West was taught... but to an audience of passionate believers. Now, of course, as a result of the dissolution of the Soviet Empire... the institutional support for Marxist philosophy... must depend for its survival on the efforts of its devotees in the universities of the West.[51]

That many professors are smitten with, or slavishly adapt to, radical ideology should not be surprising. Venerated Chinese writer Ba Jin recalled the professorial victims of communist Cultural Revolutions. Those who were murdered, in contrast to the majority, were intellectually heroic since they alone "did not succumb to the oppressive power of the day..."[52] And Arno Mayer responds to ordinary persons who may be dismayed by Heidegger's paean to the new Nazi order because he was such a knowledgeable philosopher. He reminds us that Heidegger was "no less supererogatory than the oath of allegiance to Hitler which seven hundred university and college professors signed in November 1933."[53]

Western educators who relate increasing education to an increasing liberal to Left perspective beg a question: Is the perspective due to a *liberal education* or to a surreptitious *subjugation* of education to political ideology. Disguised as science or infused into it, ideology can be coupled to courses

---

[51] A. Kenny, Ed., *The Oxford History of Western Philosophy* (Oxford: Oxford University Press, 1994), p. 368.

[52] See Tongqi Lin, "A Search for China's Soul," *Daedalus: Journal of the American Academy of Arts* 122 (1993) 171-188.

[53] A. J. Mayer, "Founding and Consolidation of Nazi Regime," in *Why Did the Heavens Not Darken?* (NY: Pantheon Books, 1990), p. 135.

which not only view science as debunking religion but confuse metaphysics with physics. Since the time of the scientific revolution with its origin in physics, which was exacerbated by Marx's comparison of himself to a physicist, many educators may have been inordinately influenced by a materialistic and deterministic metaphysics.

§

We are beyond a naive belief that world wars will end all wars. Yet many now think that ethnic conflicts are merely tribal. This plays into the hands of political demagogues whose quest for power stems from modern philosophical notions of human nature.

§

Ultimate faith in science raises the specter of a progressive scientific morality, even if this morality has involved a flirtation with Marxism. And while Marxism in universities of the West tends to ignore a relativism of Nietzcshe, with historical roots in the Sophists' Enlightenment, the latter has ominous similarities to our Enlightenment. No pretense can be made to either *science* when it is politicized or *rationality* when it is viewed as an ethnic-determined notion. In terms of this notion, it is denied that there is any objective truth with a truth-condition of reality. Rather, political power is held to shape ideas of reality, if not Nature and human nature themselves. We are beyond a naive belief that world wars will end all wars. Yet many think we begin the twenty-first century with ethnic conflicts which are merely tribal.

This plays into the hands of political demagogues whose quest for power stems from modern views of human nature. A new understanding of our nature is needed in place of demagogic substitutes for a metaphysics of freedom and determinism. Manifest in ideologies which undermine morality and science in the name of 'science,' the substitutes usurp objective 'truth' and are exploited for relegating it to conflicting ethnic interpretations of the world. A response to the world views is now addressed by a novel mode of reasoning.

154

Chapter 6

Truth From Nature: Getting it Right

A modern neglect of appealing to Nature for integrated and objective truth in science, theology, ethics, and politics is rooted in mischievous answers to 'Whence comes *truth* if not from metaphysics?' If a metaphysics of freedom and causal determinism are presupposed for coherent moral and scientific inquiries, but the inquiries are undercut by not knowing a truth of the metaphysics, then a basis other than metaphysics is needed for 'truth.' What or *who* were the new substitutes for metaphysical truth?

Construing truth-conditions as either deterministic classes or as willful supermen, who originate conflicting worldviews, does not merely mean that 'truth' is incoherently relative to different political classes and supermen. In beginning with new substitutes for metaphysics rather than with physics, it means that this modern approach collides head-on with a perennial understanding of metaphysics in terms of the dictum *ta meta ta phusika* (or 'things after physics').

Thus a physics of Nature was superseded by metaphysical extremes of an unfettered freedom and determinism to shape 'truth.' The extremes were incompatible despite their later entanglement in a totalitarian 'Nietzschean Marxism' whose central target was a medieval naturalism. However, in starting with an incontrovertible experience of ourselves as being limitedly both free and determined, a revitalized naturalism leads modally to Nature's God wherein human nature and Nature are as they ought to be. Subsequently, how our nature ought to be fulfilled could be both inferred from scientific descriptions of it and institutionalized politically

Before noting how this God is related modally to science, a harmony of freely-choosing and deterministic behavioral agencies is reiterated. The former agency is often called 'voluntary' and the latter 'natural.' In this respect, there is an irony: A common-sense acceptance of them was excluded by a modern causal principle which posited only natural causes and was given a so-called 'critical expression' by Hume and Kant. The following responses consist in several points as a prelude to discussing modal truth. This truth serves to unite, rather than to divide or politicize science, ethics and theology.

Complementariness of Freedom and Determinism

First, having evolved from Kant's idea that a metaphysics of freedom and determinism were not known to be true, Nietzschean and Marxian *Weltanschauungen* analyses ignore what are complementary human agencies. A disregard of these dual agencies by the worldviews results in an imposition of unnatural political policies on citizens. And the imposition results in their psychobiological dysfunction, unhappiness, and lack of productivity.

Precisely, these pathologies induce a collapse of unnatural policies of a politicized science. Scientists can no more viably deny that the free will of persons to fall is consistent with calculating their falling velocities than ethicists can cogently deny that gravity determines velocities of suicides whose behavior they evaluate morally.

Surely, assessments in Newtonian mechanics disregard the free will of persons falling, where the fall, kinematically, is $mg = md^2/sdt^2$. At the same time, forensic investigations in criminal science acknowledge free will since, without being facetious, cries of 'No, no, no!' or 'My problems are over!' evidence an unchosen homicide or a freely-chosen suicide. Thus free will is not merely relevant to morality but to human science as well. And viewing persons ideologically as causally determined phenomena, mechanically or dialectically, is as senseless as viewing phenomena to be merely subject to our free will: Both freedom and determinism, as ambiguous as they are, must be acknowledged for an intelligibility of morality and science without which societies cannot be sustained.

156

Kant was correct that freedom is presupposed by a moral praise and blame which may be understood in the context of traditional moral theories. Having said that, a post-Kantian inability to ascribe truth to the theories does not imply that they are not true.

§

The perennial effectiveness of traditional moral theories, in rendering happiness and pro- ductivity, invites the point that they might rival theories of social science in predicting a fate of societies.

§

Thus in regard to modern moral theories with seeds in ancient-medieval ones, the following is noted: Deontologists hold that moral reasons have their status as reasons in virtue of our rational nature, which is a nature reminiscent of a Platonic virtue ethics; consequentialists specify that moral rules have a demonstrable utility in producing happiness, which brings to mind the end of happiness (*eudaimonia*) in Aristotle's more empirical approach; and theologians tend to hold, without inconsistency, that conscience and notions of 'unconscionable laws' are based on God's eternal laws which are 'written in the human heart.'

While a metaphysics of moral theories is not empirically or logically true, how is their perennial adoption sustained if they are not effective? And how can they be effective when they do not reflect our moral nature?

A Modal Defense of Moral Truth

Second, a familiar objection that traditional moral theories are conditioned by societal indoctrination is peculiar. Why did the propaganda and reeducation of ideological communism, not to mention a Watsonian psychology used by Nazi propaganda minister Joseph Goebbels, fail in Eastern Europe, the Soviet Union, and China? knee-jerk responses that such countries are not genuinely Marxist is irrelevant to their having employed, systematically, an indoctrination which pales any putative

157

one of open societies in the West. Many *Marxist Hitlers*, to use words applied to Rumania's Ceausescu and East Germany's Henver Hoxa in the 1980s, were charged by their own citizens with crimes against humanity in terms of a traditional morality which was denied ideologically.

The effectiveness of traditional moral theories invites the point that they might rival the theories of social science in predicting a fate of societies in virtue of a morally relevant history, or, in Aristotelian terms, an 'experience of ages.' Could moral theories, in addressing a moral nature which complements our physical nature, have been consulted not only for human rights violations but for predictions about the results of the 'cultural revolutions' and 'great leaps forward' of closed societies now collapsed?

In regard to collapsed societies, the predictions are not made by a formalized scientific reasoning which coordinates empirical and theoretical terms. Still, the predictions bear on societies which cannot survive if they have institutionalized agenda which do not fulfill human nature, as specified by traditional moral theories. There is an impossibility of it being false that the theories reflect how our nature is fulfilled when it is true that their violation by institutionalized agenda results in a collapse of society: Necessarily if the violation of moral theories by institutionalized agenda results in a collapse of society (V), then those theories reflect how our nature is fulfilled (R). That is, $R \Rightarrow V$. The latter is taken with R for an analogue of modus ponens: $R \wedge (R \Rightarrow V) / \therefore V$.[1]

In response to an objection that the argument begs for another premise, *e.g.* which bears on the point that predictive success cannot be explained unless the theories reflect our nature, a *reductio* of the denial of $R \Rightarrow V$ may illustrate its patent truth:[2] Absurdly, moral theories might not reflect how our nature is fulfilled when a lack of the fulfillment by a

---

[1] *Cf.* H. Kahane and P. Tidman, for the symbol '/∴' which may be used in modal reasoning, in *Logic and Philosophy* (CA: Wadsworth Publishing Co., 1995), pp. 385, 387.

[2] The *reductio* may, in place of another premise, hold for other predictive conditionals. See R. B. Marcus, *Modalities* (NY: Oxford University Press, 1993), p. 171.

society results in its collapse. Or, our nature is not *necessarily* fulfilled in terms of traditional moral theories which, when violated by a society, results in its downfall. Though the necessity is not logical but modal, it needs to be said that the conditional $R \Rightarrow V$ is a truth that is stronger epistemologically than one that is known by material implication — empirically or factually; say, if *as a matter of fact* society X collapsed, X had norms injurious to traditional nuclear families. Here, it is modally possible that X did not suffer these particular pathological norms even if X collapsed. If the conditional is true, it is true as a matter of fact.

§

When philosophers express logically possible doubt, do they evidence doubt by their behavior? And when their behavior reveals genuine doubt, do they express a pedantic doubt that is logically possible?

§

The modal reasoning expresses a naturalistic ethics which accords with traditional modes of scientific realism: To say a moral theory is true is to say it reflects how human nature *ought* to be fulfilled on the basis of how it *is* in light of scientific descriptions, *viz.* psychology, sociology, political science and so on. Human nature remains the truth-condition for 'truth.' An objection that the inferred truth commits a Naturalistic Fallacy holds only if, as examined later, there is no principle of divine will or intelligence which makes human nature both how it is and ought to be.

Modal Defense of Scientific Truth

Third, it seems more than reasonable to ascribe limited truth to theories of physics in virtue of their systematic success. The success could *not* be explained unless the theories reflect what physical reality is approximately like. A modal truth of scientific principles, such as a law of thermodynamics, has already been noted. But a relevant reasoning holds prima facie for an impossibility that 'Well established scientific theories are approximately true *(T)*' is false when it is true that 'They

159

have systematic predictive and manipulative success *(S)*.' That
is, *(S ⇨ T) ∧ S /∴ T.*

Conceding that theories are approximately true, contrasts
to virtual truisms in the philosophy of science: *Truth implies
success, but success does not imply truth* and *Nature never
says 'yes' to theories, but it may say 'no.'* The dictums suppose
a material implication wherein a first premise *S → T* is true if
as a *matter of fact T* is not false when *S* is true. But *S ⇨ T*
reveals a modal inference which is not acknowledged by
admitting of merely empirical and logically necessary truth.
Hence, a misguided confinement to such truth evokes the
supposition that there is no logical necessity in *T* following
from *S* so that, when *S* obtains, there is not a warranted
inference to the truth of *T*.

However, the scientific theories in *T* are applied to life-
risking pursuits. For example, the pursuits include space flights
to the moon by astronauts who express little practical doubt
and virtually no theoretical doubt. Or they include engineers
who design structures which are inhabited by skeptical
philosophers in the tradition of Hume and Kant. Their logical
skepticism, illustrated by a material-implication reasoning, is
belied by their confident behavior.

When they express a logically possible truth-functional
doubt, do they evidence genuine doubt by their behavior? And
when their behavior evidences genuine doubt, say about a
building's safety in an earthquake, do they have a pedantic
logically possible doubt? Such considerations indicate that
there is no practical doubt about a truth of the scientific
theories. Belief in theoretical truth is not expressed by a truth-
valueless metaphysics but rather by, what may be called, a
metaphysico-modal reasoning. This reasoning is rooted in an
experience of human nature and Nature.

Both Truths Grounded in Nature

Fourth, the modal reasoning needs to not only integrate
notions of causal determinism and freedom but relate them to
a morally relevant human nature and Nature. This need seems
to have been recognized by even Nietzsche and Marx. But the
development of a Marxian 'teleology' or a Nietzschean

'*telos*' (desire) into scientific descriptions for evoking morally relevant prescriptions, by a progressive dialectics or an organismic desire for power, has no affinity with a revitalized naturalistic ethics. The traditional ethics suggested, herein, is at least intelligible.

Herein, a naturalistic ethics posits scientific descriptions of our nature for making the following points: Our obvious morphological design, natural instincts, and capacities which spring from them evoke natural desires for sexual relationships of males and females; biological offspring bonded by families; and familial unities evolving into communities and nations that result in more than national institutions which merely enhance tribal dominance.

§

Afro-American pulitzer-prize winner William Raspberry reveals that his liberalism is not blind ideology when he refers to empirical studies which show that politicized theories of sex and family are leading to cultural suicide.

§

In terms of some degree of continuity in our classical, medieval and modern traditions — their *ethike* or *ethos*, if not the idea of metaphysics as something after physics, our institutions have fostered international as well as national cooperation in artistic, economic, and scientific endeavors. These endeavors reveal that our common capacities and natural desires do not need to be forced by any *securitate* parasitic upon a productivity it destroys.

By contrast, promoting now what had been called 'unnatural sexual behavior' has, at a foundational psychobiological level, led biologically to epidemics of virulent sexual diseases and to disintegrating families with morally relevant national consequences. Afro-American pulitzer-prize winner William Raspberry reveals that his liberalism is not blind ideology when he refers to empirical studies which show that politicized theories of sex and family are leading to cultural suicide: "a

161

decrease in individual happiness — growing economic insecurity for women, increased isolation for men and sadness, rage
and neglect for children."[3] Is not the cultural suicide predictable, given our nature?

Whereas post-Kantian ideologies base how our nature *is*
on a politicized teleology that shapes facts rather than admits
of them, naturalism roots moral claims of how we ought to
fulfill our nature in our nature. For example, an Aristotelian
naturalism stemmed from scientific notions of human nature
and Nature. The notions explained essential natures in terms
of formal causes. In virtue of the causes, forms were
conceptually related to a Formal Cause (*Nous*) of the world's
substance. In this capacity, the Cause was an efficient and
final cause *qua* God whose thinking produced morally desirable
motion (*Metaphysics* 1072[a]).

Prima facie, with no circularity or Naturalistic Fallacy,
scientific descriptions permit moral prescriptions with an
integrity of scientific laws intact that, even in a formalized
physics, yield a historically generated sequence of nested
domains. For instance, Einstein's laws were indebted to those
of Newton, his laws to those of Galileo, and they to the laws
of Aristotle. Such a metaphysical and physical continuity is
defended by physicists Rohrlich and Hardin in terms of
historically nested domains. The domains are typically so well
tested that their turning out to be false would require a radical
change in the structure of Nature.[4]

By contrast, a Nietzschean ideology makes no pretense to
scientific objectivity and well defended criticisms of Marxian
science reveal that, unlike empirically tested scientific
theories, it permits no facts to count against it. Imre Lakatos
observes that "auxiliary hypotheses were all cooked up after
the [falsely predicted] event to protect Marxian theory from
the facts."[5] He adds that "The Newtonian programme led to

---

[3] W. Raspberry, "Divorce Revolution is a Failure," *TCE*, 2 April 1995, G2.

[4] F. Rohrlich and L. Hardin, "Established Theories," *Philosophy of Science*
50 (1983) 603-17.

[5] See I. Lakatos, *The Methodology of Scientific Research Programmes*
(London: Cambridge University Press, 1980), p. 6, for both quotes.

novel facts; the Marxian lagged behind the facts and has been running to catch up ever since." An upshot of the fourth point is the following.

Though physicists may sometimes assume a metaphysico-modal reasoning of only physical causes for limited purposes, it is notable that their purposes presuppose freedom and that the causes are consistent with a morally relevant principle Cause. The Cause *qua* God is consistent with both naked-eye and instrument-aided observation of interrelated phenomena whose external intelligibility has been held perennialy to imply an internal intelligence.

§

Expressed by the modality 'It is impossible for there to be natural and voluntary causes when there is no uncaused Cause' — for a traditional Creator, the reasoning was abandoned by accepting only natural causes. A limitation to them made incoherent scientific and moral truth.

§

As a principle of intelligence to explain the intelligibility of the cosmos, the intelligence is inescapably brought to mind by recent findings such as *COBE-Satellite* data which corroborated an inflationary big-bang theory and led to claims that the "currently existing structure of the universe, including the laws of physics, could very well have been spontaneously generated after Planck time..." with evidently "natural processes of self-organization and... a kind of Darwinian natural selection among... possibilities."[6]

In being conceptually related to biophysical phenomena that adapt to physical systems and subsystems from which they evolve, in terms of purposes to sustain equilibrium, such selected possibilities clearly suggest a teleological naturalism. Expressed by the modality 'It is impossible for there to be dependent natural and voluntary caused causes when there is no Uncaused Cause,'[7] the naturalism was abandoned by

---

[6] See astronomer V. J. Stenger's "The Face of Chaos," *Free Inquiry* 13 (1993) 14, which actually argues against theological considerations.

[7] See Thomas' "Second Way," *Summa Theologica*, I, 2, 3.

restricting the modern causal principle to natural causes. The restriction rendered untenable scientific and moral truth.

Nature's Cause: Its Forgotten Basis in Modal Logic

Having discussed deterministic and freely-choosing agencies of our nature, their relation to Nature and Nature's God is noted after recalling how they bear on scientific truth. Besides the truth's tie to freedom, it bears on theories: 'Necessarily if their predictions are systematically true in given domains (*P*), then the theories are roughly true in the domains (*T*).' That is, $(P \Rightarrow T) \wedge P / \therefore T$

Importantly, to accept a truth of the theories is to affirm the truth of a presupposed causal principle — as by analogy we would accept either 'It is necessarily true that if a door is open, then there is a door' or 'It is impossible that there is not the presupposed door when it is true the door is open.' Thus, besides a straightforward case for the causal principle's truth in terms of an impossibility that there is no cause when there is an event, *i.e.* necessarily if there is an event, there's a cause, the causal principle's truth is strictly implied by an accepted truth of scientific theories.

At the same time, the truth of a causal principle is related to our free will. For to be conscious of our thinking that it is impossible for there to be no cause when there is an event is to have an incontrovertible consciousness of our freedom to think or not to think of the impossibility — including a self-refuting thought that all thoughts are caused. Alas, however, although a causal determinism of science is related modally to our freedom in this manner, an understanding of the freedom begs for a more liberal notion of causality.

In a classical-medieval understanding, causality includes both voluntary and natural causes. Hence, to say that it is necessarily the case that all events have causes is to admit that any given cause includes both. In contrast to a modern interpretation of the principle which permits only natural or material causes, this liberality makes patently good sense because it renders coherent ordinary truth-claims such as that 'Chris lifts his arm' as opposed to 'His arm is lifted'; as if his

164

free choice of will played no role in the action. So, how does this broad notion of 'causality' fit into the context of modern scientific discourse?

Given that everything has a cause, what is the 'cause' of freedom? Though our free will *per se* is not caused in a modern sense of that word, since freedom would not be free if it was caused, it does not come from nothing. It is causally dependent, among other things, on reproductive causes of our coming into the world and those causes on others and so on. In other words, natural causality is a necessary but not sufficient condition for explicating most human behavior. Free will is also involved, although it needs to be appreciated in terms of a Greek concept of *'aitia.'* This term ranges in meaning from a brute sequence of material events, such a one pool ball striking another, to our psychobiological nature 'inspiring' us to behave in distinctively human ways to our physiology and environment being 'necessary conditions' for behavior such as thinking or speaking.

§

New substitutes for a metaphysical Creator were superior men who freely created 'truth' and dominating classes who determine it. Since moral truth was relative to whoever had power, there was an apologetics for heinous crimes.

§

To speak or think is to be conscious of our freedom to do them. In light of these considerations, while our freedom is a caused cause, its agency is as effective as a natural cause. For example, free will is a cause of our moving into the shade when our skin is being burned by the sun. The sun is a natural cause of the burn, the burn a cause of dermatological pathologies and so forth. And these considerations show that the modern causal principle, which admits only of natural causes, is limitedly true. However, it also shows that we are self-conscious voluntary agencies by which scientific as well as moral truth is rendered coherent. One's mind might boggle at a modern assumption that such causal agencies are only

165

metaphysical — in the most pejoratively speculative sense of that term. We have seen how an ensuing anti-metaphysics bears on practical politics.

New substitutes for metaphysics were fascist dictators who freely created 'truth' and dominating classes who determined it. Since moral and scientific truth was relative to whoever had power, an apologetics for mass murder arose which left over sixty million persons dead in the first half of the twentieth century alone. Having evoked Truman's assertion that it was easy to kill tyrants in comparison to killing the ideas making them possible, his assertion was born out from the killing fields of the Khmer-Rouge to China's cultural revolutions to Soviet gulags and liquidations.[8]

There is, then, dramatic import for a metaphysics of freedom and determinism being revitalized in terms of complementary causes. For a scientific notion that all the causes are causally dependent leads modally to a theological one of an Uncaused Cause *qua* God. And this fact preempts the question 'Whence comes truth if not from metaphysics?' The question is replaced by a stunning specter that theology and science are not only *not* at odds but, positively, logically and phenomenologically connected.

In reasoning to an Uncaused Cause by a causal dependence, there might be no better example than a submicroscopic black hole. Its quantum fluctuation or Big Bang at Planck time 10^{-45} has triggered inquiries into this hole's sheer energy as a cause of our universe. In having maximum entropy or chaos, the energy can be understood as the condition for an unpredictable fluctuation in terms of Heisenberg's indeterminacy principle and Einstein's physics for a conversion of the energy into the present mass of the universe. A novel problem involves a specter of the hole being caused by a prior collapsed universe and it by another and so for a series of causes ad infinitum.

Korner aptly notes that an infinite series, as a finite one, consists of a totality or "plurality of individuals which either is itself an individual or is in some respect like one."[9] The

[8] H. Truman, *Years of Decision* (NY: Doubleday & Co., 1955) p. 411.

[9] S. Korner, *Experience and Theory* (London: Routledge & Kegan Paul, 1966), p. 115.

assumption that a totality *qua* infinite cosmos begs for a cause is both presupposed by astrophysical inquiry and natural in terms of the cosmos having a primordial nature, like the phenomena composing it, that makes it subject to scientific inquiry. With no fallacy of composition any more than concluding that a fence composed of white parts is white, a conclusion ensues that the cosmos is insufficient to cause itself. The causal insufficiency means that it is itself a second cause and that an uncaused First Cause is necessary: Necessarily if there is no First Cause (~*F*), there are no second causes *(~S)*. Taken with *S*, there is an analogue of *modus tollens: (~F ⇨ ~S) ∧ S /∴ F*

§

Both Wittgenstein and Heidegger were not only astonished by there being anything rather than nothing, giving credence to the reasoning, but related it to a divine Being "making the world" and to "God himself, the increate creator."

§

In noting that *F* requires no revelation and is not strictly a Judeo-Christian God, its not being dependent on anything has a striking affinity to the prophetic words "I AM THAT I AM". The most influential contemporary thinkers did not quibble about the religio-moral status of the Cause. Wittgenstein and Heidegger were not only astonished by there being anything rather than nothing,[10] giving credence to the modal reasoning, but related it to a divine Being "making the world"[11] and to "God himself, the increate creator."[12] Surely, the notion that this creating cause was God went beyond a Greek tradition from Thales to Plato. But Aristotle noted in his first book of

---

[10] Wittgenstein said "How extraordinary... anything should exist!," and Heidegger asked "Why are there... [existents] rather than nothing?" See N. Malcolm, *Ludwig Wittgenstein: A Memoir* (NY: Oxford University Press, 1984), p. 59, and M. Heidegger, *An Introduction to Metaphysics*, Tr. R. Manheim (NY: Doubleday, 1961), p. 3.

[11] Malcolm, *Ludwig Wittgenstein*, p. 59.

[12] Heidegger, *An Introduction to Metaphysics*, p. 6.

the *Metaphysics* that their search for this Cause was one for both Wisdom and God. And Thomas distinguished faith from reason, based on experience, as well as reasoned modally to a first cause as Creator.

Thomas states in his second way that "in efficient causes it is not possible to go on to infinity." Prefacing $\sim F \Rightarrow \sim S$, the impossibility may be recast as this conditional. He brings to mind Aristotle's *Prior* and *Posterior Analytics* (43^b, 87^a): "*A* cannot inhere in *B* when *B* inheres in *C*, with an inference that *A* inheres in *C*, and this is a known impossibility" and "It is necessary indeed, if animal follows man,... all these also [follow as predicates]."

The impossibilities and necessities were studiously ignored by Kant when he made his analytic-synthetic distinction. By his and his followers' examples, the dichotomy became an epistemic paradigm of physics. Though there was a revolution in physics, its metaphysics was disguised as an addendum to physics. In the case of Marx, the addendum was not progressive but actually reactionary. It resembled a Sophistic relativism and deterministic materialism of Atomism.

Logic Strengthened by Modal Scientific Truth

Modern science may itself fortify the premise $\sim F \Rightarrow \sim S$. Given a basic nature of second-cause phenomena, all sciences address them by rudimentary principles or laws which reflect modal necessities. The necessities may be captured in the premise, without skewing its meaning, by denoting S as 'S_m'. Before noting its import, consider some necessities.

The necessities S_m include: 'Necessarily if a periodically functioning machine has no outside energy source *(~O)*, its work does not exceed its internal energy *(~W)*' for $\sim O \Rightarrow \sim W$, where the work is causally dependent on the sources;[13] 'Necessarily if metamorphic processes do not occur *(~M)*, certain rocks will not be produced *(~R)*' for $\sim M \Rightarrow \sim R$, where the rocks depend on processes; 'Necessarily if there are no

---

13 *Cf.* B. M. Yavorsky and Yu. A Seleznev, *Physics*, Tr. from the Russian by G. Leib with contributions by N. Boguslavskaya (Moscow: MIR Publishers, 1979), p. 165, emphasis added.

prior reproductive processes *(~P)*, a person is not conceived *(~C)*' for *~P* ⇨ *~C*, where the conception depends on the processes; and 'Necessarily if bacteria do not radically mutate *(~M)*, then their environment did not suddenly change *(~S)*' for *~M* ⇨ *~S* and so on.[14]

§

Science bears on ethics with no Naturalistic Fallacy. Given a Creator of Nature and natural processes of purposive self-organization, scientific descriptions of our nature are the basis for its fulfillment. And the fulfillment should be institutionalized politically.

§

In bearing on a strong modal truth *~F* ⇨ *~S_m*, *S_m* expresses modal scientific laws whose epistemological strength exceeds an ordinary empirical truth of laws and theories whose denials are typically admitted to be possible. Despite gradual modifications with scientific developments, *S_m* sets parameters for what is admitted as reasonable empirical truth. Astrophysicist Victor Stenger suggests that claims about a quantum fluctuation, which produced the structured cosmos, *must* be consistent with a thermodynamic law. These laws posit impossibilities such as that it is impossible for physical systems to evolve from disorder to order: It is *impossible* for there to be the currently ordered universe when there was no purposive self-organization generated spontaneously at Planck time by a black hole with peak disorder.[15]

Precisely, an impossibility of *S* when *~F*, though recast as *~F* ⇨ *~S_m*, can be viewed as a causal principle writ large. It specifies a causal dependency of both second causes and a causal series which is the cosmos. In contrast to either a logical possibility of an infinite cosmos not being caused or a finite cosmos coming into existence from nothing—excluding

---

14 *Cf.* medical researchers at Tuft University Medical School who state that "It is *not possible* that resistance won't occur," in L. Garrett, "Drugs Barely Keep Ahead of Bacteria," *Newsday-Ky Enq* 13 March 1995, No. 338.
15 *Cf.* Stenger, "The Face of Chaos," pp. 13-14.

the cosmos from scientific inquiry, the principle includes the cosmos in the scope of science as well as integrates science and natural theology.

Science bears on ethics with no Naturalistic Fallacy. Given a Creator of Nature and natural self-organizations, scientific descriptions of our nature are the basis for its fulfillment.[16] The fulfillment and its political incorporation may be rooted in the modal scientific laws in $\sim F \Rightarrow \sim S_m$: To acknowledge $\sim F \Rightarrow \sim S_m$ is to acknowledge that it cannot be false when S_m is true — and S_m reflects that which is necessarily true: $S_m \Rightarrow (\sim F \Rightarrow \sim S_m)$. For, prima facie, the latter and $\sim F \Rightarrow \sim S_m$ are equivalent. Consider the tables:

S_m	$\Rightarrow$	$(\sim F$	$\Rightarrow$	$\sim S_m)$		$\sim F$	$\Rightarrow$	$\sim S_m$
T	**T**	f t	T	f t		f	**T**	f
T	**F**	t f	F	f t		t	**F**	f
F	**T**	f t	T	t f		f	**T**	t
F	**T**	t f	T	t f		t	**T**	t

Though these truth-tables may not strictly certify the equivalence because modalities are not truth-functional, the tables do afford two points. First, the second rows disclose logical possibilities that the modal scientific laws S_m may be true when $\sim F \Rightarrow \sim S_m$ is false and that F may be false when S_m is true. But these logical possibilities violate a causal dependency, presupposed by science, which scientists would be loathe to accept. Second, since the falsities of S_m in the third and fourth rows are not acceptable, an import of the modally relevant first row is patent. To accept S_m is to accept that it cannot obtain without a First Cause ($\sim F \Rightarrow \sim S_m$). This is to say that $S_m \wedge [S_m \Rightarrow (\sim F \Rightarrow \sim S_m)] / \therefore (\sim F \Rightarrow \sim S_m)$.

Also, there is a modal argument for a Necessary Being, in Thomas' *third proof*, which compares to his second way proof for a First Cause and underlines its reasoning. The following is sufficient to capture the reasoning in the *Summa* (I, 2, 3):[17]

---

16 *Cf.* Peter Kreeft, *Summa of the Summa* (San Francisco: St. Ignatius Press, 1990), p. 70, fn. 31. Professor Kreeft states that "The natural and human sciences of themselves need not raise questions of ultimate origin." In my argument, science is inextricably related to the origin with clear implications for ethics and politics.

17 *Ibid*, pp. 67-68. Emphasis added.

We find in nature things that are possible to be and not to be... Therefore, if everything is possible not to be, then at one time there could have been nothing in existence. Now if this were true, even now there would be nothing in existence, because that which does not exist only begins to exist by *something already existing*... Therefore... there *must* exist something the existence of which is necessary.

§

While scientists may assume that it is logically *possible* that phenomena are not caused, a truth of the presupposition begs for a modal *impossibility*. Modally, not either individual phenomena or phenomena collectively can come from nothing.

§

In the above passage, the proposition that there is a Necessary Being may be denoted 'N', that there exist experienced possible beings 'P', and that there is a prior series of possible beings 'P_1'. And in specifying that there exist second causes (S) and a prior series of causes (S_1), the argument's comparison to proving a First Cause ('F') can be roughly outlined:

1. We infer from our experience of Nature that P (S), in having a truth which depends on P_1 (S_1), cannot be true when $\sim P_1$ $(\sim S_1)$.
2. $\sim P_1$ $(\sim S_1)$ $\Rightarrow$ $\sim P$ $(\sim S)$
3. P_1 (S_1), modus-tollens analogue: 1, 2.
4. In being a dependent truth, P_1 (S_1) cannot be true when $\sim N$ $(\sim F)$.
5. $\sim N$ $(\sim F)$ $\Rightarrow$ $\sim P_1$ $(\sim S_1)$
6. $\sim N$ $(\sim F)$ $\Rightarrow$ $\sim P$ $(\sim S)$, analogue of hypothetical syllogism: 2, 5.
7. N (F), modus-tollens analogue: 1, 6.

In the context of science, $\sim N \Rightarrow \sim P$ and $\sim F \Rightarrow \sim S$ may be supported by a *reductio ad absurdum*: To deny them is to affirm paradoxically that *no* phenomena depend on something which is not dependent and that *all* phenomena are dependent. The dependence reflects a causal principle presupposed by scientific inquiry. While those who conduct the inquiry may assume that it is logically possible that events are not caused, a truth of the presupposition begs for a modal impossibility. Events are understood in terms of phenomena and, modally, not either individual phenomena or phenomena collectively can come from nothing.

Collectively, to say that the series of phenomena is itself a dependent phenomenon no more commits a fallacy of composition than to say a phenomenon composed of particles of mass has mass. This point lends itself, straightforwardly, to reasoning from the visible world: Necessarily if there are possible beings ($P \Rightarrow$), they cannot exist ($\sim P$) when there is no Necessary Being ($\sim N$): $P \Rightarrow (\sim N \Rightarrow \sim P)$. Or, Necessarily if there are second causes ($S \Rightarrow$), they cannot exist ($\sim S$) when there is no First Cause ($\sim F$): $S \Rightarrow (\sim F \Rightarrow \sim S)$.

A Harmony of the Truth and Revelation

The foregoing points put a novel theologico-scientific spin on revelations which pertain to Jews, Muslims, and Christians. Either a First Cause or a Necessary Being (in terms of F or N) create and sustain possible beings by being in two realms simultaneously. Thus, for example, God is said to reveal "I fill heaven and earth" in Jeremiah (23:24). In quoting these words, St. Augustine adds that "He is wholly in heaven and... on earth; and He is in both simultaneously... which is utterly *impossible*... [for] any material substance.[18]

What is modally impossible for matter may be possible for God. To admit of an analogous possibility in physics may be to admit, prima facie, of the possibility at hand: It is possible for the classical equation

$$P_i = m_i v_i$$

for calculating the momentum of a point particle, to bear simultaneously on macrophysical and microphysical realms. But it is impossible for any quantum equation to apply to the

---

18 St. Augustine, *City of God*, Tr. by G. Walsh, S.J., D. Zema, S.J., G. Monahan, O.S.U., and D. Honan (NY: Doubleday & Co., Inc., 1958), p. 536. Emphasis added.

former realm. For the quantum equations bear on phenomena within limits of 10^{-15} to 10^{-10} m with coordinates characterizing their positions on an axis determined only within an accuracy to quantity Δx. This limitation is called the "uncertainty in the coordinate of the particle."[19]

Finally, with a caveat that Wittgenstein was more open-minded than his followers, there is more import for revelation. After saying that only in certain "circumstances does a reasonable person doubt..." and that a statement "someone came into the world without parents [with no biological intervention] wouldn't ever be taken into consideration," he states: "There are cases where doubt is unreasonable, but others where it seems logically impossible... [and] there seems to be no clear boundary between them."[20]

§

Besides resolving knotty epistemological problems of a deterministic materialism for the coherence of scientific and moral truth, a causal Creator is a principle of intelligibility which at least renders intelligible ascriptions of 'truth' to scientific theories.

§

Wittgenstein suggests that to accept an impossibility which borders what is logically inconceivable and empirically unreasonable, even if unclearly, is to accept a modality which skirts empirical and logically necessary truth. Accordingly, a denial of its truth is *more* than unreasonable.

Beyond this point, he indicates that inasmuch as it is modally impossible to not have two biological parents when there is no medical intervention, the impossibility renders significant a believer's faith that Jesus had only one, *e.g.*, his mother. If Jesus had been conceived like other men, what would be the point of faith in his being the Son of God?

---

[19] Cf. Yavorsky and Seleznev, *Physics*, pp. 474, 486. $P_i = m_i v_i$ for overlapping domains, where Planck's constant being small, does not obviate the point.

[20] L. Wittgenstein, *On Certainty*, Ed. by G. E. M. Anscombe and G. H. von Wright (NY: Harper & Row, 1972), pp. 42, 59.

Insofar as disbelievers permit truth which is only logically or empirically possible — and thus permit a possibility of Jesus having only one biological parent, how can faith be dismissed *a priori* as irrational? An irrationality of the dichotomized truth is exacerbated by a disregard of modal truth in regard to an uncaused Cause. The Cause is related modally to a causal principle presupposed by scientific inquiry. And attention to the inquiry returns us to Nature's God.

Further Import of Nature's Cause

Despite a gender neutral Necessary Being in $\sim N \Rightarrow \sim P$, the word 'He' is used traditionally for a Creator, or Nature's God, without being overly anthropocentric and despite feminist attempts to erase masculine-feminine distinctions. In contrast to females who bear progeny, males beget them — which in this case is the world by cosmological analogy.

Also, males determine the gender or, what had been called, biophysical essential forms of offspring (*rationes seminales*). Such forms are rational principles and ends in speaking of a necessary first, or a possible second, cause. Further, in accord with this causality, recent biological research affirms the male's chromosomal cause of gender as well as "fundamental [chromosomal] differences between men and women."[21] And this research does not either diminish genetic contributions of females or confuse difference with superiority.

Ironically, some feminists such as Val Plumwood denounce modern mechanistic views of the world. In reflecting typical male attempts to dominate Nature like a machine, she says, the views are lacking "agency and teleology."[22] And a notable medical researcher is not atypical in asserting that Nature's built-in wisdom is "born of a vast clinical experience over millions of years" in terms of which we must seek our "cues and clues and norms from the operations of nature."[23]

---

[21] C. Ezzel, "Clues to the Sex Chromosome Gender Gap," *Science News* 142 (December 1992) 327.

[22] V. Plumwood, "Nature, Self, and Gender," in *Environmental Philosophy*, Ed. by M. E. Zimmerman et al (NJ: Prentice Hall, 1993), p. 286.

[23] H. Ratner, M.D., *The Family Bed* (NJ: Avery Publishing Gp, 1987), p. xii.

These notions of Nature raise a specter of our cosmic origins. If physical systems of astrophysics are viewed as self-organizing phenomena with teleological adaptabilities,[24] scientists are warranted *a fortiori* in thus construing biological systems. For physical systems are their ontological origin and physics their epistemological and methodological model. The model is acknowledged in biosocial models having a *telos* (purpose or choice of persons) when it is stated that a "person is not a... passive recipient of social forces" but rather part of dynamic-impact models whose analysis in "physics can be found in... 'Statistical Mechanics of Social Impact' [*Physical Review A* (1981) 45]."[25]

§

'*Angst*' denotes despair over a purposeless world and why it exists rather than nothing. A specter of 'nothing' is ameliorated by a traditional reasoning. There never was nothing but always something — a Being who created the world.

§

Thus besides resolving knotty epistemological problems of a mechanico-deterministic materialism for the coherence of scientific and moral truth, a causal Creator is a principle of intelligibility which at least renders intelligible ascriptions of 'truth' to scientific theories. And a Creator is consistent with modern mathematico-theoretical expressions for properties and processes in virtue of creating the natures of things. A Creator thereby provides a basis for both how Nature ought to be fulfilled environmentally and our natures morally.

There is no Humean Naturalistic Fallacy. What *ought* to *be* is not deduced simply from scientific descriptions of what *is* the case with no morally relevant import. The way in which *is* human nature is the truth-condition for truth-claims of the human sciences, *viz.* from medicine to psychology and social

---

24 Stenger, "The Face of Chaos," p. 14.

25 See D. MacPhee, "Directed Evolution Reconsidered," *American Scientist* 81 (1993) 554.

science. Thus the sciences provide a basis for descriptions of natural desires which are desirable. There are desirable pursuits of 'truth' whereby cultures have perennially either institutionalized education or established informal pedagogical traditions. Moreover, natural desires that are desirable include pursuits of sexual relationships for propagating our species and fulfilling our needs for natural affection. And they also include creations of art and practical artifacts as well as the development of scientific theories for the subjugation as well as stewardship of the world.

All of these things are grounds for our relationship to God, as a voluntary uncaused Cause, to which we are analogical. An *anological* relation means we are both like and unlike God. By contrast, a *univocal* relation means we are the same and an *equivocal* one specifies that we are different. The relations have poignant significance.

On the one hand, fascist and communist demagogues, who liken themselves to gods, bring to mind a *univocal* relation to God. One need only recall that Wagner's son-in-law compared himself to John the Baptist because he supposedly discovered Hitler as 'Savior.' And communist dictators were viewed as god-like prophets. Having larger than life portraits on banners and 'little red books' read like Bibles, the dictators had models from Lenin to Mao Tse-tung.

On the other, social scientist Stephan Goldberg expresses an opposite or *equivocal* relation. He laments that the world is disturbingly inhabited by the irrelevant effects of an infinite number of causes.[26] Though some causes may be 'alive' in the case of persons, they have no free will or purpose. Ironically, persons as voluntary purposeful agencies were included in the medieval efficient causality from which was derived a modern causal principle which disturbs him.

Indeed, an existentialist term '*angst*' has been absorbed into twentieth-century popular jargon. The word denotes despair over both a purposeless world and why it exists rather than nothing. The specter of 'nothing,' if not human dignity,

---

[26] *Cf.* the eminent social scientist S. Goldberg, "Bob Dylan and the Poetry of Salvation," *National Forum* 69 (1979) 20.

is ameliorated by a traditional modal reasoning. There never was nothing, the reasoning specifies, but always a necessary being or first cause who created the world.

Finally, straw man objections to a Creator or First Cause includes viewing them in terms of an archaic rationalism. The objections might contrast rational philosophies of science, from Plato to Descartes, to 'cutting-edge' relativistic philosophies of science in a genre of the previously noted Nietzschean Marxism. For example, it is noted about David Bloor's popular philosophy of science that "objectivity and rationality are... a [mere] reflection of power relations within society... Protagoras the relativist has returned to haunt the Platonic realists."27

§

When scientific realists criticize contemporary relativists such as Kuhn or Feyerabend, who are heirs of a "neo-Kantian Nietzschean pragmatism," they are not advancing an anti-relativistic rationalism but rather rejecting irrationalism.

§

Realism is not rationalism. Their conflation, exploited for a relativistic politicization of 'truth,' self-servingly obfuscates scientific realism. But its confusion with rationalism should not be underestimated by Realists. They should no more avoid experienced phenomena for inferring modalities than impose rational norms on reality such as the Laws of Thought by Popper in response to a supposed 'Protagorian relativism' in quantum physics. A scientific methodology which is rational, as opposed to rationalism per se, begins with an experience of reality from naked-eye observation to experimental setups as truth-conditions for 'truth.'

When scientific realists criticize contemporary relativists such as Kuhn or Feyerabend, who are heirs of a "neo-Kantian Nietzschean pragmatism," they are not advancing an anti-

---

27 J. McGuire, "Scientific Change," *Introduction to Philosophy of Science* (NJ: Prentice Hall, 1992), p. 164.

relativistic rationalism but rather rejecting irrationalism.[28] As specified in *The Rationality of Science*, for instance, there is a rejection of the irrational thesis "It is possible that sentence '*S*' is true in ϕ and false in φ," where 'ϕ' and 'φ' are whatever that to which 'truth' is relative.[29]

The realist holds that this relativistic thesis, exploited most notoriously by radical feminists for a 'social construct-ionism,'[30] is either trivial or logically incoherent. For '*S*' may be either incoherent, in being both true and false by having the same truth-condition, or interpreted trivially in terms of different truth-conditions. Typically, both sorts of conditions are specified by things such as political ideology, scientific conventions, paradigms, and revolutionaries. Clearly, the latter are inconsistent with a created Nature that *is* as it *is* apart from our will, wish, or thought and in which what is thought, say about 'mass,' may become truer with theoretical developments from Newton to Einstein.

The Cause and Modern Pessimism

Having reasoned modally to an uncaused cause, which eludes an epistemological pessimism by providing a basis for moral and scientific truth, we note that most philosophers are not familiar with modal logic.

Also, many logicians familiar with it seem to construe advanced modal systems as being too controversial to amend knotty problems of 'truth.' After noting that modal logic capture's differences of necessity for the Laws of Thought and of Nature, Tidman and Kahane note a controversy over

---

[28] Cf. F. Suppe, Ed., *The Structure of Scientific Theories* (Chicago: UI Press, 1977), pp. 126-27, fn. 258, for a neo-Kantian Nietzscheanism. Also, see K. Parsons' pioneering feminism in terms of Kuhn and Nietzsche in "Nietzsche and Moral Change," *Nietzsche: A Collection of Critical Essays*, Ed. by R. C. Solomon (NY: Anchor Books, 1973), pp. 169-193.

[29] W. H. Newton-Smith, *The Rationality of Science* (London: Routledge & Kegan Paul, 1981), p. 35.

[30] Cf. Daphne Patai and Noretta Koertge's *Professing Feminism: Caution-ary Tales From the Strange World of Women's Studies* (NY: BasicBooks, 1994), 138.

modal predicate systems.[31] But these systems are not appealed
to in our reasoning, though the reasoning is not necessarily
inconsistent with the systems. And their controversy, in any
case, is paled by difficulties of accepting only empirical and
logically necessary truth.

Moreover, the difficulties are worsened by anachronistic
impositions of that 'truth'— and by mathematical in contrast
to causal concepts of formal logic — on the entire history of
philosophy. In terms of icons such as Leibniz and Russell, as
profound as many of their insights were, the problems are
even further compounded by a surreptitious supposition that
anything which is less than a fully mathematized or functional
linguistic calculus *(calculus ratiocinator)* has merely a second-
class epistemological status.

§

**There are obvious problems of capturing concepts
such as relationships of 'love' by modern logicians who, oriented to a reasoning of mathematics, have quite neglected causal
relationships as well.**

§

Some of these points become clear by noting how often it
is held that an argument for a First Cause may, without any
analysis of 'cause,' be shown to be invalid by modern symbolic
logic.[32] The argument is sometimes said to have a premise
'For every x there is a single thing y such that x relates C to y
$[(x)(\exists y)\,(Cyx)]$ where 'Everything which occurs has a cause'
yields the conclusion 'There is one y such that for every x, x
relates C to y $[(\exists)(x)Cyx)]$: 'There is a first cause of everything.' The argument's invalidity is supposedly evident with
other instances of premises and conclusions such as 'Everyone
loves someone, so there is someone whom everyone loves.'

But there are obvious problems of capturing concepts such
as relationships of 'love' by modern logicians who, oriented
to a reasoning of mathematics, have quite neglected causal

---

31 Tidman and Kahane, *Logic & Philosophy*, pp. 384, 389.

32 *Cf.* M. Salmon, *Introduction to Logic and Critical Thinking* (NY: HBJ
Publishers, 1989), pp. 317, 356.

relationships as well. In addition to ignoring modalities, they disregard that the expression 'everything which happens has a cause' begs for both an adequate formalization in formal logic and a distinction of propositions which are causal hypotheticals *(p* because *q)* from those which express, say, an idea of efficient causality.[33]

In keeping in mind the problem of imposing symbolic logic on historical causal arguments, we might briefly follow R. B. Marcus' pioneering work on modalities for purposes of contrast and for expanding on several points.[34] She considers an Aristotelian essentialism, in accord with a Thomistic one, that may be related to a first-cause argument. To hold that anything x is essentially a kind of thing F is to hold that x is F necessarily: $(x)(F(x) \rightarrow NF(x))$, so that a thing being gold, for example, is not accidental.

That is, s is gold *[G(s)]* yields $NG(s)$. With the definition of a causal conditional 'N$(S \rightarrow P) =_{df} S \rightarrow_c P$' and the modal principle $(P \rightarrow_c Q) \rightarrow_c (NP \rightarrow_c NQ)$, there is the instantiation $G(s) \rightarrow_c (R(s) \rightarrow D(s))$. This is read 'Necessarily if s is gold, then if s is immersed in aqua regia, s will dissolve.' From this there is inferred $R(s) \rightarrow_c D(s)$. In expanding on the significance of modal logic for the conditionals, Marcus states that there are "*No metaphysical mysteries*. Such essences are dispositional properties of a very special kind: if an object had such a property and ceased to have it, it would have ceased to exist or it would have changed into something else."[35]

What can Marcus mean other than that everything has necessary essential properties which, in being dispositional, necessarily dispose them to cause other kinds of things? For otherwise things could not have either properties or existence. In acknowledging this meaning, there is acknowledgement prima facie that the existence of everything is dependent because there is a dependence of all essential properties on the property dispositions of other things. One may object that, while quantified modal logic is controversial, the notion

33 Cf. P. Geach, *God and the Soul* (NY: Schocken Books, 1969), p. 82.
34 Marcus, *Modalities,* pp. 67-68.
35 *Ibid.*, p. 69, emphasis aaded.

'everything is dependent' still begs for quantification. But there is not merely an evident need for simple modalities to be admitted for various causal relations as opposed to relations of the notoriously vague term 'love.' In addition, there needs to be a reminder that many logicians seem to make the questionable assumption that anything less than a language subject to the predicate calculus, or something similar to it, is less than rational.

§

A First Cause bears on moral and scientific truth that was politicized. Objections to the politicization, and to a political correctness in open societies, will not have much force as long as there is a false dichotomy of empirical and logically necessary truth.

§

The assumption may simply show, however, how informal logic bears on an irrationality in regard to ignoring a mode of acceptable reasoning when it is not formulated in terms of a predicate logic. When one is ignorant about the logic's application, but a conclusion is inferred — say that a First Cause is not validly concluded, an Appeal to Ignorance is committed (*argumentum ad ignorantiam*). Geach touches on this in his criticism of a modern view of rationality:

> It may even be rational... to accept some such proof [for the existence of God as a First Cause] as valid before a satisfactory logical analysis has been worked out: mathematical proofs were valid and rationally acceptable long before logicians could give a rigorous account of them.[36]

An account of the first-cause argument is not captured by inferring 'There is some glorified single cause S of everything' from 'Everything has a single cause S.' S is not either a mere physical event or a natural cause, in the tradition of Hume and Kant. And a denial of the actual inference is not empirically or logically false. A falsity of the denied inference is modal, skirting those epistemic extremes, with a modal impossibility

---

[36] Geach, *God and the Soul* (NY: Schocken Books, 1969), p. 85.

that there exist causally dependent second causes which are both natural and voluntary when there is no voluntary First Cause which is not dependent.

The causal argument for a First Cause underscores that the universe begs modally, not logically by trivial definitions or empirically by banal possibilities, for an uncaused Cause which caused it. The argument does not involve a reasoning of physics but rather a metaphysico-modal reasoning. Its neglect explains why Wittgenstein and Heidegger were astonished that there is a world rather than nothing.[37] Also by contrast, the reasoning explains why Aristotle and Thomas, unburdened by the false dichotomy of an analytic-synthetic distinction, reasoned to a First Mover and Cause.

Attention to this Cause returns us to a metaphysical freedom and determinism. In recalling Marx's proclamation that as "the revolution... began in the brain of the *monk*, now it begins in... the *philosopher*,"[38] the question ensues of whether he was correct even if most philosophers have not succumbed to Marxism. We have seen how a First Cause bears on moral and scientific truth which was politicized. Objections to the politicization — and to political correctness in open societies — will not have much force as long as there is a false dichotomy of empirical and logically necessary truth.

Now a *reductio ad absurdum* can be used on a Marxist or Nietzschean relativism, as was done by Chalmers and others on its cold-war heirs in the philosophy of science in open societies.[39] However, the objections are hampered because a reduction of relativism to absurdity, though making it more rational to accept realism, does not imply the 'truth' of realist

---

[37] See Norman Malcolm's *Ludwig Wittgenstein: A Memoir* (NY: Oxford University Press, 1984), p. 59, and Martin Heidegger, *An Introduction to Metaphysics*, Tr. by R. Manheim (NY: Doubleday & Co., Inc., 1961), p. 3.

[38] Karl Marx, *Toward a Critique of Hegel's Philosophy of Right*, from *Marx*, Ed. by A. W. Wood (NY: Macmillan Publishing Co., 1988), p. 29.

[39] E.g. Alan Chalmers, *Science and Its Fabrication* (MN: University of Minnesota Press, 1990) p. 112, 113; Larry Lauden, *Science and Relativism* (London: The University of Chicago Press, 1990), pp. 162, 163; Newton-Smith, *The Rationality of Science*, pp. 34-37; Suppe, *The Structure of Scientific Theories*, pp. 125-217, and others.

construals — at least as they are traditionally expressed. In short, the absurdity of relativsm has not led to an articulation by realists, in the tradition of Hume and Kant, of any 'truth' in general science which has not been dismissed as a mere matter of metaphysics. And these realists have not explained how science bears on ethics and politics. Indeed, there has been such obstruction by an anti-metaphysical infrastructure that, it sometimes seems, the wind has been quite taken out of their sails.[40]

§

Though Marx and Nietzsche veered off in radical directions from the mainstream, they are relatives of the same post-Kantian family. This family has an *anti-metaphysical blood* which is thicker than the *meta-physical water*.

§

A philosophical malady needs to be acknowledged before it can be cured. Mainstream philosophy is so entangled with an anti-metaphysical establishment that the challenge may simply induce an epistemological vertigo. A central difficulty is this: While Marx and Nietzsche veered off in radical direct-ions from the mainstream — to its Left and Right, they are relatives of the same post-Kantian family. This family has an anti-metaphysical blood which is thicker than a metaphysical water of traditional Western culture.

---

[40] This is not to say all philosophers. Besides the National Association of Scholars, those who have courageously spoken against politicized 'truth,' which is a legacy of a 1960s New Left, include Daphne Patai, Noretta Koertge, Christina Sommers, Susan Haack, Michael Levin, Margarita Levin, Sydney Hook, John Gray (Oxford), and Nicholas Rescher. And sadly in a relevant respect, Ralph McInerny, Michael P. Grace Professor of Medieval Studies at the University of Notre Dame, noted that many Catholic Universities were missing the 'moment' when they could make a unique contribution to contemporary philosophy.

Chapter 7

Afterword: Reasoning to Nature's God Stubbornly Resisted

With a caveat that the following illustrates only some resistance to scientific truth, related to Nature's God, it is central to a Humean-Kantian tradition.[1] This tradition has obstructed a scientific realism, with which those who resist often express sympathy, wherein theories are approximately true in virtue of reflecting reality. In defending a weak realism, Popper is one of the most influential of this genre. His deference to Hume's case against induction, *e.g.* of true universal laws from observation, led with especially pessimistic developments to an idea of uninducted bold conjectures.

On one the hand, Popper held that scientists begin with universal theory-like conjectures and try to falsify them by predictions. For by a reasoning of material implication, true predictions do not imply true conjectures. If there is any knowledge, it is not that conjectures are true but rather that they are false because false predictions *do* imply false conjectures. On the other hand, while a truth of conjectures could not be strictly known, they could enjoy a *verisimilitude* or truth-likeness in virtue of an Inverse-Probability Thesis. In understanding conjectures as new laws or theories, this Thesis holds that the more *improbable* the predictions of theories, the more their truth-likeness is *probable*. But the probability

---

[1] This chapter was the basis of my presentation, invited by Professor of Physics Maria Falbo-Kenkel, to the Scientific Research Society of Sigma Xi on October 8, 1997, at the NKU Natural Sciences Center.

faced a self-refuting appeal to rejected inductions. And this problem only deepened the pessimism.

A Core Pessimism about Science

Vertical inductions which proceed upward from observation to generalizations would have to convert the generalizations into formalized laws and theories with complex theoretical properties and processes. Thus in addition to the problem that the initial generalizations are universal and all things are not observed, the properties and processes tend to be perceptually enigmatic. And thus observational inductions are admittedly untenable. Still, one may object that an inductivist approach is effective elsewhere. *Horizontal inductions* from theories (T_o) to observed predictions (P), by a verisimilar reasoning $T_o \rightarrow P$, might be viable. However, this strategy faces the skepticism of a pessimistic induction.[2]

§

Marxian scientists explained rising living standards of the working class by a theory of imperialism and so on. But their auxiliary hypotheses were all cooked up after the facts.

§

To accept an induction, based on a past supersession of theories falsified by predictions, is to accept that theory A at any given historical time will turn out to be false. And it will be superseded by theory B which will itself be falsified and superseded and so on. That is, A and B can in principle have truth-values of false, but not a truth or truth-likeness, ascribed to them when they are construed as conjunctive propositions. The conjuncts would be laws, say Newtonian theory regarded as a conjunction of three laws 'L'; that is, $L_1 \wedge L_2 \wedge L_3$. For example, the second law (L_2) is $f = ma$ and its interpretations such as $mg = md^2/sdt^2$ for free fall.

---

2 *Cf.* W. H. Newton-Smith, *The Rationality of Science* (Oxford: Oxford University Press, 1980), p. 14: "all physical theories in the past have had their heyday and have eventually been rejected as false. Indeed, there is inductive support for a *pessimistic induction*: any theory will be discovered to be false..."

Stubborn Resistance

In light of this point, an inductive pessimism is worsened by D. Miller and P. Tichy who argue, for instance,[3] that when A and B are false, one cannot have more verisimilitude than the other: B cannot have more truth-likeness than A and vice versa. That is, the proof concludes, in regard to verisimilitude, that there cannot be a rational choice between two false theories. For those who wish to skip the technicalities, this is an important point even if one knows only that A is false because it is inductively rational to believe that at least one conjunct of B is false:

1. Assume that two false theories A and B are distinct and comparable, *i.e.* $C(A) \leq C(B)$ or $C(B) \leq C(A)$.
2. Writing "___ $<_V$ ___" for "___ has less verisimilitude than ___," Popper's verisimilitude is defined thus: $A <_V B$ if and only if *(i)* $A_T < B_T$ and $B_F \leq A_F$ or *(ii)* $A_T \leq B_T$ and $B_F < A_F$.
3. Let $p \in A_F$ *(i.e. p is false and p is a consequence of A)* and let $q \in B_F$. Thus $(p \lor q)$ is false and $(p \lor q) \in C(A)$ and $(p \lor q) \in C(B)$.
4. Assume $A_T < B_T$ and $B_F \leq A_F$.
    Let $r \in B_T$ and $r \notin A_T$.
    Then $r \& (p \lor q) \in B_F$.
    If $r \& (p \lor q) \in A_F$ then $r \in A_F$. But r is true.
    $\therefore r \& (p \lor q) \notin A_F$.
    B_F The assumption is false that $B_F \leq A_F$.
5. Assume $A_T \leq B_T$ and $B_F < A_F$. Let $s \notin B_F$ and $s \in A_F$. s is false and $\sim(p \lor q)$ is true. $\therefore s \lor \sim(p \lor q) \in A_T$.
    $\therefore (p \lor q) \to \in A_T$. If $(p \lor q) \in B_T$, then $s \in B_F$. But $s \notin B_F$. $\therefore (p \lor q) \to s \notin B_F$. $\therefore$ It is false that $A_T \leq B_T$
    $\therefore$ It is false that $B_F \leq A_F$ contrary to assuming $A_T \leq B_T$.
6. Hence, both possibilities in (2) lead to contradiction, so it is false that $A <_V B$ and that $B <_V A$. And thus there is not a verisimilar comparability between two false theories.

---

[3] *Ibid.*, p. 58. See D. Miller's "Popper's Qualitative Theory of Verisimilitude" and P. Tichy's "On Popper's Definition of Verisimilitude" in the *British Journal for the Philosophy of Science* 25 (1974) pp. 178-88 and 155-60. Cf. Newton-Smith's *The Rationality of Science*, p. 58.

Scientific Success and Politics

Having noted these developments, some scholars tried to salvage optimism from the pessimism by contrasting scientific methodology to political ideology. Imre Lakatos focuses on success, for example, since successful research programs may obtain even if there is pessimism about comparing two false theories.[4] Theoretical *success* contrasts to ideological *failures* such as that of Marxism.

§

But science operates in different political contexts which make a difference. Only certain groups of citizens are encouraged to obtain research degrees, and politics determines which kind of research receives how much funding and so on.

§

The "Marxists," notes Imre Lakatos, "explained all their failures... the rising living standards of the working class by devising a theory of imperialism; why the first socialist revolution occurred in industrially backward Russia... the Russian-Chinese conflict [and so on]."[5] But, he adds, "their auxiliary hypotheses were all cooked up... after the event to protect Marxian theory from the facts."[6]

Insofar as facts count against scientific theories which also predict them, something is odd about their disassociation from truth. In considering $B <_v A$ in which theory B has less verisimilitude than A, the oddity might be ameliorated by initially denoting A's laws as 'L'; that is, $L_{A1} \wedge L_{A2} \wedge L_{A3}$. Accordingly, we may illustrate how theory A can be preferred rationally to B in terms of the laws $L_{B1} \wedge L_{B2} \wedge L_{B3}$. The preference may be articulated by letting L_{B2} and L_{B3} both be false in theory B but only L_{A3} in theory A. Here, A and B are not *equally false* even

---

[4] Imre Lakatos, "Falsification and Methodology of Scientific Research Programmes," *Philosophy of Science*, Ed. by A. Zucker (NJ: Prentice Hall, 1996), pp. 169-172.

[5] Imre Lakatos, *The methodology of scientific research programmes*, Ed. J. Worrall and G. Curries (NY: Cambridge University Press, 1980), p. 6.

[6] *Ibid.*, p. 6.

if they are both false in terms of propositional logic.[7] Notwithstanding this logic, is it not more rational to choose A than B? This consideration brings us back to how reasoning about science may correlate success to 'truth.' Consider the modal sentence: It is impossible that the consequent 'Theory A is approximately true (T)' is not the case when it is the case in the antecedent that 'The predictions of A are systematically successful (P).'

§

To say that truth obtained by research favors certain political groups is not to say 'truth' is relative to whichever group has power; notwithstanding that power may be harnessed wrongfully in the interests of certain parties.

§

Expressed '$P \Rightarrow T$,' the sentence is not countered prima facie by a question-begging objection that we may reasonably suppose that A is false in view of past falsifications. For the question ensues of whether the falsifications hold in given domains. Physicists Rohrlich and Hardin suggest the modal impossibility that a historical sequence of domain-nested theories will turn out to be entirely false.

A more than unreasonable supposition of the falsity is undergirded by a fundamental nature of phenomena in terms of such things as a metamorphic and reproductive nature of phenomena about which ordinary empirical denials would not be admitted as possible. Given the nature of marble, for example, it is impossible for it to be formed when there are not metamorphic processes of great heat and pressure. Or, for instance, given the reproductive nature of human beings, it is impossible for them to be conceived reproductively when there are not certain prior biological processes.

To admit of such modalities in natural science, which are so patently true that they are seldom noticed, is to admit of the supposition about Nature. We may more than rationally suppose that such 'truth,' and therefore Nature, will not

---

[7] I am beholden to Professor Emeritus James Kimble, the University of Colorado at Boulder, for this metalogical consideration.

radically change.[8] *Pari passu* to reject the change is to accept domain nested truth. Truth would hold within a Newtonian domain, for instance, in which phenomena do not approach light speed and Planck's constant is small. But these points may be challenged politically.

Politico-Scientific Truth

'Truth' is not needed merely for a strong rationality of science. In addition, it is necessary for relating science to ethics as well as to a politics which does not politicize it. Yet support for a politicized ethics and science may ensue by various objections. These include that science does not function in a vacuum. Rather, science operates in a more epistemologically liberal context in which a difference of political setups makes a difference, for example, in which select groups of citizens are encouraged to obtain research degrees in science as well as which kind of research receives what amount of funding and so on.

§

The import of an incontrovertible experience of ourselves as being limitedly both free and causally determined is clear if for no other reason than it fosters moderation in place of a political polarization.

§

First, it might be objected that those who dominate patriarchal Western societies are usually heterosexual white males whose research serves their interests. These males are not as interested in conducting research into AIDS, to take a paradigm example, as they are into lung cancer or in ameliorating poverty as much as in the space program. However, despite their ostensibly dominating all Western institutions, Daphne Patai's *Heterophobia* makes the case that, in point of fact, "hostile environment" actions are based on a subjective experience of what is offensive to minorities. Thus, contrary

---

[8] F. Rohrlich and L. Hardin, "Established Theories," *Philosophy in Science* 50 (1983) 603-617.

to American judicial practice, the burden of proof rests with accused heterosexual white males.[9] Professor Patai asks: "Are most of the men passively accepting this? Wonder where the 'patriarchy' is in all this... it doesn't seem to be defending its bastions."[10] Further, more funds go to AIDS research than to breast, lung, and prostrate cancer combined.[11] Ironically, while AIDS is largely self-inflicted by drugs or sex outside traditional marriage, research funds for lung cancer are notoriously scarce because the disease is self-inflicted by smokers, for whom there is little sympathy, who comprise almost ninety percent of the patients.[12] And in regard to the space program, it was initiated by an American President who was a liberal icon of most minorities.

§

In terms of human nature evolving from Nature, politics should further nurture our nature's fulfillment. Inexact details of the fulfillment accords with a creative intelligence of which we conscious.

§

Having addressed such issues, there is the epistemological one. One may admit that truths obtained by research favor certain political groups without admitting that 'truth' is relative to whichever group has power; notwithstanding that such power may be harnessed wrongfully in the interests of certain parties. This leads to a second point.

---

[9] D. Patai, *Heterophobia: Sexual Harassment and the Future of Feminism* (MD: Rowman & Littlefield, 2000). Wellsley College Professor Mary Lefkowitz states in her review: "Patai shows in detail how women's reasonable desire for a 'hands-off' workplace has now been transformed into a witch-hunt, where men are the devils, and guilty until proven innocent. This book demonstrates how in universities today the postmodern approach to reality has affected... our bodies as well as our minds."

[10] Daphne Patai, professional correspondence, October 26, 2000.

[11] "Lung Cancer Awareness Week," *CancerCare*, 12-18 Nov. 2000, p. 3: Lung cancer receives $900 per death, breast cancer $9,000 per death, prostrate cancer $3, 500 per death, and AIDS nearly $34,000 per death.

[12] "Robert Miller: Something Must Change," *CancerCare*, p. 1.

Second, in speaking of epistemology, is not a defense of politicized 'truth' in agreement with Aristotle's own caution not to expect exact truth from less rigorous sciences such as those of politics and ethics? At the same time, it will be objected, he held that physics investigates causes of moving bodies, ethics causes of the 'good,' and political science causes of good government. However, it might be insisted, modern philosophy reveals that such causes are metaphysical and that a metaphysics of causality and freedom is largely avoided in today's controversial problems. Problems of rigor are regarded after one of metaphysics.

§

Science and theology are logically reciprocal, not merely consistent. And they render coherent an evolution of our limitedly deterministic and freely-choosing nature from Nature.

§

A causal principle may not avert successful predictions as it does true theories in the reasoning of *non-modal* modern logic. But besides the fact that this logic does not even afford ascriptions of 'truth' to well established theories, which led to politicized truth in the first place, modern intellectuals often assume a truth-valueless metaphysics of freedom and causality in even their social-political views. So, let us expand momentarily on these views. They presuppose causally conditioned behavior in the case of liberals and responsibility in that of conservatives. For example, these groups perennially debate retributive and rehabilitative norms of punishment which rest on the behavioral interpretations.

The interpretations are clear in Einstein's view of a Block Universe and Whitehead's cosmology of Real Possibilities.[13] The Block Universe stems from a deterministic metaphysics of relativistic physics, wherein causes are exactly measured, and the view that measured phenomena are inexact since they permit real possibilities follows from an indeterminism of

---

13 Donald Sherburne, "Responsibility, Punishment, & Whitehead's Theory of Self," *Alfred NorthWhitehead,* Ed. by G. L.Kline (NJ: Prentice-Hall, 1963), pp. 179-188.

quantum physics. A deterministic *weltanschauung* proscribes such things as capital punishment and the indeterministic worldview prescribes it. That the views have been politicized is obvious. The *ad hominem* is used by liberals to attack their opponents as 'right-wing' and by conservatives to assault their rivals as 'left-wing.'

§

In undercutting a Naturalistic Fallacy, which is now a virtual truism, reasoning to God from Nature will be resisted strenuously with further tragic cultural consequences.

§

However, with the conflation of metaphysics and physics as well as a prestige of physical theories over religio-moral theories, liberals seem to have gone more left of the political center than conservatives have to its right. Liberals have assumed more increasingly that there are 'root causes' of our behavior, in terms of science-oriented liberal democratic to Marxian views, than conservatives have assumed either free will or a will-to-power in terms of blindly conservative to fascist views. Invariably, the metaphysical conflict is held to be irreconcilable. In the aftermath of a Kantian critique of metaphysics, the metaphysical worldviews are understood as sorts of *a priori* lenses wherein empirical facts count no more against physics than the metaphysics.

Precisely, the import of our limitedly having behavior which is voluntary and causally determined is clear if for no other reason than it fosters moderation in place of a political polarization. The polarization has been discussed in light of a modal truth that we have both, not just one or another, behavioral agencies. The agencies reflect our being analogous to a Creator as either first causes dependent on a voluntary First Cause or possible beings who beg for a voluntary Being who is Necessary: It is necessarily the case that if there is no Necessary Being $(\sim N)$, there are no possible beings $(\sim P)$, for the conditional $\sim N \Rightarrow \sim P$. The '$N$' posits the existence of God in virtue of representing a voluntary Agency or Creator who governs a cosmic psycho-biophysical evolution.

The reasoning *(i)* shows a logical and phenomenological reciprocity of science and theology, not merely their possible consistency;[14] *(ii)* renders intelligible an evolution of our limitedly caused and voluntary nature from Nature — Nature is not understood deterministically and materialistically which makes incoherent the concept of 'truth' and relegates both freedom and God to possible realities; *(iii)* fosters political moderation in virtue of being related to freely choosing and deterministic human agencies whose extremes are presupposed by radical ideologies; *(iv)* surmounts a K-K Thesis wherein scientific and moral knowledge presuppose a metaphysics that is not known; and *(v)* affords inferences from scientific descriptions of our nature, which *is* implicitly as it *ought* to be, to moral truth-claims regarding how it *ought* to be fulfilled.

Exactly, in terms of the evolution of human nature from Nature, the point of developing political institutions is to increasingly nurture our nature's fulfillment. Inexact specifications of truth about the fulfillment accords with a creativity of our reflexive intelligence of which we are immediately, incontrovertibly, and phenomenologically conscious. And in view of the human species having *one* nature, the inexact specifications explain why *many* cultural modes permit its consummation. These insights capture Aristotle's caution against expecting rigorous inferences from certain sciences such as ethics and politics. But in undercutting entrenched philosophies and a Naturalistic Fallacy, which is now a virtual truism, reasoning to God on the basis of our experience of Nature will be resisted strenuously with further tragic cultural consequences despite its explanatory power and cogency.

---

14 Compare the logical interrelatedness, for example, to Israeli physicist Gerald Schroeder's *The Science of God: The Convergence of Scientific and Biblical Wisdom* (Broadway Books, 1998) and to Dr. Hugh Ross' *Beyond the Cosmos: The Extra-Dimentionality of God: What Recent Discoveries in Astronomy and Physics reveal about the Nature of God* (NavPress Publishing Group, 1996). With a proviso that both works admirably apply science to religion, their connections are less logically rigorous in the sense that Jeffrey argues that science and the Bible have 'consistent sets of data' and Ross that God's existence is scientifically probable.

Bibliography

Adams, E. M. "Accountability of Religious Discourse." *International Journal of Religion* 18 (1985) 3-17.

Addis, L. "Memorial Minutes." *Proceedings and Addresses of the American Philosophical Association* 61 (1987) 165.

Aiken, H., ed. *Age of Ideology: The 19th Century Philosophers*. New York: New American Library of World Literature, Inc., 1957.

Aquinas, T., St. *Summa Theologica. From A Shorter Summa*. Ed. By P. Kreeft. San Francisco: Ignatius Press, 1993.

Augustine, St. *On Free Choice of the Will*. Tr. by A. Benjamin and L. Hackstaff. London: Collier Macmillan Publishers, 1986.

Ayer, A. J. *The Foundations of Empirical Knowledge*. New York: St. Martin's Press, 1962.

Ayer, A. J. *Logical Positivism*. New York: The Free Press of Glencoe, 1958.

Ayer, A. J. *Language, Truth and Logic*. New York: Dover Publications, Inc., 1946.

Bahm, A. ed. *Directory of American Philosophers*. Bowling Green, Ohio: Philosophy Documentation Center, 1988-89.

Baird, E. and Kaufmann, W. eds. *Medieval Philosophy: Philosophical Classics*. 2nd Ed., Vol. II. New York: Prentice-Hall, Inc., 1997.

Barnes, H. *An Existentialist Ethics*. Chicago: University of Chicago Press, 1978.

Berkeley, G. *Principles of Human Knowledge and Three Dialogues Between Hylas and Philonous*. Cleveland: The World Publishing Co., 1963.

Birken, L. *Hitler as Philosophe*. New York: Praeger Publishers, 1995.

Bourque, S. "Book Reviews." *Signs: Journal of Women in Culture and Society* (1997) 453-456.

Chalmers, A. *Science and Its Fabrication*. University of Minneapolis Press, 1990.

Primary and Secondary Works

Cooper, J. N. and Smith, A. W. *Elements of Physics*. New York: Mc-Graw-Hill, 1979.

Damasio, A. R. *Descartes' Error: Emotion, Reason, and the Human Brain*. New York: G. P. Putnam's Sons, 1994.

De George, R. T. "Theological Ethics and Business Ethics." *Journal of Business Ethics* (1986) 421-432.

Descartes, R. *Meditations on First Philosophy*. From M. C. Beardsley, ed., The European Philosophers. New York: Random House, Inc., 1960.

Descartes, R. *Descartes' Conversation with Burman*. Tr. by J. Cottingham. Oxford: Oxford University Press, 1976.

Descartes, R. *Descartes: Philosophical Letters*. Tr. and ed. by A. Kenny. Oxford: Oxford University Press, 1970.

Descartes, R. *Descartes: Philosophical Writings*. Tr. and ed. by E. G. M. Anscombe & P. Geach. New York: The Macmillan Co., 1971.

Descartes, R. *Oeuvres de Descartes*. 11 volumes. Ed. by C. Adam and P. tannery. Paris: Librairie Philosophique J. Vrin and Le Centre National de la Recherche Scientifique, 1964-76.

Dewey, J. *Quest for Certainty*. New York: Capricorn Books, G. P. Putnam's Sons, 1960.

Dicker, G. *Descartes: An Analytical & Historical Introduction*. New York: Oxford University Press, 1993.

Edel, A. "Romanell Lecture." *Proceedings of the American Philosophical Association* (1987) 823-840.

Evans, M. B. "Newton and the Cause of Gravity." *The American Journal of Physics* 26 (1958) 619-24.

Ezzel, C. "Clues to the Sex Chromosome Gender Gap." *Science News* 142 (1992) 327.

Feyerabend, P. *Against Method*. London: New Left Books, 1975.

Fulenwider, C. *Feminism in American Politics*. New York: Praeger Publishers, 1980.

Geach, P. *God and Soul*. New York: Schocken Books, 1969.

Gier, N. *Wittgenstein and Phenomenology*. New York: State University of New York Press, 1981.

Goldberg, S. "Bob Dylan & the Poetry of Salvation." *National Forum* 69 (1979) 20.

Greer, G. *The Female Eunuch*. New York: McGraw-Hill Publishers, 1970.

Gross, P. and Levitt, N. *Higher Superstition: The American Left and Its Quarrels with Science*. MD: The John's Hopkins University Press, 1994.

Gross, P. R. and Lewis, M. W. *The Flight From Reason*. New York: Proceedings of the NY Academy of Sciences. Vol. 775, 1996.

196

Primary and Secondary Works

Haack, S. *Philosophy of Logics*. London: Cambridge University Press, 1978.

Halliday, D. and Resnick, R. *Fundamentals of Physics*. New York: John Wiley & Sons, 1988.

Heidegger, M. *An Introduction to Metaphysics*. Tr. by R. Manheim. New York: Doubleday & Company, Inc., 1961.

Heidegger, M. "Deutsche Studenten," November 3, 1933. From K. Harries, "Heidegger as a Political Thinker." *Heidegger and Modern Philosophy*. Ed. by M. Murray. New Haven: Yale University Press, 1978.

Heller, M., Stoeger, W., and Zycinski, J. "Editorial Note." *Philosophy in Science* V (1993).

Herrick, P. *The Many Worlds of Logic*. New York: Harcourt Brace & Co., 1994.

Hook, S. "Invited Address." *Proceedings and Addresses of the American Philosophical Association* 60 (1987) 511-12.

Hubner, K. *Critique of Scientific Reason*. Tr. by P. Dixon and H. Dixon. Chicago: University of Chicago Press, 1985.

Hume, D. *A Treatise of Human Nature*. Ed. L. A. Selby-Bigge. Oxford: Clarendon Press, 1967.

Hume, D. *Enquiries Concerning Human Understanding and Concerning the Principles of Morals*. Introduction by L. A. Selby-Bigge. Oxford: Clarendon Press, 1975.

Hume, D. *Dialogues Concerning Natural Religion*. New York: The Liberal Arts Press, Inc., 1962.

Hume, D. *Hume's Moral and Political Philosophy*. Hafner Publishing Co., Inc., 1948.

Jacob, M. C. *Living the Enlightenment*. New York: Oxford University Press, 1991.

Jaki, S. L. "The Last Word in Physics." *Philosophy in Science* V (1993) 9 -32.

James, W. *Essays in Pragmatism*. New York: Hafner Publishing Co., Inc., 1948

Jean, C. *Beyond the Eurocentric Veil: The Search for African Realities*. MA: University of Massachusetts Press, 1992.

Jones, W. T. *The Medieval Mind*. New York: Harcourt Brace Jovanovich Publishers, 1969.

Kahane, H. and Tidman, P. *Logic and Philosophy*. Belmont, CA: Wadsworth Publishing Co., 1995.

Kant, I. *Critique of Pure Reason*. Tr. N. K. Smith. Unabridge Edition. New York: Macmillan & Co., 1965.

Kant, I. *Critique of Practical Reason*. Tr. by L. W. Beck. Indianapolis: Bobbs-Merrill, 1956.

Kant, I. *Anthropology from a Pragmatic Point of View*. Tr. by L. W. Beck. Indianapolis: Bobbs-Merill, 1956.

Kant, I. *Critique of Judgment*. Tr. by J. H. Bernard. New York: Hafner Publishing Co., 1968.

Kant, I. *The Critique of the Faculties*. Tr. by M. J. Gregor and R. E. Anchor. New York: Abaris Books, 1979.

Kaufmann, W. *Philosophical Classics*. Vol. I. New Jersey: Prentice-Hall, 1968.

Kaufmann, W. *Nietzsche: Philosopher, Psychologist, Anti-Christ*. New York: Meridan Books. The World Publishing Co., 1964.

Kenny, A., ed. *The Oxford History of Western Philosophy*. Oxford: Oxford University Press, 1994.

Korner, S. *Experience and Theory: An Essay in the Philosophy of Science*. London: Routledge & Kegan Paul, 1966.

Kuhn, T. *The Structure of Scientific Revolutions*. Chicago, Ill: University of Chicago Press, 1970.

Kuhn, T. *The Copernican Revolution*. New York: Random House, 1959.

Lafleur, L. J. *Philosophical Essays*. New York: The Liberal Arts Press, Inc., 1964.

Lakatos, I. *Methodology of Scientific Research Programmes*. Ed. J. Worrall and G. Currie. Cambridge University Press, 1980.

Laudan, L. *Science and Relativism: Some Key Controversies in the Philosophy of Science*. University of Chicago Press, 1990.

Leibniz, G. W. *Philosophical Papers and Letters*. Ed. by L. Loemker. New York: D. Reidel, Dordrecht, 1970.

Levin, M. *Feminism and Freedom*. New Jersey: Transaction Press, Rutgers –The State University, 1987.

Lewis, D. *Counterfactuals*. Cambridge, MA: Harvard University Press, 1973.

Lewontin, R. C. *Biology as Ideology*. New York: Harpers Collins Publishers, 1997.

Lin, T. "A Search for China's Soul." *Daedalus: Journal of the American Academy of Arts* 122 (1993) 171-188.

Livingston, D. W. *Philosophical Melancholy and Delirium: Hume's Pathology of Philosophy*. Chicago: University of Chicago Press, 1998.

Locke, J. *Essay Concerning Human Understanding*. Two volumes. New York: Dover Publications, Inc., 1894.

Logan, J. "The Critical Mass." *American Scientist,* Vol. 84 (1996) 263-277.

Lynch, F. *Invisible Victims*. New York: Praeger Publishers, 1991.

MacPhee, D. "Directed Evolution Reconsidered." *American Scientist*, 81 (1993) 554.

Magee, B. *Modern British Philosophy: Dialogues with A. J. Ayer et al.* New York: St. Martin's Press, 1971.

Malcolm, N. *Ludwig Wittgenstein: A Memoir.* New York: Oxford University Press, 1984.

MacKinnon, E. A. *The Problem of Scientific Realism.* New York: Appleton-Century Crofts, 1972.

Marcus, R. B. *Modalities: Philosophical Essays.* New York: Oxford University Press, 1993.

Marschall, L. A. "Newton's Principia for the Common Reader." *The New York Academy of Sciences* 35 (1995) 45-46.

Marx, K. *Capital: A Critique of Political Economy I.* From *Marx: Selections.* Ed. by A. Wood. New York: Macmillan Publishing Co., 1988.

Marx, K. *Toward a Critique of Hegel's Philosophy of Right.* Tr. by L. Easton and K. Guddat. From *Marx: Selections.* Ed. by A. W. Wood. New York: Macmillan Publishing Co.,1988.

Marx, K. *The Poverty of Philosophy.* From *Karl Marx: Selected Writings.* New York: Oxford University Press, 1987.

Marx, K. *The Revolutions of 1848.* Ed. by D. Ferbach. Pelican Marx Library. New York: Random House, 1973.

Mayer, A. J. "Founding and Consolidation of the Nazi Regime." *Why Did The Heavens Not Darken?* New York: Pantheon Books, 1990.

McGuire, J. "Scientific Change." *Introduction to the Philosophy of Science:* A Text by Members of the Department of the History and Philosophy of Science at the University of Pittsburgh. New Jersey: Prentice Hall, 1992.

Melchert, N. *The Great Conversation: A Historical Philosophy.* Toronto: Mayfield Publishing, 1991.

Merleau-Ponty, M. *Phenomenology of Perception.* Tr. by C. Smith. London: Routledge & Kegan Paul, 1978.

Merleau-Ponty, M. *Visible and the Invisible.* Tr. by A. Lingis. Evanston, Ill: Northwestern University Press, 1968.

Methvin, E.H. "The Unquiet Ghosts of Stalin's Victims." *National Review* 41 (1989) 24-52.

Miller, D. "Popper's Qualitative Theory of Verisimilitude." *British Journal for the Philosophy of Science* 25 (1974) 178-188.

Monk, R. *Ludwig Wittgenstein: The Duty of Genius.* London: Penguin Books Ltd., 1990.

Moody, A. E. *Studies in Medieval Philosophy, Science, and Logic.* Berkeley: University of California Press, 1975.

Primary and Secondary Works

Moore, B. N. and Parker, R. *Critical Thinking*. Toronto: Mayfield Publishing Co., 1998.

Moore, E. G. and H. J. McCann and J. McCann. *Creative and Critical Thinking*. Boston: Houghton Mifflin Co., 1985.

Mosley, I., Ed. *Dumbing Down: Culture, Politics and the Mass Media*. Devon, UK: Imprint Academic, 2000.

Newton-Smith, W. H. *The Rationality of Science*. London: Routledge & Kegan Paul, 1981.

Nietzsche, F. *The Will to Power*. Tr. by W. Kaufmann and R. J. Holindale. New York: Random House, 1968.

Nietzsche, F. *Early Greek Philosophy and Other Essays*. Tr. by M. A. Muegge. London: Foulis, 1911.

Nietzsche, F. *Beyond Good and Evil*. Tr. W. Kaufmann. Chicago: Regnery-Gateway, 1955.

Nietzsche, F. *The Antichrist*. Tr. by R. J. Hollingdale. Baltimore: Maryland: Penguin Books, 1968.

Nolt, N. *Logics*. Belmont, CA: Wadsworth Publishing Co., 1997.

O'Brien, C. C. *On the Eve of the Millennium: The Future of Democracy Through an Age of Unreason*. New York: Free Press, 1996.

O'dea, T. et al. "Religion in the Year 2000." *Philosophy Looks to the Future*. Ed. P. Richter and W. Fogg. Ill: Waveland Press, 1985.

Panichas, G. "The Incubus of Deconstruction — An Editorial." *Modern Age* (32 (1989) 290-293.

Papineau, D., ed. *The Philosophy of Science*. Oxford Readings in Philosophy. Oxford: Oxford University Press, 1996.

Parsons, K. P. "Nietzsche and Moral Change." *Nietzsche: A Collection of Essays*. Ed. by R. Solomon. New Jersey: Anchor Books, 1973.

Patai, D. and Koertge, N. *Professing Feminism: Cautionary Tales From the Strange World of Women's Studies*. New York: Basic Books, 1995.

Patai, D. *Heterophobia: Sexual Harassment and the Future of Feminism*. Lanham, MD: Rowman & Littlefield, 2000.

Payne, R. *Life and Death of Adolf Hitler*. New York: Praeger, 1971.

Peacock, J. "Multiculturalism in the USA." *AnArchaey Notes II* (1994) 4.

Pine, R. C. *Science & the Human Prospect*. Belmont, CA: Wadsworth Publishing Co., 1989.

Pitkin, H. F. *Wittgenstein and Justice: On the Significance of Ludwig Wittgenstein for Social and Political Thought*. Berkeley: University of California Press, 1972.

Plumwood, V. "Nature, Self, and Gender: Feminism, Environmental Philosophy, and the Critique of Rationality." *Environmental Philosophy: From Animal Rights to Radical Ecology*. Ed. by M. E. Zimmerman et al. Englewood Cliffs, NY: Prentice-Hall, 1993.

Popper, K., Sir. *Realism and the Aim of Science.* Totowa, NJ: Rowman and Littlefield, 1983.

Popper, K., Sir. *Quantum Theory and the Schism in Physics.* From *Postscript to the Logic of Scientific Discovery.* Ed. by W. W. Bartley, III. Totowa, New Jersey: Rowman and Littlefield, 1982.

Popper, K., Sir. *The Logic of Scientific Discovery.* London: Hutchinson, 1968.

Popper, K., Sir. *Conjectures and Refutations.* London: Routledge & Kegan Paul, 1963.

Putnam, H. "Philosophers & Human Understanding." *Scientific Explanation.* Ed. A. Heath. Oxford: Clarendon Press, 1981.

Redpath, P. *Masquerade of the Dream Walkers: Prophetic Theology from the Cartesians to Hegel.* GA: Rodopi, Editions, BV, 1998.

Rescher, N. "Where Wise Men Fear to Tread," *American Philosophical Quarterly* 27 (1990) 259.

Rohrlich, F. and Hardin, L. "Established Theories." *Philosophy of Science* 50 (1983) 603-617.

Rozemond, M. "The Role of the Intellect in Descartes' Case for the Incorporality of the Mind." From *Essays on the Philosophy and Science of Rene Descartes.* Ed. by S. Voss. New York: Oxford University Press, 1993.

Rothman, M. A. *A Physicists Guide to Skepticism.* New York: Promethius Books, 1988.

Russell, B. *The Autobiography of Bertrand Russell.* Boston: Little, Brown and Company, 1967.

Salmon, M. H. *Introduction to Logic and Critical Thinking.* New York: Harcourt Brace Jovanovich Publishers, 1989.

Saleci, R. *The Spoils of Freedom.* New York: Routledge, 1995.

Sargent, L.T. *Contemporary Political Ideologies.* Chicago: The Dorsey Press, 1987.

Sartre, J-P. *Being and Nothingness.* Tr. by H. Barnes. New York: Philosophical Library, Inc., 1956.

Schlipp, P. A., ed. *The Philosophy of Karl Popper.* La Salle, Illinois: Open Court, 1974.

Schramm, P. E. *Hitler: The Man and the Military Leader.* Malabar, Fla: Robert E. Krieger Publishing Co., 1986.

Schutte, O. "Nietzsche, Mariategui, & Socialism: A Case of Nietzschean Marxism in Peru." *Social Theory and Change* 14 (1988).

Scott, E. C. "Monkey Business." *The Sciences: The New York Academy of Science* 36 (1996) 20-25.

Sherburne, D. "Responsibility, Punishment, and Whitehead's Theory of Self." *Alfred North Whitehead.* Ed. by G. L. Kline. New Jersey: Prentice Hall, 1963.

Primary and Secondary Works

Sluga, H. and Stern, D. G., eds. *The Cambridge Companion to Wittgenstein.* Cambridge: Cambridge University Press, 1996.

Smith, J. *The Spirit of American Philosophy.* New York: State University of New York Press, 1983.

Sommers, C. H. "Feminism and Resentment." *Reason Papers* 18 (19-93) 1-15.

Sommers, C. H. "Argumentum Ad Feminam." *Journal of Social Philosophy* 22 (1991) 5-19.

Spinoza, B. *Chief Works.* Two vols. New York: Dover Publications, Inc., 1962.

Stalin, J. *Dialectical and Historical Materialism.* New York: International Publishers Co., Inc., 1940.

Stenger, V. J. "The Face of Chaos." *Free Inquiry* 13 (1993) 12-15.

Suppe, F., ed. *The Structure of Scientific Theories.* Chicago: University of Illinois Press, 1979.

Thevin, T. *The Family Bed.* Wayne, NJ: Avery Publishing Group, Inc., 1987.

Tichy, P. "On Popper's Definition of Verisimilitude." *British Journal for the Philosophy of Science* 25 (1974) 155-160.

Toulmin, S. *Human Understanding. Vol. I.* Princeton, NJ: Princeton University Press, 1972.

Trotsky, L. "Socialism and the Human Future." *Marxism and Spirituality: An International Anthology.* Ed. by B. Page. Ct: Greenwood Publishing Group, 1993.

Truman, H. S., *Years of Decisions.* Vol. I. New York: Doubleday and Co., 1955.

Trundle, R. C. "San Agustin y el Dios del filosofo moderno." *Augustinus: Revista Trimestral Publicada* XLV (Sum 2000) 215-225.

Trundle, R. C. *Medieval Modal Logic & Modern Science: Augustine on Scientific Truth & Thomas on its Impossibility without a First Cause.* Lanham, MD: UP of America, 1999.

Trundle, R. C. "Thomas' 2nd & 3rd Ways by Modern Science," *Aquinas: Revista Internazionale di Filosofia* 42, N0. 3 (1999) 541-548.

Trundle, R. C. "Cold-War Ideology: An Apologetics for Global Ethnic Conflict?" *Res Publica: Leuven Politologisch Instituut* 37 (1996) 61-84.

Trundle, R. C. "Twentieth-Century Despair and Thomas' Sound Argument for God." *Laval Theologique et Philosophique* 52 (1996) 101-125.

Trundle, R. C. "Thomas' 2nd Way: A Defense by Modal Scientific Reasoning." *Logique et Analyse* 146 (1994) 145-168.

Trundle, R. C. "Applied Logic: An Aristotelian Organon for Critical Thinking." *Philosophy in Science* V (1993) 117-140.

Primary and Secondary Works

Trundle, R. C. "Physics and Phenomenology." *New Horizons in the Philosophy of Science*. Ed. by D. Lamb. London: Ashgate Publishing Co., 1992.

Trundle, R. C. "Business, Ethics, & Business Ethics: Second Thoughts on the Business-Ethics Revolution." *Thought: A Review of Culture and Idea* 66 (1991) 297-309.

Vance, E. P. *Modern Algebra and Trigonometry*. London: Addison-Wesley Publishing Co., Inc., 1962.

Vitale, R. "Modern Europe: Free Integrations Vs. Centre-Bound Unity." *History of European Ideas* (1995) 661-666.

Waller, B. N. *Critical Thinking: Consider the Verdict*. New Jersey: Prentice Hall, 1998.

Wittgenstein, L. "On Heidegger on Being and Dread." From *Heidegger and Modern Philosophy*. Ed. by M. Murray. New Haven: Yale University Press, 1978.

Wittgenstein, L. *On Certainty*. Ed. by G. E. M. Anscombe and G. H. von Wright. New York: Harper & Row Publishers, 1972.

Wittgenstein, L. *Philosophical Investigations*. Tr. by G. E. M. Anscombe. New York: The Macmillan Co., 1971.

Wolf, Diane L. Ed. *Feminist Dilemmas in Fieldwork*. With a Forword by Carmen Diana Deere. Boulder: Westview Press, 1996.

Yavorsky, B. M. and Seleznev, Yu. A. *Physics: A Refresher Course*. Tr. from the Russian by G. Leib with contributions by N. Boguslavskaya. Moscow: MIR Publishers, 1979.

Youssef, S. "Is Quantum Mechanics An Exotic Probability Theory?," *Fundamental Problems in Quantum Theory*. A Conference Held in Honor of Professor John A. Wheeler. Ed. by D. M. Greenberger and A. Zeilinger. New York: Annals of the New York Academy of Sciences, 1995.

Index

Index

Levitt, N. 25
Lewis, M. 25
Lewontin, R. 14
Liberal to Left 88, 124-139, 143,
    148, 153, 154 *See also*
    Liberalism, Marx, and New
    Left
Liberalism 88, 120, 122, 124,
    125, 129, 130, 152-154, 161,
    191-193
Locke, John 49
Logic
    Aristotelian propoositions 102
    Fallacy of Against the Person
        (*ad hominem*) 80 fn. 2,
        129, 144, 149, 153, 193
    Fallacy of Appeal to Ignorance
        181
    Fallacy of Begging the Question
        30, 44, 66, 67, 75, 92,
        189
    Fallacy of Composition 3, 167
    Fallacy of Missing the Point
        65
    Fallacy of Reductionism 4, 19,
        113
    Fallacy of the Straw Man 73
    Falsificationism 70, 71, 90
    Hypothetical judgment 100
    Hypothetico-deduction 23, 24,
        105
    Inductive reasoning 55-57, 65,
        67-71, 113, 185-187
    Laws of thought 177, 179
    Material conditional 3, 19, 40,
        62-64, 160, 185
    Modal conditional 3, 19, 40,
        63, 75-77, 158, 160,
        164, 167-172, 189
    Modal reasoning 3, 19, 40, 45,
        46, 56, 62, 63, 75-77,
        92, 112, 158-160, 163,
        164, 167-173, 181, 189

Modern logic 3, 19, 179
Modus ponens 100
Modus tollens 70, 171
Principle of Excluded Middle
    99
Principle of Noncontradiction
    91, 92, 115
Propositional logic 62, 64,
    189
Simplification 36
Square of opposition 68, 69
    See also Naturalistic Fallacy;
    Truth-condition; and Truth,
    modal
Logical positivism 11, 12, 54,
    55, 64, 141, 145
Logan, J. 151
Lynch, F. R. 126, 149

M

Magee, Bryan 17
Marcus, Ruth Barcan 180, 181
Marx (Marxian theory) 6, 7, 14,
    16, 33, 77, 80 fn. 2, 81, 82,
    88, 96, 97, 118-120, 126, 128,
    131-134, 141, 144-148, 151-
    154, 160-163, 168, 182, 183,
    188, 193 *See also* Ideology and
    Liberal to Left
Marxist Hitlers 158
Materialism 3-5, 24, 38, 113,
    154, 175
Mathematics 5, 24, 26, 27, 32,
    110, 111, 179
Mayer, Arno 153
Medieval thought 1, 3, 23, 40,
    42, 61, 82, 111, 142, 164, 165
Melchert, N. 143
Mendel, Gregor 21
Merleau-Ponty, Maurice 21, 31,
    55 *See also* Existentialism and
    Phenomenology
Metaphysical substitutes 117, 155